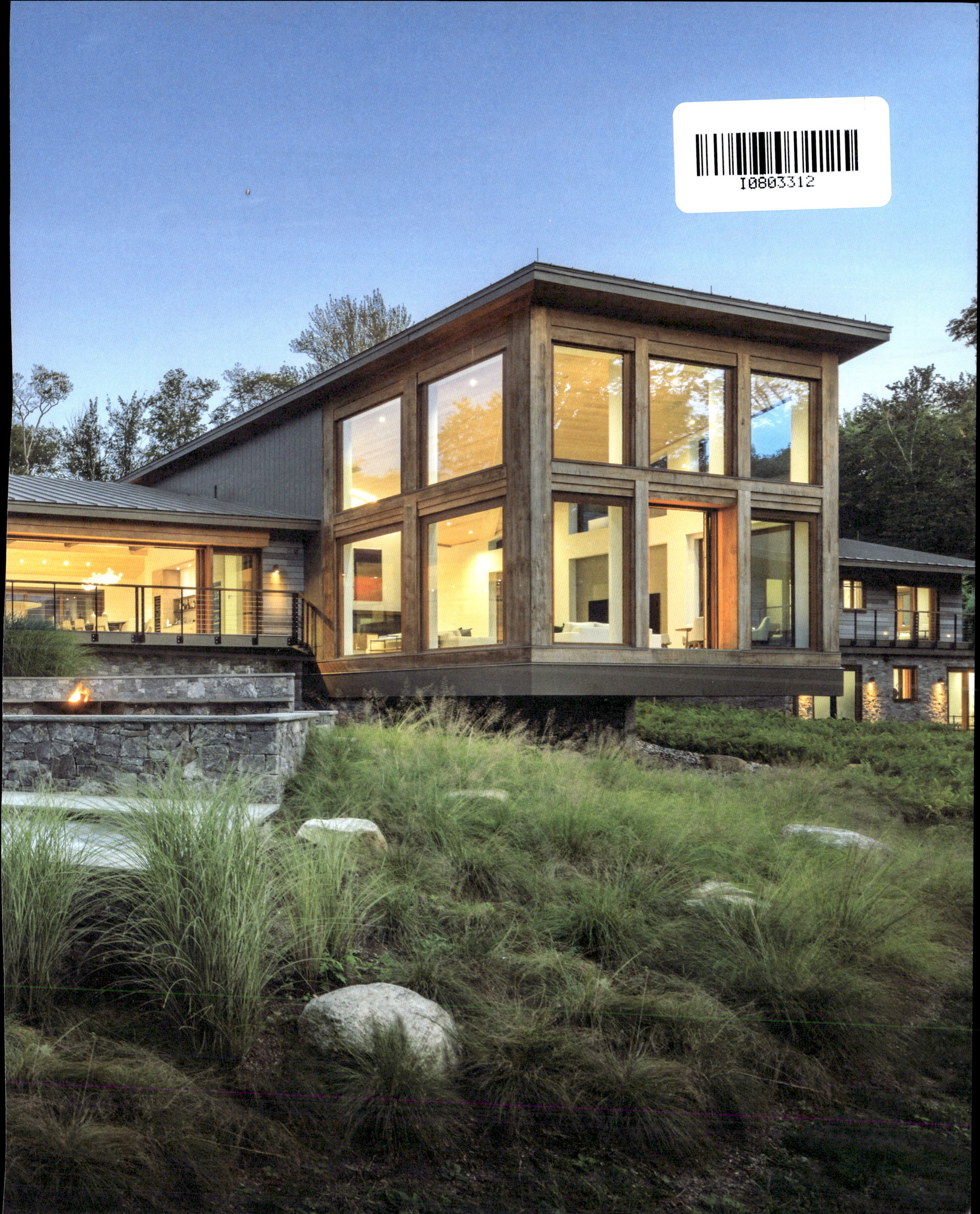
I0803312

Editorial project:
2025 © **booq** publishing, S.L.
c/ Domènech, 7-9, 2º 1ª
08012 Barcelona, Spain
T: +34 93 268 80 88
www.booqpublishing.com

ISBN: 978-84-9936-614-2 [EN]
ISBN: 978-84-9936-592-3 [ES]

© Éditions du Layeur
Dépôt Légal : Janvier 2025
Espagne, en janvier 2025

ISBN : 978-2-38378-076-2

Editorial coordinator:
Claudia Martínez Alonso

Art director:
Mireia Casanovas Soley

Editor and layout:
Francesc Zamora Mola

Translation:
© **booq** publishing, S.L.

Printing in China

This exploration of single-family house design showcases how architecture can seamlessly integrate with the stunning landscapes of New England, Québec, and the Maritime provinces. These regions, known for their picturesque natural beauty, serve as the canvas for homes that are thoughtfully designed to reflect the environment and the cultural heritage of each locale. Whether nestled in a forest, near the Atlantic coast, or in an urban setting, each home embodies a deep respect for its surroundings and carefully considers the challenges posed by the regional climate, including harsh winters and varying seasonal conditions.

Often incorporating locally sourced materials and traditional techniques, these homes honor the land and its cultural heritage while embracing the conveniences of contemporary living. Central to this design philosophy is regionalism — the idea that architecture should resonate with the distinct identity of its location. Whether in an urban setting or surrounded by nature, these homes evoke a strong sense of place. This approach preserves and enhances the essence of place while blending timeless aesthetics and modern functionality.

Sustainability is a key focus, with many architects prioritizing eco-conscious practices, such as energy-efficient technologies and sustainable construction methods aimed at reducing environmental impact without compromising modern comforts.

Another significant theme is the seamless indoor-outdoor integration. Many projects feature large windows, sliding doors, and site-sensitive layouts that blur the boundaries between interior spaces and the surrounding environment, making the outdoors an integral part of the home.

A common feature across many of these designs is the balance between traditional and modern elements. By blending historic architectural features with contemporary requirements, these homes honor their past while meeting today's expectations for functionality and sustainability. Each design reflects the individual vision and lifestyle of its occupants, resulting in a harmonious fusion of heritage and modern living.

Together, these shared values — regionalism, sustainability, indoor-outdoor connectivity, and the fusion of traditional and modern design — highlight a collective approach to creating homes that are environmentally conscious, deeply connected to their surroundings, and tailored to modern living. These homes offer a glimpse into a world where architecture, nature, and culture coexist in harmony.

Diese Untersuchung der Einfamilienhausarchitektur zeigt, wie sich Architektur nahtlos in die atemberaubenden Landschaften von Neuengland, Québec und den Seeprovinzen integrieren kann. Diese Regionen, bekannt für ihre malerische Naturschönheit, dienen als Leinwand für Häuser, die mit Bedacht entworfen wurden, um die Umwelt und das kulturelle Erbe jedes Ortes widerzuspiegeln. Ob eingebettet in einen Wald, in der Nähe der Atlantikküste oder in einer städtischen Umgebung – jedes Haus verkörpert einen tiefen Respekt für seine Umgebung und berücksichtigt sorgfältig die Herausforderungen, die das regionale Klima mit sich bringt, einschließlich strenger Winter und wechselnder saisonaler Bedingungen.

Oft unter Verwendung lokal bezogener Materialien und traditioneller Techniken ehren diese Häuser das Land und sein kulturelles Erbe, während sie gleichzeitig die Annehmlichkeiten des modernen Lebens integrieren. Im Zentrum dieser Designphilosophie steht der Regionalismus – die Idee, dass Architektur im Einklang mit der unverwechselbaren Identität ihres Standorts stehen sollte. Ob in einer städtischen Umgebung oder von der Natur umgeben, diese Häuser vermitteln ein starkes Gefühl von Verbundenheit mit ihrem Ort. Dieser Ansatz bewahrt und verstärkt das Wesen des Ortes, indem er zeitlose Ästhetik und moderne Funktionalität miteinander verbindet.

Nachhaltigkeit ist ein zentrales Thema, wobei viele Architekten umweltbewusste Praktiken wie energieeffiziente Technologien und nachhaltige Baumethoden priorisieren, um die Umweltauswirkungen zu reduzieren, ohne auf modernen Komfort zu verzichten.

Ein weiteres bedeutendes Thema ist die nahtlose Integration von Innen- und Außenbereichen. Viele Projekte verfügen über große Fenster, Schiebetüren und ortsbezogene Grundrisse, die die Grenzen zwischen Innenräumen und der umliegenden Natur verwischen und die Außenwelt zu einem integralen Bestandteil des Hauses machen.

Ein gemeinsames Merkmal vieler dieser Designs ist das Gleichgewicht zwischen traditionellen und modernen Elementen. Durch die Verbindung historischer architektonischer Merkmale mit zeitgenössischen Anforderungen ehren diese Häuser ihre Vergangenheit, während sie den heutigen Erwartungen an Funktionalität und Nachhaltigkeit gerecht werden. Jedes Design spiegelt die individuelle Vision und den Lebensstil seiner Bewohner wider und führt zu einer harmonischen Verschmelzung von Erbe und modernem Wohnen.

Diese gemeinsamen Werte – Regionalismus, Nachhaltigkeit, Innen-Außen-Verbindung und die Verschmelzung von traditionellem und modernem Design – unterstreichen einen kollektiven Ansatz zur Schaffung von Häusern, die umweltbewusst sind, tief mit ihrer Umgebung verbunden und auf das moderne Leben zugeschnitten. Diese Häuser bieten einen Einblick in eine Welt, in der Architektur, Natur und Kultur in Harmonie koexistieren.

Cette exploration de la conception de maisons unifamiliales met en lumière la manière dont l'architecture peut s'intégrer harmonieusement aux paysages magnifiques de la Nouvelle-Angleterre, du Québec et des provinces maritimes. Ces régions, reconnues pour leur beauté naturelle pittoresque, servent de toile de fond à des maisons conçues avec soin pour refléter l'environnement et le patrimoine culturel de chaque lieu. Qu'elles soient nichées dans une forêt, près de la côte atlantique ou en milieu urbain, chaque maison incarne un profond respect pour son cadre et prend en compte les défis posés par le climat régional, notamment les hivers rigoureux et les conditions saisonnières changeantes.

Souvent construites avec des matériaux locaux et des techniques traditionnelles, ces maisons honorent la terre et son patrimoine culturel tout en embrassant les commodités de la vie contemporaine. Au cœur de cette philosophie de conception se trouve le régionalisme — l'idée que l'architecture doit résonner avec l'identité distincte de son emplacement. Que ce soit en milieu urbain ou entourées par la nature, ces maisons évoquent un fort sentiment d'appartenance. Cette approche permet de préserver et d'enrichir l'essence du lieu tout en combinant une esthétique intemporelle avec une fonctionnalité moderne.

La durabilité est un axe majeur, de nombreux architectes privilégiant des pratiques éco-responsables, telles que des technologies écoénergétiques et des méthodes de construction durables, visant à réduire l'impact environnemental sans compromettre le confort moderne.

Un autre thème important est l'intégration fluide entre l'intérieur et l'extérieur. De nombreux projets comportent de grandes fenêtres, des portes coulissantes et des agencements sensibles au site, qui estompent les frontières entre les espaces intérieurs et l'environnement extérieur, faisant de la nature une partie intégrante de la maison.

Un trait commun à de nombreuses conceptions est l'équilibre entre éléments traditionnels et modernes. En mêlant des caractéristiques architecturales historiques aux exigences contemporaines, ces maisons honorent leur passé tout en répondant aux attentes actuelles en termes de fonctionnalité et de durabilité. Chaque conception reflète la vision individuelle et le mode de vie de ses occupants, résultant en une fusion harmonieuse entre patrimoine et vie moderne.

Ensemble, ces valeurs partagées — le régionalisme, la durabilité, la connexion entre intérieur et extérieur, et la fusion du design traditionnel et moderne — illustrent une approche collective de la création de maisons à la fois respectueuses de l'environnement, profondément connectées à leur cadre et adaptées à la vie moderne. Ces maisons offrent un aperçu d'un monde où architecture, nature et culture coexistent en harmonie.

Esta exploración del diseño de casas unifamiliares muestra cómo la arquitectura puede integrarse perfectamente con los impresionantes paisajes de Nueva Inglaterra, Québec y las provincias marítimas. Estas regiones, conocidas por su pintoresca belleza natural, sirven de lienzo para hogares que han sido diseñados cuidadosamente para reflejar el entorno y el patrimonio cultural de cada lugar. Ya sea enclavadas en un bosque, cerca de la costa atlántica o en un entorno urbano, cada vivienda encarna un profundo respeto por su entorno y considera cuidadosamente los desafíos que presenta el clima regional, incluidas las rigurosas condiciones invernales y las variadas estaciones del año.

A menudo incorporando materiales locales y técnicas tradicionales, estas casas honran la tierra y su herencia cultural, al mismo tiempo que abrazan las comodidades de la vida contemporánea. En el centro de esta filosofía de diseño está el regionalismo, la idea de que la arquitectura debe resonar con la identidad distintiva de su ubicación. Ya sea en un entorno urbano o rodeado de naturaleza, estas casas evocan un fuerte sentido de lugar. Este enfoque preserva y mejora la esencia del sitio, fusionando estéticas atemporales con la funcionalidad moderna.

La sostenibilidad es un enfoque clave, con muchos arquitectos priorizando prácticas ecológicas, como tecnologías energéticamente eficientes y métodos de construcción sostenibles que buscan reducir el impacto ambiental sin comprometer las comodidades modernas.

Otro tema importante es la integración fluida entre el interior y el exterior. Muchos proyectos presentan grandes ventanales, puertas corredizas y diseños sensibles al entorno que difuminan los límites entre los espacios interiores y el entorno circundante, haciendo que el exterior sea una parte integral del hogar.

Una característica común en muchos de estos diseños es el equilibrio entre elementos tradicionales y modernos. Al combinar características arquitectónicas históricas con las necesidades contemporáneas, estas casas honran su pasado al tiempo que satisfacen las expectativas actuales de funcionalidad y sostenibilidad. Cada diseño refleja la visión individual y el estilo de vida de sus ocupantes, resultando en una fusión armoniosa entre el patrimonio y la vida moderna.

En conjunto, estos valores compartidos —regionalismo, ecología, conectividad interior-exterior y la fusión de diseños tradicionales y modernos— destacan un enfoque colectivo para crear hogares conscientes del medio ambiente, profundamente conectados con su entorno y adaptados a la vida moderna. Estas casas ofrecen una visión de un mundo donde la arquitectura, la naturaleza y la cultura coexisten en armonía.

AUSTIN PATTERSON DISSTON
ARCHITECTURE & DESIGN

"Intimate scale and meticulous detail."

Austin Patterson Disston Architecture & Design is an award-winning architectural and planning firm with offices in Norwalk, Connecticut, and Quogue, New York. The firm was founded in 1982 by David Austin, AIA, and McKee Patterson, AIA. It is currently led by Senior Principal Stuart Disston, AIA, LEED GA, and Principal Joshua Rosensweig, Associate AIA. The firm specializes in bespoke residential, hospitality, and private club projects, demonstrating expertise in renovations, restorations, additions, apartments, and new residences. Their design approach respects the unique built and natural surroundings of each site, ensuring harmony with the surrounding neighborhood and historical frameworks. The team combines a deep understanding of architectural history with innovative design solutions tailored to each project's context, while being responsive to the clients' needs and aspirations.

Austin Patterson Disston Architecture & Design ist ein preisgekröntes Architekturbüro mit Büros in Norwalk, Connecticut, und Quogue, New York. Das Büro wurde 1982 von David Austin, AIA, und McKee Patterson, AIA, gegründet. Derzeit wird es von Senior Principal Stuart Disston, AIA, LEED GA, und Principal Joshua Rosensweig, Associate AIA, geleitet. Es spezialisiert sich auf maßgeschneiderte Wohn-, Gastgewerbe- und Clubprojekte und demonstriert Fachwissen in Renovierungen, Restaurierungen, Erweiterungen, Apartments und neuen Residenzen. Ihr Designansatz respektiert die einzigartigen gebauten und natürlichen Umgebungen jedes Standorts und gewährleistet Harmonie mit der Nachbarschaft und den historischen Rahmenbedingungen. Das Team kombiniert ein tiefes Verständnis der Architekturgeschichte mit innovativen Designlösungen, die auf den Kontext jedes Projekts abgestimmt sind, und reagiert auf die Wünsche der Kunden.

Austin Patterson Disston Architecture & Design est une agence d'architecture et de planification primée avec des bureaux à Norwalk, Connecticut, et Quogue, New York. L'agence a été fondée en 1982 par David Austin, AIA, et McKee Patterson, AIA. Elle est actuellement dirigée par le Directeur Principal Stuart Disston, AIA, LEED GA, et le Directeur Joshua Rosensweig, Associé AIA. L'agence se spécialise dans des projets résidentiels, d'hospitalité et de clubs privés sur mesure, démontrant une expertise en rénovations, restaurations, extensions, appartements et nouvelles résidences. Leur approche de conception respecte les environnements bâtis et naturels uniques de chaque site, garantissant l'harmonie avec le quartier environnant et les cadres historiques. L'équipe combine une compréhension approfondie de l'histoire architecturale avec des solutions de design innovantes adaptées au contexte de chaque projet, tout en répondant aux besoins et aux aspirations des clients.

Austin Patterson Disston Architecture & Design es una firma de arquitectura y planificación galardonada con oficinas en Norwalk, Connecticut, y Quogue, Nueva York. La firma fue fundada en 1982 por David Austin, AIA, y McKee Patterson, AIA. Actualmente está dirigida por el Socio Principal Stuart Disston, AIA, LEED GA, y el Principal Joshua Rosensweig, Asociado AIA. La firma se especializa en proyectos residenciales, de hospitalidad y de clubes privados a medida, demostrando experiencia en renovaciones, restauraciones, ampliaciones, apartamentos y nuevas residencias. Su enfoque de diseño respeta el entorno construido y natural único de cada sitio, asegurando la armonía con el vecindario circundante y los marcos históricos. El equipo combina una profunda comprensión de la historia arquitectónica con soluciones de diseño innovadoras adaptadas al contexto de cada proyecto, mientras responde a las necesidades y aspiraciones de los clientes.

apdarchitects apdarchitects.com

OLD STONE NEW LIGHT

HOUSE ON THE POND

OLD STONE NEW LIGHT

Norwalk, Connecticut, United States // Lot area: 46,368 sq ft; house area: 4,500 sq ft + garage: 460 sq ft

Site plan

This project exemplifies APD Architecture & Design's mission to honor the built and natural contexts of each site, preserving the original Gothic Stone Carriage house and remnants of a rose garden. The historic cottage, although one-third the size of the new addition, forms the foundation of the entire build. By integrating the original structure through entryways and stair circulation, the transition from exterior to interior is seamless. This thoughtful design grounds the staircase in the home's history, making it a striking centerpiece as the space evolves from old to new. The new structure features a modern aesthetic with clean lines and large industrial sash windows, flooding the interiors with natural light and offering sweeping views of the garden, nearby saltwater pond, and harbor. The auto court complements the cottage gable by mirroring its shape in the detached garage. Set amidst lush greenery, this home is a luxurious blend of old and new, home and garden, classic and modern.

Dieses Projekt veranschaulicht die Mission von APD Architecture & Design, den gebauten und natürlichen Kontext jedes Standorts zu ehren, indem das gotische Steinhaus für Kutschen und die Überreste eines Rosengartens erhalten bleiben. Das historische Cottage, nur ein Drittel so groß wie der neue Anbau, bildet das Fundament des gesamten Baus. Durch die Integration der ursprünglichen Struktur über Eingänge und Treppenzirkulation wird der Übergang von außen nach innen nahtlos. Dieses durchdachte Design verankert die Treppe in der Geschichte des Hauses und macht sie zu einem auffälligen Mittelpunkt, während sich der Raum von alt zu neu entwickelt. Die neue Struktur zeigt eine moderne Ästhetik mit klaren Linien und großen Schiebefenstern, die die Innenräume mit Licht fluten und weite Blicke auf den Garten, den Salzwasserteich und den Hafen bieten. Der Autohof ergänzt den Giebel des Cottages, indem er dessen Form im freistehenden Garagengebäude spiegelt. Eingebettet in üppiges Grün ist dieses Haus eine luxuriöse Mischung aus Alt und Neu, Haus und Garten, Klassik und Moderne.

North elevation

East elevation

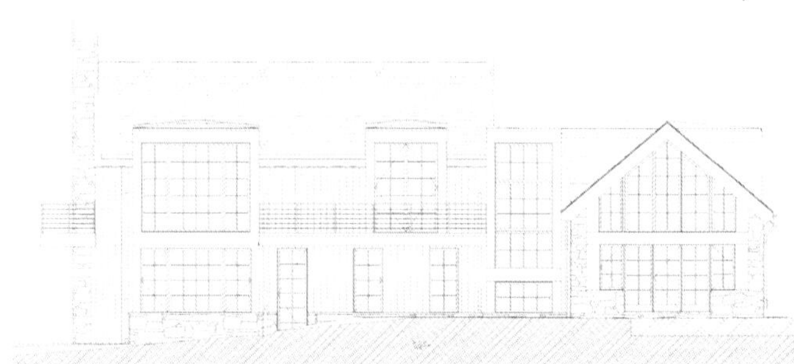

South elevation

West elevation

Ce projet illustre la mission de APD Architecture & Design d'honorer les contextes bâtis et naturels de chaque site, en préservant la maison gothique en pierre et les vestiges d'un jardin de roses. Le cottage historique, bien qu'il ne fasse qu'un tiers de la taille de la nouvelle extension, forme la base de l'ensemble. En intégrant la structure d'origine à travers les entrées et la circulation des escaliers, la transition entre l'extérieur et l'intérieur est fluide. Ce design ancre l'escalier dans l'histoire de la maison, en faisant une pièce maîtresse saisissante à mesure que l'espace évolue. La nouvelle structure présente une esthétique moderne avec des lignes épurées et de grandes fenêtres industrielles, inondant les intérieurs de lumière naturelle et offrant des vues sur le jardin, l'étang d'eau salée et le port. La cour automobile complète le pignon du cottage en reproduisant sa forme dans le garage. Située au milieu d'une verdure luxuriante, cette maison est un mélange luxueux d'ancien et de nouveau, de maison et de jardin, de classique et de moderne.

Este proyecto ejemplifica la misión de APD Architecture & Design de honrar los contextos construidos y naturales de cada sitio, preservando la casa gótica de piedra y los restos de un jardín de rosas. La cabaña histórica, aunque es un tercio del tamaño de la nueva adición, forma la base de toda la construcción. Al integrar la estructura original a través de entradas y escaleras, la transición del exterior al interior es perfecta. Este diseño conecta la escalera con la historia de la casa, convirtiéndola en una pieza central impactante a medida que el espacio evoluciona de lo antiguo a lo nuevo. La nueva estructura presenta una estética moderna con líneas limpias y grandes ventanas industriales, inundando los interiores de luz natural y ofreciendo vistas del jardín, el estanque de agua salada y el puerto. El patio de automóviles complementa el hastial de la cabaña al reflejar su forma en el garaje independiente. Situada en medio de exuberante vegetación, esta casa es una lujosa combinación de lo antiguo y lo nuevo, de la casa y el jardín, de lo clásico y lo moderno.

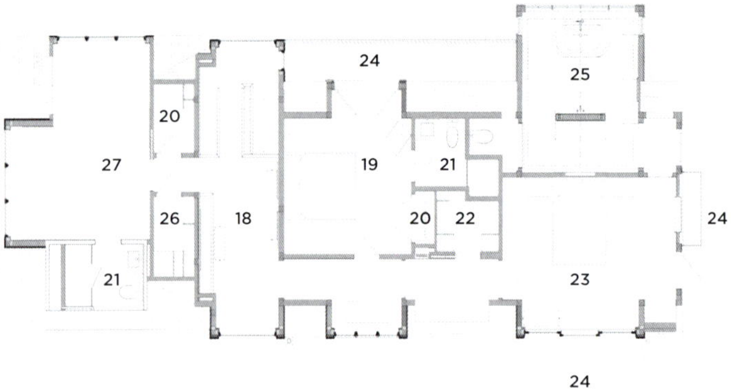

Second Level floor plan

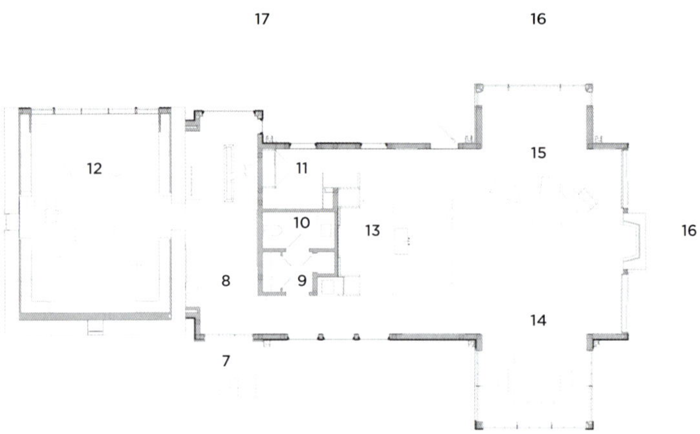

Ground level floor plan

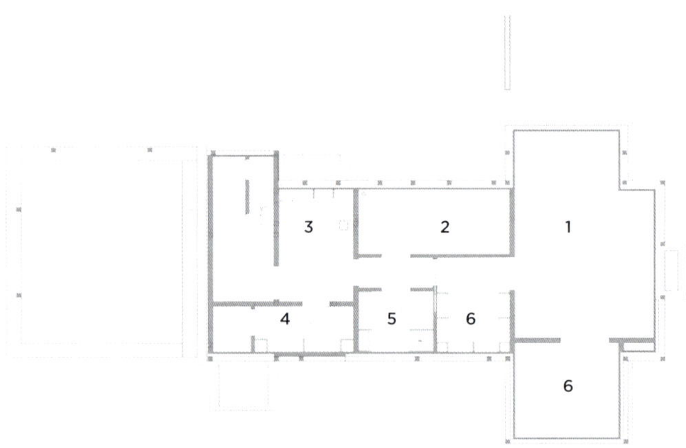

Basement level floor plan

1. Exercise room
2. Mechanical room and storage
3. Boot room
4. Cedar closet
5. Wine room
6. Storage
7. Entry
8. Entry foyer
9. Coat closet
10. Powder room
11. Pantry
12. Library
13. Kitchen
14. Dining area
15. Living area
16. Terrace
17. Rose garden
18. Staircase second floor landing
19. Bedroom
20. Closet
21. Bathroom
22. Walk-in closet
23. Primary bedroom
24. Balcony
25. Primary bathroom
26. Laundry room
27. Study/guest bedroom

HOUSE ON THE POND

Hamptons, New York, United States // Lot area: 53,162 sq ft; house area: 4,794 sq ft + garage: 502 sq ft

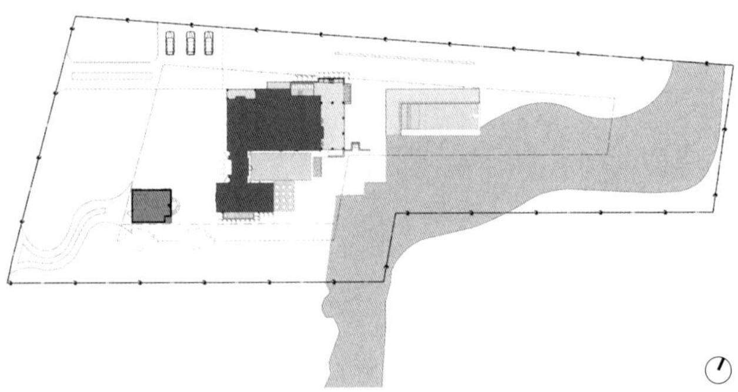

Site plan

North elevation

East elevation

South elevation

West elevation

Situated by a man-made pond from the 1890s, this art collectors' home is designed to maximize both the water setting and the display of artwork. The entry features an eight-foot wide, sixteen-foot high connector offering immediate pond views. Turning left reveals a sculptural staircase leading to an intimate study through an arched opening. To the right is the light-filled, twelve-foot-high dining and living area, with a kitchen tucked away for a cozy atmosphere. The space is arranged to showcase artwork and offers views through a gracious porch and pool, which appears to spill directly into the pond. The twelve-foot ceilings provide ample light and wall space for art. The staircase connects second-floor bedrooms via a gallery overlooking the stairs, dining/living area, and out to the porch, pool, and pond. In this home, the eye continually dances between the artwork and the picturesque pond views.

Diese Kunstsammler-Residenz, die sich neben einem künstlichen Teich aus den 1890er Jahren befindet, wurde entworfen, um sowohl die Wasserlandschaft als auch die Ausstellung von Kunstwerken zu maximieren. Der Eingangsbereich verfügt über einen acht Fuß breiten und sechzehn Fuß hohen Durchgang, der sofortige Blicke auf den Teich bietet. Links offenbart sich eine skulpturale Treppe, die durch eine bogenförmige Öffnung in ein intimes Arbeitszimmer führt. Rechts befindet sich der lichtdurchflutete Speise- und Wohnbereich mit zwölf Fuß hohen Decken und einer gemütlich eingerichteten Küche. Der Raum ist so gestaltet, dass Kunstwerke zur Schau gestellt werden können und bietet Ausblicke durch eine elegante Veranda und einen Pool, der scheinbar direkt in den Teich fließt. Die zwölf Fuß hohen Decken bieten reichlich Licht und Wandfläche für Kunstwerke. Die Treppe verbindet die Schlafzimmer im zweiten Stock über eine Galerie, die die Treppe, den Speise-/Wohnbereich und den Ausblick auf die Veranda, den Pool und den Teich überblickt. In diesem Haus tanzt der Blick ständig zwischen den Kunstwerken und den malerischen Teichansichten.

Située près d'un étang artificiel des années 1890, cette maison de collectionneurs est conçue pour maximiser le cadre aquatique et l'exposition des œuvres d'art. L'entrée, avec un connecteur de huit pieds de large et seize pieds de haut, offre une vue immédiate sur l'étang. À gauche, un escalier sculptural mène à un bureau intime via une arche, tandis qu'à droite, la salle à manger et le salon, éclairés naturellement, bénéficient de plafonds de 3,5 m de haut. La cuisine, nichée à côté, crée une ambiance cosy. L'espace met en valeur les œuvres d'art tout en offrant des vues sur un porche élégant et une piscine qui semble se fondre dans l'étang. Les plafonds de douze pieds procurent lumière et espace mural pour l'art. L'escalier relie les chambres du deuxième étage via une galerie qui surplombe les espaces de vie et s'ouvre sur le porche et la piscine. Le regard circule constamment entre les œuvres d'art et les vues pittoresques de l'étang.

Situada junto a un estanque artificial de la década de 1890, esta casa de coleccionistas de arte está diseñada para maximizar el entorno acuático y la exhibición de obras de arte. La entrada tiene un conector de ocho pies de ancho y dieciséis de alto, ofreciendo vistas inmediatas al estanque. A la izquierda, una escalera escultórica conduce a un estudio íntimo a través de una abertura arqueada. A la derecha, el comedor y la sala de estar, con techos de 3,5 m, están bañados de luz, con una cocina escondida para crear un ambiente acogedor. El espacio exhibe obras de arte y ofrece vistas a través de un elegante porche y una piscina que parece verterse en el estanque. Los techos de doce pies proporcionan luz abundante y espacio para arte. La escalera conecta los dormitorios del segundo piso mediante una galería que domina los espacios de vida y se abre al porche y la piscina. Aquí, la vista alterna entre las obras de arte y las pintorescas vistas del estanque.

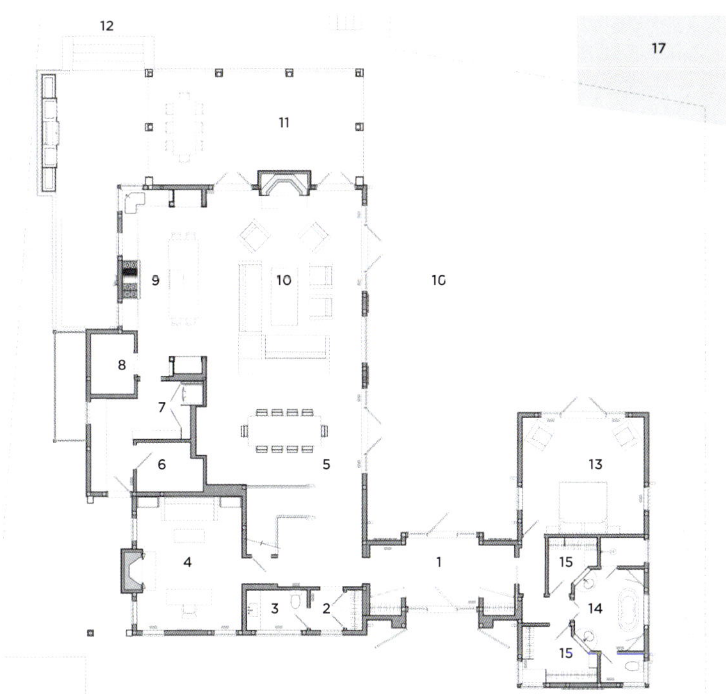

Ground level floor plan

Second level floor plan

1. Entry
2. Coat closet
3. Powder room
4. Study
5. Dining area
6. Mechanical room
7. Mudroom
8. Pantry
9. Kitchen
10. Living area
11. Porch
12. Stairs down to pool and pond
13. Primary bedroom
14. Primary bathroom
15. Closet
16. Terrace
17. Pond
18. Gallery
19. Connector/bridge
20. Guest bathroom
21. Guest bedroom
22. Bedroom
23. Bathroom
24. Laundry room
25. Sitting area
26. Deck/balcony

VALLAURIS
1951
EXPOSITION

DOYLE | COFFIN ARCHITECTURE

"Blending luxury and functionality into ageless architectural design."

Doyle | Coffin Architecture has delivered top-tier architectural design services to residential and commercial clients across Fairfield County, New York, and Greater New England for over fifty years. Based in Ridgefield, Connecticut, with two partners and a staff of ten, the studio also operate satellite offices in Dover, New Hampshire, West Dover, Vermont, and Block Island, Rhode Island. Doyle | Coffin Architecture specializes in timeless design that blends beauty and function, working closely with clients to bring their visions to life. Their portfolio includes custom new residences, additions, and renovations, all marked by their unwavering commitment to excellence in design and service.

Doyle | Coffin Architecture hat seit über fünfzig Jahren erstklassige architektonische Design-Dienstleistungen für private und gewerbliche Kunden in Fairfield County, New York und Greater New England erbracht. Das Studio mit Sitz in Ridgefield, Connecticut, zwei Partnern und einem zehnköpfigen Team betreibt auch Satellitenbüros in Dover, New Hampshire, West Dover, Vermont und Block Island, Rhode Island. Doyle | Coffin Architecture ist spezialisiert auf zeitloses Design, das Schönheit und Funktion vereint und arbeitet eng mit den Kunden zusammen, um ihre Visionen zu verwirklichen. Ihr Portfolio umfasst maßgeschneiderte Neubauten, Erweiterungen und Renovierungen, die alle durch ihr unerschütterliches Engagement für Exzellenz in Design und Service gekennzeichnet sind.

Doyle | Coffin Architecture a offert des services de conception architecturale de premier ordre à des clients résidentiels et commerciaux dans le comté de Fairfield, à New York et en Nouvelle-Angleterre depuis plus de cinquante ans. Basé à Ridgefield, Connecticut, avec deux partenaires et une équipe de dix personnes, le studio opère également des bureaux satellites à Dover, New Hampshire, West Dover, Vermont, et Block Island, Rhode Island. Doyle | Coffin Architecture se spécialise dans la conception intemporelle qui allie beauté et fonctionnalité, travaillant en étroite collaboration avec les clients pour donner vie à leurs visions. Leur portefeuille comprend des résidences personnalisées, des extensions et des rénovations, toutes marquées par leur engagement indéfectible envers l'excellence en matière de conception et de service.

Doyle | Coffin Architecture ha ofrecido servicios de diseño arquitectónico de primer nivel a clientes residenciales y comerciales en el condado de Fairfield, Nueva York y Nueva Inglaterra durante más de cincuenta años. Con sede en Ridgefield, Connecticut, con dos socios y un equipo de diez personas, el estudio también opera oficinas satélite en Dover, New Hampshire, West Dover, Vermont, y Block Island, Rhode Island. Doyle | Coffin Architecture se especializa en un diseño atemporal que combina belleza y funcionalidad, trabajando estrechamente con los clientes para dar vida a sus visiones. Su portafolio incluye residencias nuevas personalizadas, ampliaciones y renovaciones, todas marcadas por su inquebrantable compromiso con la excelencia en el diseño y el servicio.

doylecoffin

doylecoffinarchitecture.com

MODERN FARMHOUSE

WATERFRONT POST AND BEAM

MODERN FARMHOUSE

Connecticut, United States // Building area: 4,000 sq ft

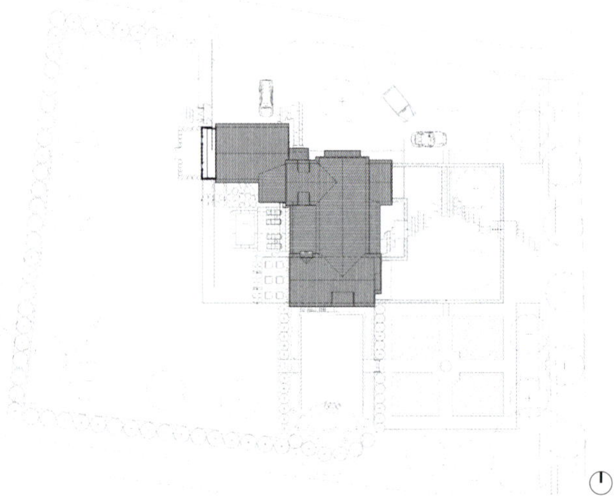

Site plan

This modern farmhouse draws inspiration from its flat site and blends modern lines with the local vernacular. While facing a busy street, it achieves a balance between a welcoming street view and family privacy. The residence is nestled among three garden rooms: the "Front Lawn Entry Court," the "Meadow Room," and the "Spa Room," each engaging with different house areas. Designed for a casual farmhouse feel, the house supports large family gatherings with a first floor extending into outdoor rooms showcasing New England's changing seasons. Finishes blend modern and traditional elements with rift oak kitchen cabinetry, balanced lighting, black steel glass doors, and harmonious textures and colors in furnishings. This farmhouse embodies modern living while incorporating sustainable practices with super-insulated walls and roof, locally sourced materials, and a Heat Recovery Ventilation (HRV) system, creating an eco-friendly and comfortable home.

Dieses moderne Bauernhaus, inspiriert von seinem flachen Standort, verbindet moderne Linien mit lokaler Bauweise. Trotz der Lage an einer belebten Straße findet es ein Gleichgewicht zwischen einladender Straßenansicht und familiärer Privatsphäre. Die Residenz liegt zwischen drei Gartenräumen: dem „Vorgarten-Eingangsplatz", dem „Wiesenzimmer" und dem „Spa-Raum", die jeweils mit verschiedenen Bereichen des Hauses interagieren. Das Haus fördert ein entspanntes Farmhausgefühl und eignet sich für große Familientreffen, mit einem Erdgeschoss, das in Außenräume übergeht und die wechselnden Jahreszeiten Neuenglands zeigt. Die Oberflächen kombinieren moderne und traditionelle Elemente wie Eichenholz-Küchenschränke, ausgewogene Beleuchtung, schwarze Stahltüren und harmonische Möbeltexturen und -farben. Das Bauernhaus verkörpert modernes Wohnen und integriert nachhaltige Praktiken durch superisolierte Wände und Dächer, lokal beschaffte Materialien und ein Wärmerückgewinnungsbelüftungssystem (HRV), was ein umweltfreundliches und komfortables Zuhause schafft.

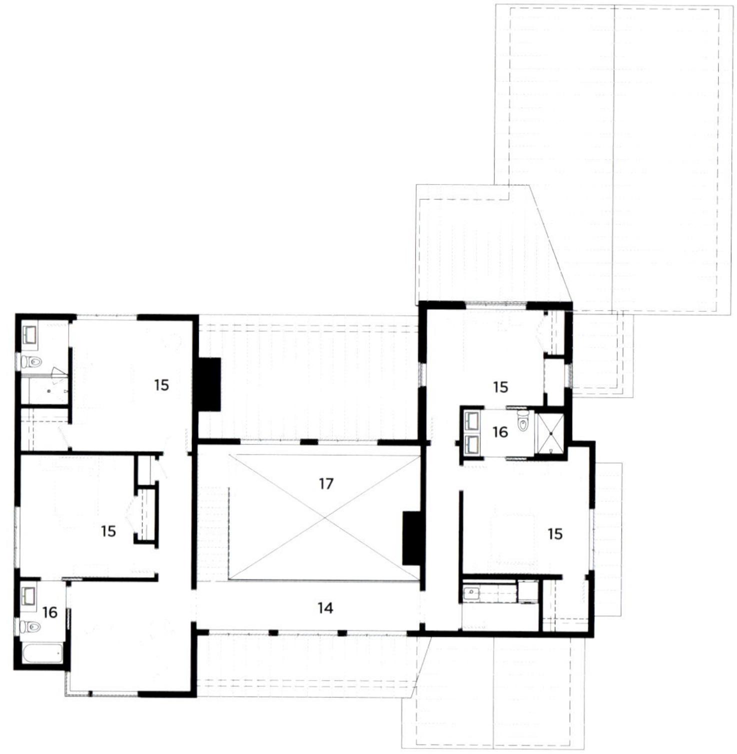

Second level floor plan

Cette ferme moderne s'inspire de son site plat et mélange des lignes modernes avec le style vernaculaire local. Tout en faisant face à une rue animée, elle parvient à un équilibre entre une vue accueillante sur la rue et l'intimité familiale. La résidence est nichée parmi trois jardins : la « Cour d'entrée de la pelouse avant », la « Salle de la prairie » et la « Salle de spa », chacun interagissant avec différentes zones de la maison. Conçue pour une ambiance décontractée de ferme, la maison soutient de grandes réunions familiales avec un rez-de-chaussée qui s'étend dans des pièces extérieures mettant en valeur les saisons changeantes de la Nouvelle-Angleterre. Les finitions mélangent des éléments modernes et traditionnels avec des armoires de cuisine en chêne fendu, un éclairage équilibré, des portes vitrées en acier noir et des textures et couleurs harmonieuses dans les meubles. Cette ferme incarne la vie moderne tout en intégrant des pratiques durables avec des murs et toits super isolés, des matériaux locaux et un système de ventilation à récupération de chaleur (VRC), créant une maison écologique et confortable.

Esta casa de campo moderna se inspira en su terreno plano y fusiona líneas modernas con el estilo local. Aunque está en una calle concurrida, equilibra una vista exterior acogedora con la privacidad familiar. La residencia está rodeada por tres jardines: el «Patio de Entrada del Jardín Frontal», el «Sala de la Pradera» y el «Sala de Spa», que conectan con distintas áreas de la casa. Diseñada para una atmósfera informal, facilita grandes reuniones familiares con un primer piso que se extiende hacia los espacios exteriores, mostrando las estaciones de Nueva Inglaterra. Los acabados combinan elementos modernos y tradicionales con muebles de cocina de roble, iluminación equilibrada, puertas de vidrio con marco de acero negro, y muebles con texturas y colores armoniosos. Esta casa encarna la vida moderna e incorpora prácticas sostenibles con paredes y techos superaislados, materiales locales y un sistema de ventilación con recuperador de calor (VRC), creando un hogar ecológico y cómodo.

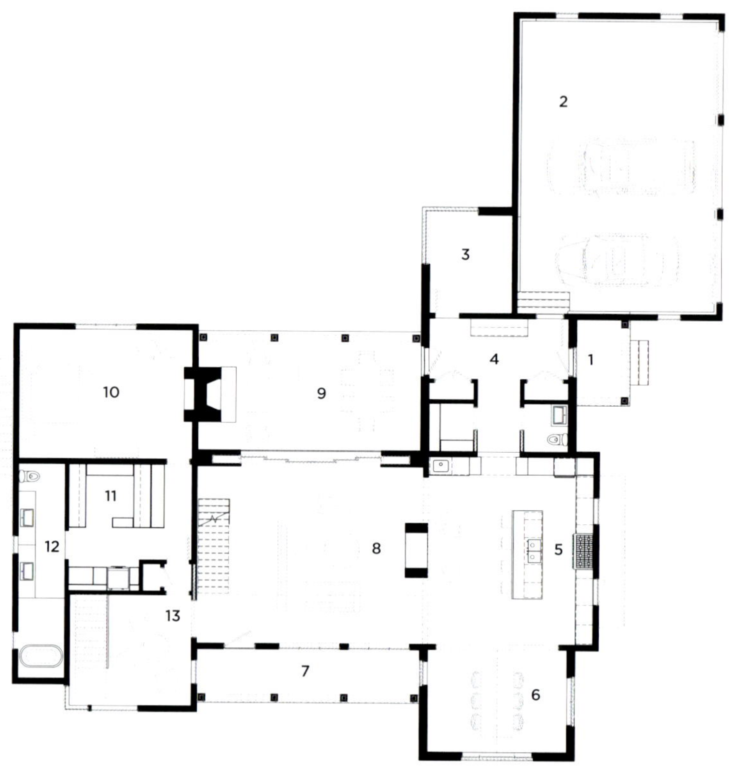

Ground level floor plan

1. Entry
2. Garage
3. Mud room
4. Entry foyer
5. Kitchen
6. Dining area
7. Porch
8. Great room
9. Family room
10. Primary bedroom
11. Dressing room
12. Primary bathroom
13. Sitting area
14. Hallway
15. Bedroom
16. Bathroom
17. Open to below

WATERFRONT POST AND BEAM

New England, United States // Building area: 8,000 sq ft

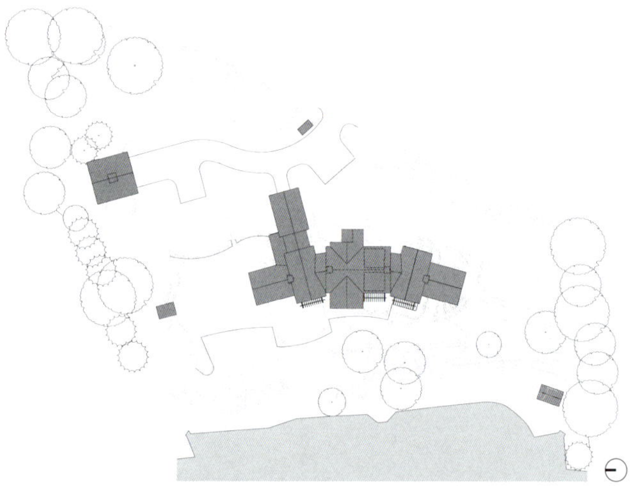

Site plan

This Adirondack-inspired residence is meticulously designed to harmonize with its picturesque lakeside surroundings. The home features interconnected volumes following the shoreline's curves, with primary living spaces in the post-and-beam structure blending seamlessly with nature. The entry leads to a cathedral family room with arching trusses and expansive windows framing serene lake views. High wood plank ceilings, stone chimneys, walnut cabinets, and white oak flooring create a warm atmosphere. Each room opens to terraces and planted spaces for quiet reflection or lakeside entertainment, while distinctive connectors serve practical and aesthetic purposes. Environmentally responsible, the home features geothermal heat, solar panels, super-insulated walls and roof, and locally sourced materials, offering comfort while minimizing environmental impact and showcasing a blend of modern living and sustainable practices.

Diese von den Adirondacks inspirierte Residenz ist sorgfältig darauf ausgelegt, mit ihrer malerischen Umgebung am Seeufer zu harmonieren. Das Haus verfügt über miteinander verbundene Volumen, die den Kurven der Uferlinie folgen, mit den Hauptwohnräumen in der Pfosten- und Balkenstruktur, die nahtlos mit der Natur verschmelzen. Der Eingang führt zu einem Kathedralsaal mit gewölbten Bindern und großen Fenstern, die ruhige Seeblicke einrahmen. Hohe Holzplankendecken, Steinkamine, Walnuss-Schränke und weißes Eichenparkett schaffen eine warme Atmosphäre. Jeder Raum öffnet sich zu Terrassen und bepflanzten Bereichen für ruhige Reflexionen oder Unterhaltung am See, während markante Verbindungen sowohl praktische als auch ästhetische Zwecke erfüllen. Umweltbewusst verfügt das Haus über Erdwärme, Solarmodule, superisolierte Wände und Dächer sowie lokal bezogene Materialien, die Komfort bieten und gleichzeitig die Umweltbelastung minimieren und eine Mischung aus modernem Leben und nachhaltigen Praktiken präsentieren.

Cette résidence inspirée des Adirondacks est conçue pour s'harmoniser avec son cadre pittoresque au bord du lac. La maison présente des volumes interconnectés suivant les courbes du rivage, avec des espaces de vie principaux dans la structure en poteaux et poutres intégrée à la nature. L'entrée mène à une salle familiale avec des fermes arquées et de grandes fenêtres offrant des vues sereines sur le lac. Les hauts plafonds en bois, les cheminées en pierre, les armoires en noyer et les planchers en chêne blanc créent une ambiance chaleureuse. Chaque pièce s'ouvre sur des terrasses et des espaces verts pour des moments de tranquillité ou des divertissements au bord du lac, tandis que des éléments distinctifs remplissent des fonctions pratiques et esthétiques. Respectueuse de l'environnement, la maison est équipée de chauffage géothermique, de panneaux solaires, de murs et toits super isolés, et de matériaux locaux, offrant confort tout en minimisant l'impact environnemental et en mettant en valeur un mélange de vie moderne et de pratiques durables.

Esta residencia inspirada en Adirondack está diseñada para armonizar con su pintoresco entorno junto al lago. La casa presenta volúmenes interconectados que siguen las curvas de la orilla, con los principales espacios de vida en una estructura de postes y vigas que se integran con la naturaleza. La entrada conduce a una sala familiar con techo a dos aguas, cerchas arqueadas y amplias ventanas que enmarcan vistas serenas al lago. Los techos altos de madera, las chimeneas de piedra, los muebles de nogal y los suelos de roble blanco crean un ambiente cálido. Cada habitación se abre a terrazas y espacios ajardinados para momentos de tranquilidad o entretenimiento junto al lago, mientras que elementos distintivos cumplen funciones prácticas y estéticas. Responsable con el medio ambiente, la casa cuenta con calefacción geotérmica, paneles solares, paredes y techos superaislados, y materiales locales, ofreciendo confort y minimizando el impacto ambiental con una combinación de vida moderna y prácticas sostenibles.

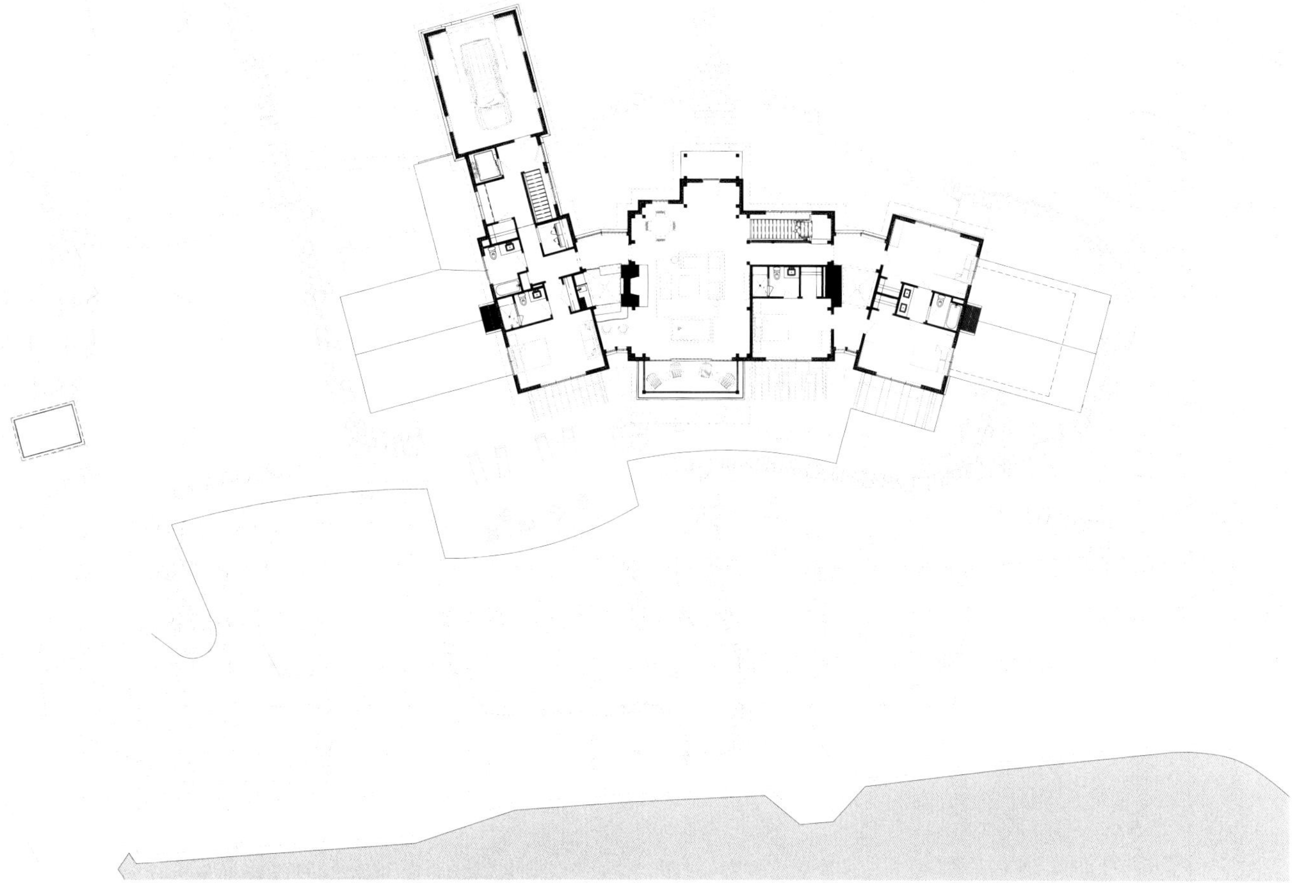

Second level floor plan

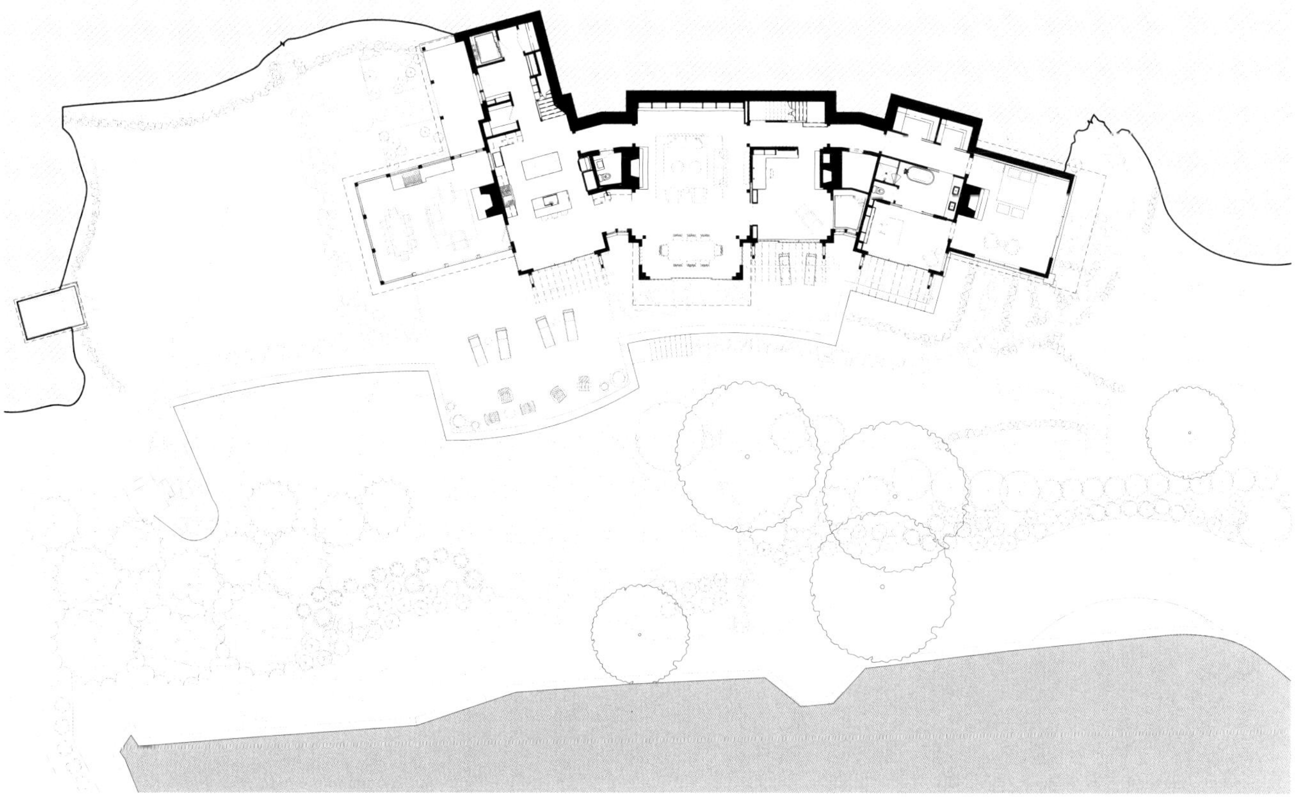

Ground level floor plan

MISIASZEK TURPIN

"Delivering design through a dynamic, inspiring, client-focused partnership."

Misiaszek Turpin is a full-service architecture and planning firm based in downtown Laconia, New Hampshire. Founded in 2004 by Sonya Misiaszek and Robert Turpin and with over sixty years of combined experience, the team includes associate partner Jared Guilmett, three studio designers, and a studio administrator. Misiaszek Turpin's portfolio includes public and private sector projects, such as historic building restoration, municipal facility renovations, and community structure designs. The firm engages all stakeholders and experienced professionals to meet project needs and aspirations. It provides comprehensive architectural services from concept to construction administration, focusing on the site and environment of each project. The team at Misiaszek Turpin is dedicated to creating distinctive structures that meet user needs and exceed client goals.

Misiaszek Turpin ist ein Architekturbüro mit umfassendem Serviceangebot mit Sitz in der Innenstadt von Laconia, New Hampshire. Gegründet 2004 von Sonya Misiaszek und Robert Turpin, bringt das Team über sechzig Jahre gemeinsame Erfahrung ein und umfasst Associate Partner Jared Guilmett, drei Studiodesigner und eine Studioadministratorin. Das Portfolio umfasst Projekte im öffentlichen und privaten Sektor, wie die Restaurierung historischer Gebäude, Renovierungen von kommunalen Einrichtungen und die Gestaltung von Gemeindestrukturen. Misiaszek Turpin bezieht alle Beteiligten und Fachleute ein, um den Projektanforderungen gerecht zu werden, und bietet umfassende architektonische Dienstleistungen vom Konzept bis zur Bauverwaltung mit Fokus auf den Standort und die Umwelt jedes Projekts. Das Team ist bestrebt, unverwechselbare Strukturen zu schaffen, die den Nutzerbedürfnissen entsprechen und die Ziele der Kunden übertreffen.

Misiaszek Turpin est un cabinet d'architecture et de planification situé au cœur de Laconia, New Hampshire. Fondé en 2004 par Sonya Misiaszek et Robert Turpin, avec plus de soixante ans d'expérience combinée, l'équipe inclut le partenaire associé Jared Guilmett, trois designers et un administrateur. Le portefeuille du cabinet couvre des projets publics et privés, tels que la restauration de bâtiments historiques, les rénovations d'installations municipales et la conception de structures communautaires. En impliquant toutes les parties prenantes et professionnels expérimentés, Misiaszek Turpin répond aux besoins des projets avec des services complets, du concept à la construction, en mettant l'accent sur le site et l'environnement. L'équipe est dédiée à créer des structures distinctives qui satisfont les utilisateurs et surpassent les objectifs des clients.

Misiaszek Turpin es un estudio de arquitectura y planificación ubicado en el centro de Laconia, New Hampshire. Fundado en 2004 por Sonya Misiaszek y Robert Turpin, el equipo combina más de sesenta años de experiencia y está encabezado por el socio adjunto Jared Guilmett, junto a tres diseñadores y un administrador. Su portafolio incluye proyectos en los sectores público y privado, como la restauración de edificios históricos, renovaciones municipales y el diseño de estructuras comunitarias. El estudio colabora estrechamente con todas las partes interesadas y profesionales para cumplir con las necesidades y aspiraciones de cada proyecto. Ofrece servicios arquitectónicos completos, desde el concepto hasta la administración de la construcción, siempre centrado en el sitio y el entorno de cada proyecto. Misiaszek Turpin se dedica a crear estructuras distintivas que satisfacen a los usuarios y superan las expectativas de los clientes.

misiaszekturpin.com

MEADOW RETREAT

MOUNTAIN HOME

MEADOW RETREAT

Lakes Region, New Hampshire, United States // Lot area: 3.14 acres; building area: 5,800 sq ft main house + 1,000 sq ft guest house

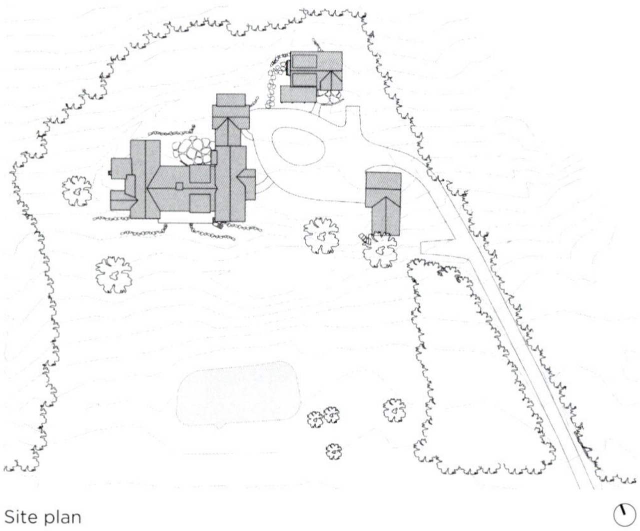

Site plan

Embodying the original family cottage, the new home emerges from surrounding gardens and sweeping vistas. The property includes a main residence, a guest house, and a storage barn with a pond for water runoff. The guest house blends with the woods using tight-matched stained vertical boards and features an airy screened porch and patio. Reflecting the original cottage and local architecture, the main house's ends are framed with painted eastern white cedar shingles, while the center is composed of a shou sugi ban timberframe with glass curtain wall infills. A shared office behind the central fireplace uses salvaged cottage windows and doors, preserving the property's history. The stone entry, built from site boulders, merges with the natural landscape. The western end hosts the primary and guest suites with hillside and garden views, while the eastern side features a four-season room with meadow views from the kitchen. A bookcase-encased stairwell leads to upper-level quarters, including a loft overlooking the rear woods and gardens.

Das neue Zuhause erhebt sich aus den umliegenden Gärten und Weitblicken und verkörpert die ursprüngliche Familienhütte. Das Anwesen umfasst die Hauptresidenz, ein Gästehaus und eine Lagerhalle mit einem Teich für Wasserabfluss. Das Gästehaus integriert sich in den Wald und verwendet gebeizte vertikale Bretter sowie eine Veranda und Terrasse mit Fliegengittern. Die Enden des Haupthauses sind mit bemalten östlichen Zederschindeln verkleidet, während das Zentrum aus einem Shou-Sugi-Ban-Holzrahmen mit Glasvorhangwänden besteht. Ein Büro hinter dem Kamin nutzt gerettete Fenster und Türen der Hütte zur Bewahrung der Geschichte. Der steinerne Eingang aus Findlingen verschmilzt mit der Landschaft. Das westliche Ende bietet Haupt- und Gästesuiten mit Blick auf den Garten, während die östliche Seite ein Ganzjahreszimmer mit Wiesenblick von der Küche hat. Ein Treppenhaus in der Bücherwand führt zu den oberen Quartieren, einschließlich eines Lofts mit Blick auf Wald und Gärten.

La nouvelle maison se distingue des jardins environnants et des vues panoramiques tout en incarnant la cabane familiale d'origine. La propriété comprend une résidence principale, une maison d'invités et un grandero avec un étang pour le ruissellement des eaux. La maison d'invités, intégrée dans les bois, utilise des planches verticales teintées et dispose d'un porche et d'une terrasse avec moustiquaire. Les extrémités de la maison principale sont bordées de bardeaux de cèdre blanc peint, tandis que le centre, en charpente Shou Sugi Ban et panneaux de verre, reflète la cabane d'origine et l'architecture locale. Un bureau derrière la cheminée centrale utilise des fenêtres et portes récupérées de la cabane, préservant l'histoire du lieu. L'entrée en pierre, faite de rochers locaux, s'intègre au paysage naturel. À l'ouest, les suites principale et d'invités offrent des vues sur la colline et le jardin, tandis que l'est dispose d'une salle quatre saisons avec vue sur la prairie depuis la cuisine. Un escalier intégré dans une bibliothèque mène aux quartiers supérieurs, incluant un loft surplombant les bois et jardins arrière.

La nueva casa surge de los jardines circundantes y vistas panorámicas, encarnando la cabaña familiar original. La propiedad incluye una residencia principal, una casa de invitados y un granero con un estanque para el drenaje pluvial. La casa de invitados se integra al bosque con tablas verticales teñidas y tiene un porche y un patio con mosquitero. Los extremos de la casa principal están enmarcados con tejas de cedro blanco oriental pintadas, mientras que el centro, de madera Shou Sugi Ban y vidrio, refleja la cabaña original y la arquitectura local. Una oficina detrás de la chimenea central utiliza ventanas y puertas recuperadas para preservar la historia del lugar. La entrada de piedra, hecha con rocas locales, se mezcla con el paisaje natural. El extremo oeste alberga las suites con vistas a la colina y al jardín, mientras que el este ofrece una sala de cuatro estaciones con vistas al prado desde la cocina. Una escalera integrada en una estantería lleva a las habitaciones superiores, incluido un loft con vistas a los bosques y jardines traseros.

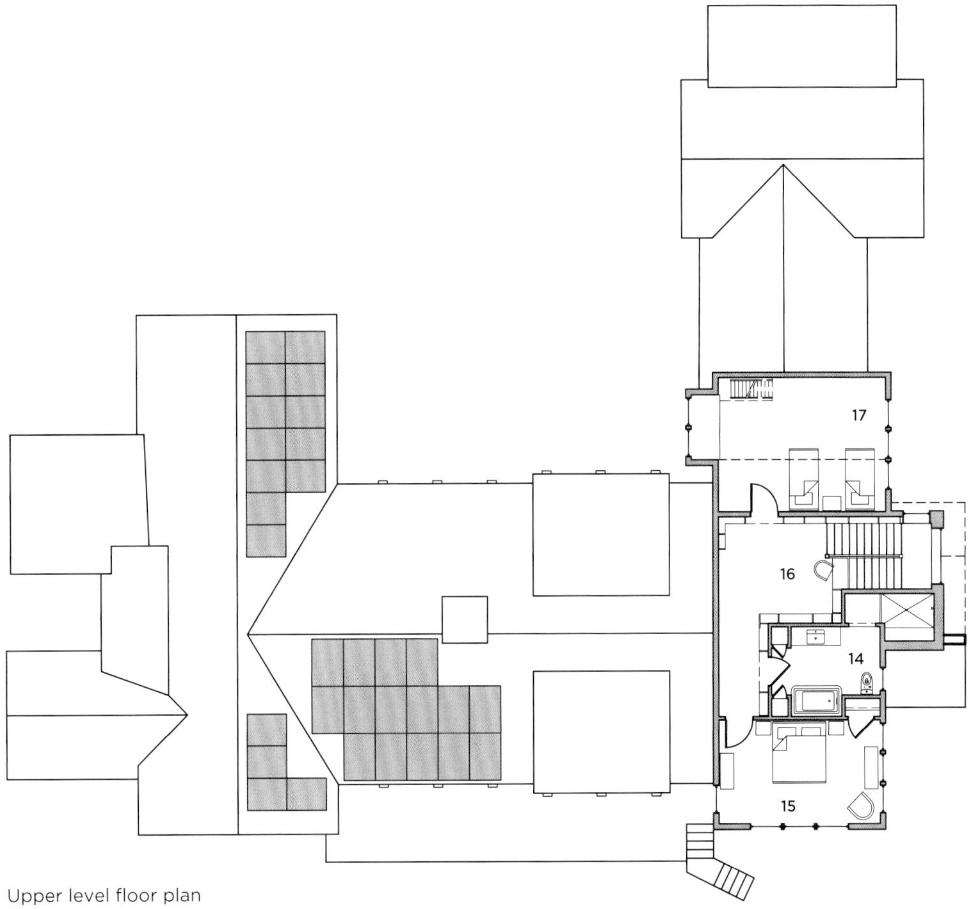

Upper level floor plan

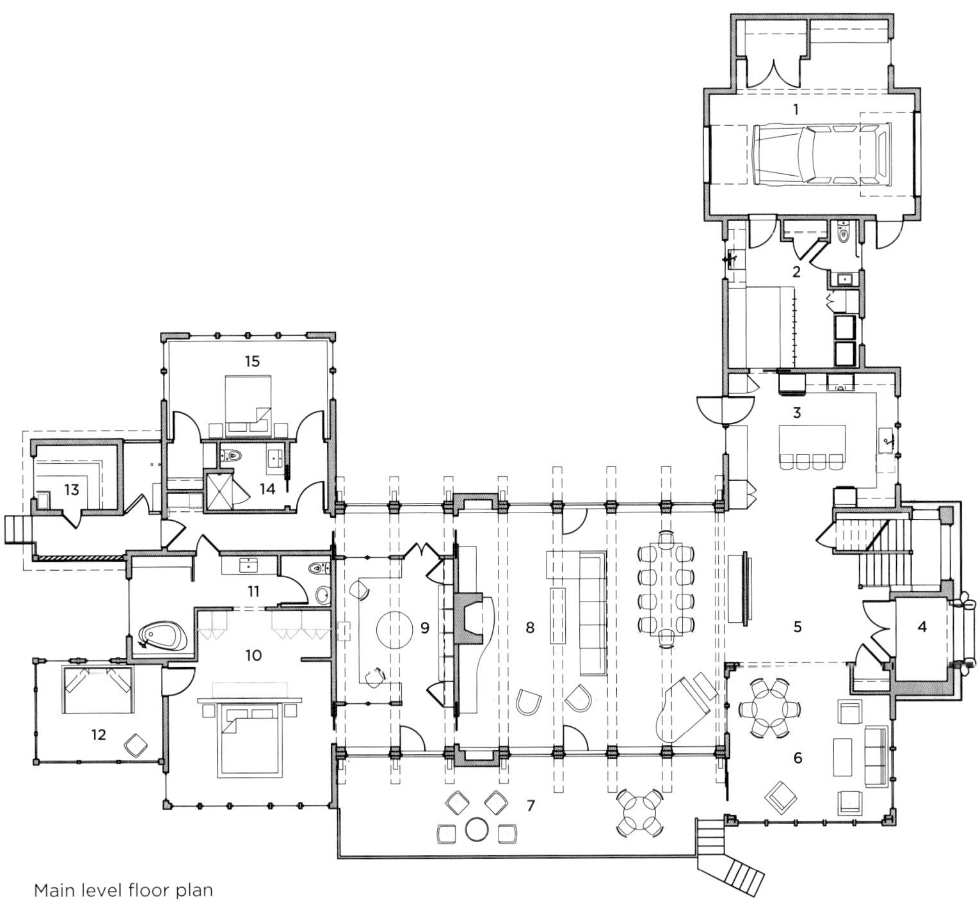

Main level floor plan

1. Garage
2. Laundry room
3. Kitchen
4. Entry porch
5. Entry foyer
6. Sun room
7. Deck
8. Great room
9. Office
10. Primary suite
11. Primary bathroom
12. Screened porch
13. Sauna
14. Bathroom
15. Bedroom
16. Upper level study
17. Loft bedroom

MOUNTAIN HOME

White Mountains, New Hampshire, United States // Lot area: 120 acres; building area: 17,500 sq ft

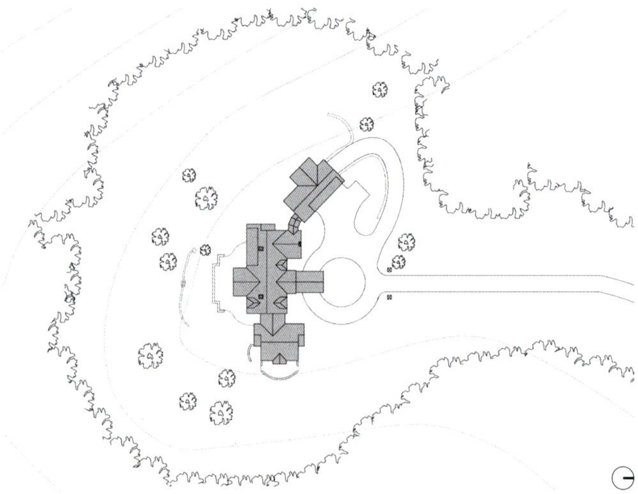

Site plan

The house sits on a partially cleared, historic logging site, perched 1,800 feet above sea level with unobstructed White Mountain views. It features three distinct volumes linked by glass connectors and anchored by a grand brick portico. The upper level integrates into the roof for a more intimate massing. The main axis of the residence is set on the east-west radial and becomes the primary organizer of the interior spaces. Rooms are arranged based on public/private use while taking advantage of the expansive mountain views and the site's daylighting patterns. The exterior blends formal Tudor and casual mountain-home styles, using red brick, natural stone, and painted cedar shingles. This mix of materials creates a tonal elegance that connects with the surrounding views. Salvaged granite blocks from an old railroad bridge define the outdoor living spaces, further integrating the home with the New Hampshire mountain landscape.

Das Haus befindet sich auf einem teilweise gerodeten, historischen Holzfällergelände, 1.800 Fuß über dem Meeresspiegel mit unverbauten Blicken auf die White Mountains. Es verfügt über drei verschiedene Volumen, die durch Glasverbindungen verbunden und durch ein großes Backsteinportikus verankert sind. Das obere Stockwerk integriert sich in das Dach für eine intimere Wirkung. Die Hauptachse der Residenz verläuft in Ost-West-Richtung und wird zum Hauptorganisator der Innenräume. Die Räume sind je nach öffentlicher/privater Nutzung angeordnet und nutzen die weitläufigen Bergblicke und die Tageslichtmuster des Standorts. Die Außenfassade verbindet formale Tudor- und lässige Berghausstile und verwendet roten Backstein, Naturstein und gestrichene Zederschindeln. Diese Materialmischung schafft eine tonale Eleganz, die sich mit den umliegenden Ausblicken verbindet. Gerettete Granitblöcke von einer alten Eisenbahnbrücke definieren die Außenwohnräume und integrieren das Haus weiter in die Berglandschaft von New Hampshire.

La maison est située sur un site historique de coupe partiellement dégagé, à 1 800 pieds au-dessus du niveau de la mer, offrant des vues dégagées sur les Montagnes Blanches. Elle se compose de trois volumes distincts reliés par des connecteurs en verre et ancrés par un grand portique en brique. Le niveau supérieur s'intègre dans le toit pour une masse plus intime. L'axe principal de la résidence est orienté est-ouest et devient l'organisateur principal des espaces intérieurs. Les pièces sont agencées en fonction de leur usage public/privé tout en profitant des vues panoramiques sur la montagne et des motifs d'éclairage naturel du site. L'extérieur mélange les styles formels Tudor et décontractés des maisons de montagne, utilisant de la brique rouge, de la pierre naturelle et des bardeaux de cèdre peints. Ce mélange de matériaux crée une élégance tonale qui se connecte aux vues environnantes. Des blocs de granit récupérés d'un ancien pont ferroviaire définissent les espaces de vie extérieurs, intégrant davantage la maison au paysage montagneux du New Hampshire.

La casa se encuentra en un sitio histórico de tala parcialmente despejado, a 550 m sobre el nivel del mar con vistas despejadas de las Montañas Blancas. Cuenta con tres volúmenes distintos conectados por conectores de vidrio y anclados por un gran pórtico de ladrillo. El nivel superior se integra en el techo para una masa más íntima. El eje principal de la residencia está ubicado en el radial este-oeste y se convierte en el organizador principal de los espacios interiores. Las habitaciones están dispuestas según su uso público/privado, aprovechando las amplias vistas a la montaña y los patrones de iluminación natural del sitio. El exterior mezcla estilos formales Tudor y casuales de casas de montaña, utilizando ladrillo rojo, piedra natural y tejas de cedro pintadas. Esta mezcla de materiales crea una elegancia tonal que se conecta con las vistas circundantes. Bloques de granito recuperados de un antiguo puente ferroviario definen los espacios de vida al aire libre, integrando aún más la casa con el paisaje montañoso de New Hampshire.

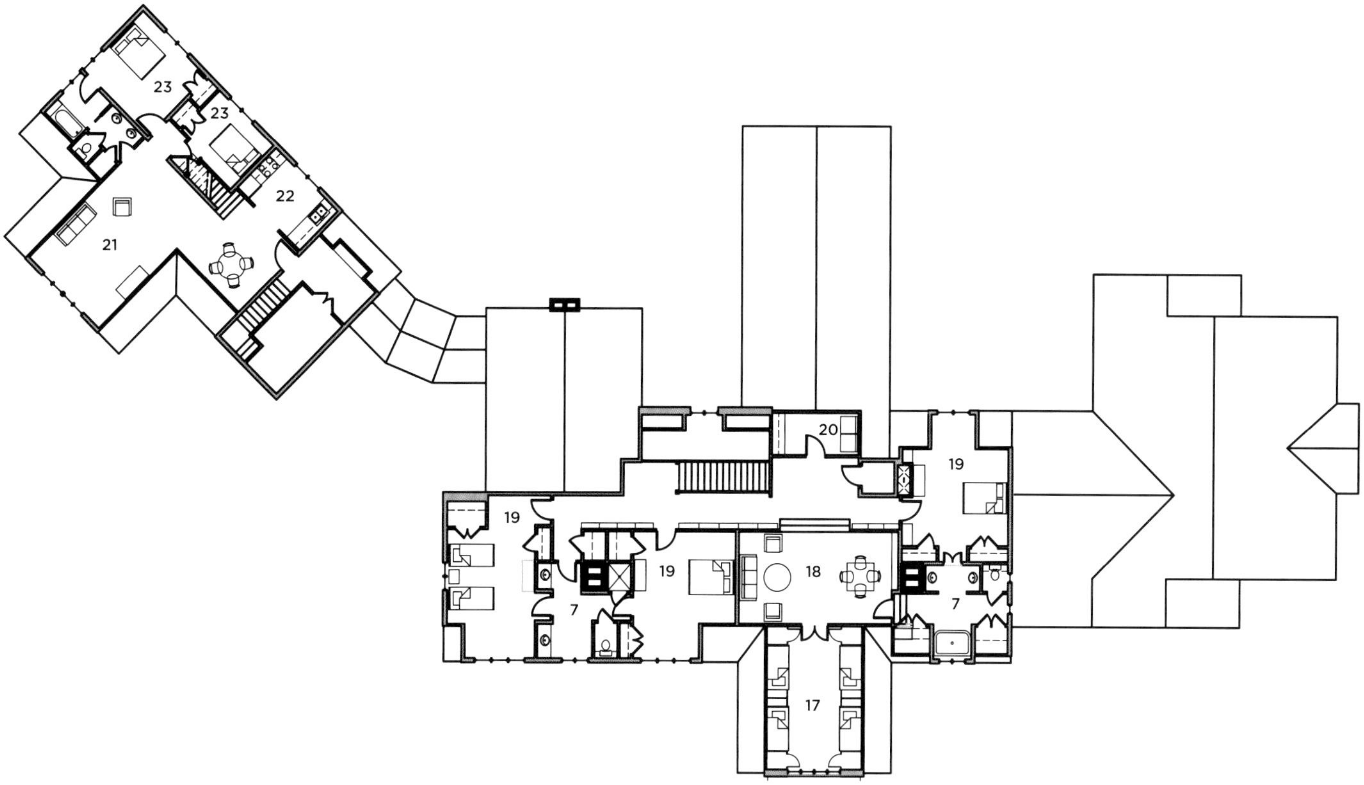

Upper level floor plan

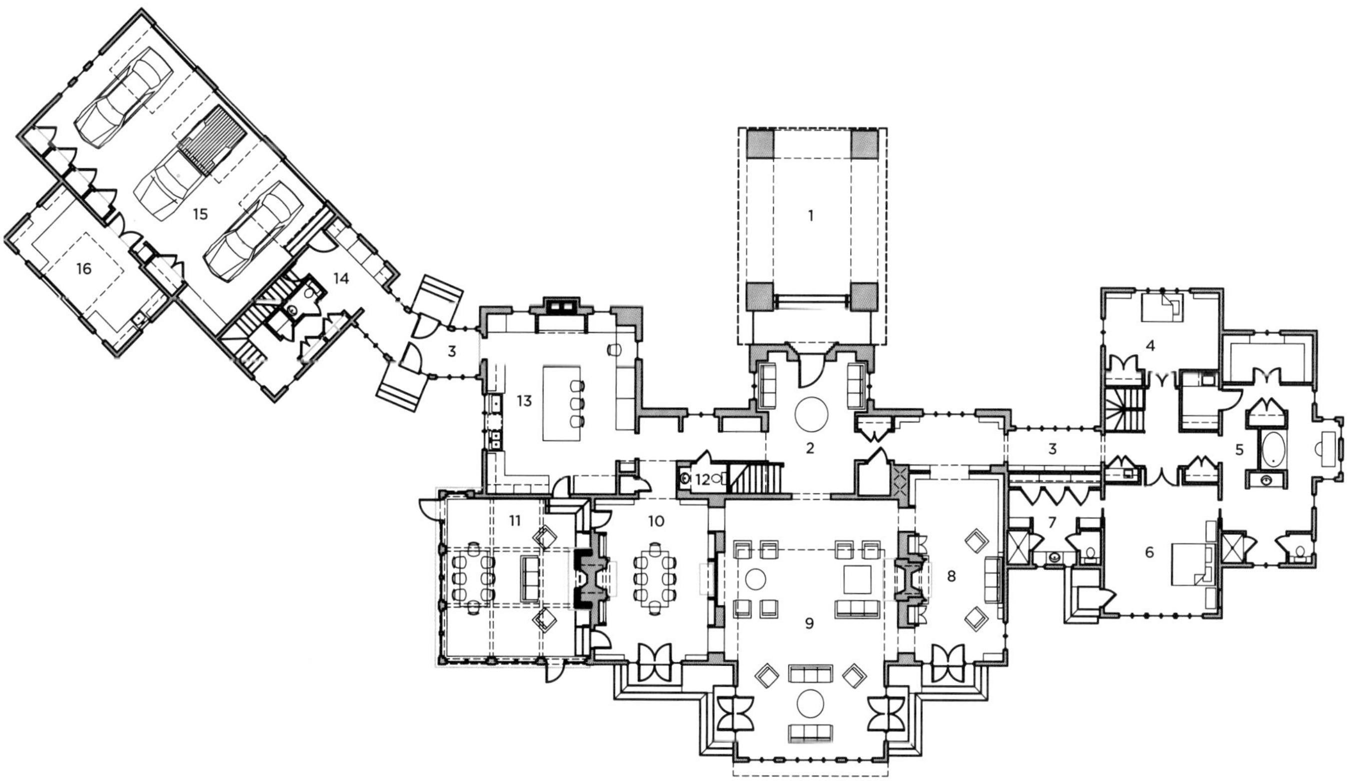

Main level floor plan

1. Entry portico
2. Entry foyer
3. Breezeway
4. Private sitting area
5. Primary bathroom
6. Primary bedroom
7. Bathroom
8. Library
9. Formal living room
10. Dining room
11. Screened porch
12. Powder room
13. Kitchen
14. Mud room
15. Garage
16. Workshop
17. Bunk room
18. Game room
19. Bedroom
20. Laundry room
21. Guest living room
22. Kitchenette
23. Guest bedrooms

SANIEE ARCHITECTS

"We believe the best architecture is context-driven, creating places rather than mere objects."

Mahdad Saniee, founder of Saniee Architects in Greenwich, Connecticut, studied Architecture at the University of Edinburgh, receiving his Master's Degree in 1983. He worked with Simpson & Brown in Edinburgh, contributing to projects recognized in the History of Scottish Architecture. In 1985, he moved to the United States, joining Centerbrook Architects. In 1995, he established his firm. Mr. Saniee's work has garnered over fifty awards and has been featured in prestigious publications. He has been named among the top ten residential architects, and his firm is among the top eight in Connecticut. Additionally, Mahdad has served as a visiting critic at the University of Hartford School of Architecture and on the boards of various architectural organizations. With a small team of just four members, his projects have reached across the US and internationally to the Far and Middle East.

Mahdad Saniee, Gründer von Saniee Architects in Greenwich, Connecticut, studierte Architektur an der Universität Edinburgh und erhielt seinen Master-Abschluss im Jahr 1983. Er arbeitete bei Simpson & Brown in Edinburgh und trug zu Projekten bei, die in der Geschichte der schottischen Architektur Anerkennung fanden. 1985 zog er in die Vereinigten Staaten und trat den Centerbrook Architects bei. 1995 gründete er sein eigenes Büro. Die Arbeit von Herrn Saniee hat über fünfzig Auszeichnungen erhalten und wurde in renommierten Publikationen vorgestellt. Er wurde unter die zehn besten Wohnarchitekten gewählt, und sein Büro gehört zu den acht besten in Connecticut. Darüber hinaus war Mahdad Gastkritiker an der University of Hartford School of Architecture und Mitglied in den Vorständen verschiedener architektonischer Organisationen. Mit einem kleinen Team von nur vier Mitgliedern haben seine Projekte die USA und international den Nahen und Mittleren Osten erreicht.

Mahdad Saniee, fondateur de Saniee Architects à Greenwich, Connecticut, a étudié l'architecture à l'Université d'Édimbourg, obtenant son diplôme de maîtrise en 1983. Il a travaillé avec Simpson & Brown à Édimbourg, contribuant à des projets reconnus dans l'histoire de l'architecture écossaise. En 1985, il a déménagé aux États-Unis, rejoignant Centerbrook Architects. En 1995, il a fondé son cabinet. Le travail de M. Saniee a remporté plus de cinquante récompenses et a été présenté dans des publications prestigieuses. Il a été nommé parmi les dix meilleurs architectes résidentiels, et son cabinet figure parmi les huit meilleurs du Connecticut. De plus, Mahdad a été critique invité à l'École d'architecture de l'Université de Hartford et a siégé aux conseils d'administration de diverses organisations architecturales. Avec une petite équipe de seulement quatre membres, ses projets ont atteint les États-Unis et, à l'international, le Moyen-Orient et l'Extrême-Orient.

Mahdad Saniee, fundador de Saniee Architects en Greenwich, Connecticut, estudió Arquitectura en la Universidad de Edimburgo, obteniendo su Maestría en 1983. Trabajó con Simpson & Brown en Edimburgo, contribuyendo a proyectos reconocidos en la Historia de la Arquitectura Escocesa. En 1985, se mudó a los Estados Unidos, uniéndose a Centerbrook Architects. En 1995, estableció su propia firma. El trabajo del Sr. Saniee ha recibido más de cincuenta premios y ha sido destacado en prestigiosas publicaciones. Ha sido nombrado entre los diez mejores arquitectos residenciales, y su firma está entre las ocho mejores de Connecticut. Además, Mahdad ha servido como crítico invitado en la Escuela de Arquitectura de la Universidad de Hartford y en las juntas de varias organizaciones arquitectónicas. Con un pequeño equipo de solo cuatro miembros, sus proyectos han alcanzado todo Estados Unidos y a nivel internacional hasta el Lejano y Medio Oriente.

sanieearchitects.com

LION HOUSE

TUDOR HOUSE

LION HOUSE

Greenwich, Connecticut, United States // Lot area: 27,000 sq ft; building area: 4,500 sq ft

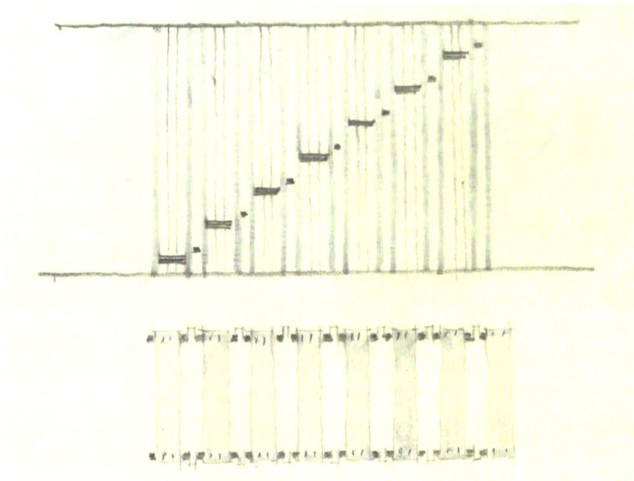

Staircase plan view and elevation

This home draws inspiration from classic New England farmhouses, celebrated for their simplicity and functionality. Its open floor plan seamlessly integrates indoor and outdoor spaces, while the understated exterior utilizes locally sourced materials for visual appeal. Despite limited space in a semi-suburban setting, the property extends to a nature conservancy land. Sustainability is prioritized through locally sourced materials, high-efficiency techniques, and strategic skylights. Inside the house, the centerpiece is the staircase, which serves as both a functional element and a striking architectural feature. Through strategic design choices, such as alternating vertical posts and protruding treads, the staircase creates a captivating visual rhythm, enhancing the overall aesthetic. This exemplifies how careful attention to detail enhances appeal and accessibility, ensuring that quality craftsmanship is accessible to all.

Dieses Haus lässt sich von klassischen Bauernhäusern in Neuengland inspirieren, die für ihre Einfachheit und Funktionalität geschätzt werden. Der offene Grundriss integriert nahtlos Innen- und Außenräume, während das dezente Äußere lokal bezogene Materialien für visuelle Attraktivität nutzt. Trotz begrenztem Platz in einer halbstädtischen Umgebung erstreckt sich das Grundstück auf ein Naturschutzgebiet. Nachhaltigkeit wird durch lokal bezogene Materialien, hocheffiziente Techniken und strategische Oberlichter priorisiert. Im Inneren des Hauses ist das Herzstück die Treppe, die sowohl ein funktionales Element als auch ein markantes architektonisches Merkmal darstellt. Durch strategische Designentscheidungen, wie das Abwechseln von vertikalen Pfosten und hervorstehenden Stufen, erzeugt die Treppe einen fesselnden visuellen Rhythmus, der die Gesamtaesthetik verbessert. Dies zeigt, wie sorgfältige Detailgenauigkeit den Reiz und die Zugänglichkeit verbessert und sicherstellt, dass qualitativ hochwertige Handwerkskunst für alle zugänglich ist.

Cette maison s'inspire des fermes classiques de la Nouvelle-Angleterre, célébrées pour leur simplicité et leur fonctionnalité. Son plan ouvert intègre parfaitement les espaces intérieurs et extérieurs, tandis que l'extérieur sobre utilise des matériaux locaux pour un attrait visuel. Malgré l'espace limité dans un cadre semi-suburbain, la propriété s'étend jusqu'à une réserve naturelle. La durabilité est priorisée grâce à des matériaux locaux, des techniques à haute efficacité et des puits de lumière stratégiques. À l'intérieur de la maison, la pièce maîtresse est l'escalier, qui sert à la fois d'élément fonctionnel et de caractéristique architecturale saisissante. Grâce à des choix de conception stratégiques, tels que des poteaux verticaux alternés et des marches saillantes, l'escalier crée un rythme visuel captivant, améliorant l'esthétique générale. Cela illustre comment une attention minutieuse aux détails améliore l'attrait et l'accessibilité, garantissant que l'artisanat de qualité est accessible à tous.

Esta casa se inspira en las clásicas casas de campo de Nueva Inglaterra, celebradas por su simplicidad y funcionalidad. Su plano de planta abierto integra perfectamente los espacios interiores y exteriores, mientras que el exterior discreto utiliza materiales locales para un atractivo visual. A pesar del espacio limitado en un entorno semi-suburbano, la propiedad se extiende hasta una reserva natural. La sostenibilidad se prioriza a través de materiales locales, técnicas de alta eficiencia y tragaluces estratégicos. Dentro de la casa, la pieza central es la escalera, que sirve tanto como un elemento funcional como una característica arquitectónica llamativa. A través de decisiones de diseño estratégicas, como postes verticales alternos y peldaños salientes, la escalera crea un ritmo visual cautivador, mejorando la estética general. Esto ejemplifica cómo la atención cuidadosa al detalle mejora el atractivo y la accesibilidad, asegurando que la calidad artesanal sea accesible para todos.

TUDOR HOUSE

Greenwich, Connecticut, United States // Lot area: 53,000 sq ft; building area: 7,200 sq ft

This project rehabilitates a late 19th-century Tudor house by Henry C. Pelton. Preserving its original residential character was vital. This project challenges misconceptions about repurposing historic houses, prioritizing preservation while meeting strict guidelines. The design expanded the home's footprint, utilizing the attic for new interior spaces and repurposing previously unused outdoor areas. Interior restoration prioritized preserving original woodwork and features while enhancing insulation and HVAC systems without altering original structures. Exterior upgrades involved replacing roofing and fenestration with matching materials, restoring brickwork and siding, and repairing trim. The remodel enhances the home's durability and sustainability while honoring its original craftsmanship.

Dieses Projekt rehabilitiert ein spätviktorianisches Tudor-Haus von Henry C. Pelton aus dem 19. Jahrhundert. Es war entscheidend, seinen ursprünglichen Wohncharakter zu bewahren. Dieses Projekt stellt Missverständnisse über die Umnutzung historischer Häuser in Frage, indem es den Erhalt priorisiert und gleichzeitig strikte Richtlinien einhält. Das Design erweiterte die Grundfläche des Hauses, indem zes den Dachboden für neue Innenräume nutzte und zuvor ungenutzte Außenbereiche umfunktionierte. Die Innenrestaurierung priorisierte die Erhaltung der originalen Holzarbeiten und Ausstattungen, während die Isolierung und die HLK-Systeme verbessert wurden, ohne die ursprünglichen Strukturen zu verändern. Zu den äußeren Verbesserungen gehörten der Austausch von Dach und Fenstern mit passenden Materialien, die Restaurierung von Mauerwerk und Verkleidung sowie die Reparatur von Zierleisten. Die Umgestaltung verbessert die Haltbarkeit und Nachhaltigkeit des Hauses, während das ursprüngliche Handwerk gewürdigt wird.

Ce projet réhabilite une maison Tudor de la fin du XIXe siècle par Henry C. Pelton. Préserver son caractère résidentiel d'origine était essentiel. Ce projet remet en question les idées reçues sur la réutilisation des maisons historiques, en donnant la priorité à la préservation tout en respectant des directives strictes. Le design a élargi l'empreinte de la maison, utilisant le grenier pour de nouveaux espaces intérieurs et réaffectant des espaces extérieurs auparavant inutilisés. La restauration intérieure a priorisé la préservation du bois et des caractéristiques d'origine tout en améliorant l'isolation et les systèmes HVAC sans altérer les structures d'origine. Les améliorations extérieures ont inclus le remplacement de la toiture et des fenêtres avec des matériaux assortis, la restauration de la maçonnerie et du bardage, et la réparation des moulures. La rénovation améliore la durabilité et la durabilité de la maison tout en honorant son savoir-faire original.

Este proyecto rehabilita una casa Tudor de finales del siglo XIX diseñada por Henry C. Pelton. Preservar su carácter residencial original era vital. Este proyecto desafía las ideas erróneas sobre la reutilización de casas históricas, priorizando la preservación mientras se cumplen estrictas directrices. El diseño amplió la huella de la casa, utilizando el ático para nuevos espacios interiores y reutilizando áreas exteriores previamente no utilizadas. La restauración interior priorizó la preservación de la carpintería y características originales, al tiempo que mejoraba el aislamiento y los sistemas HVAC sin alterar las estructuras originales. Las mejoras exteriores incluyeron la sustitución del techo y las ventanas con materiales a juego, la restauración de la mampostería y el revestimiento, y la reparación de las molduras. La remodelación mejora la durabilidad y sostenibilidad de la casa, al tiempo que honra su artesanía original.

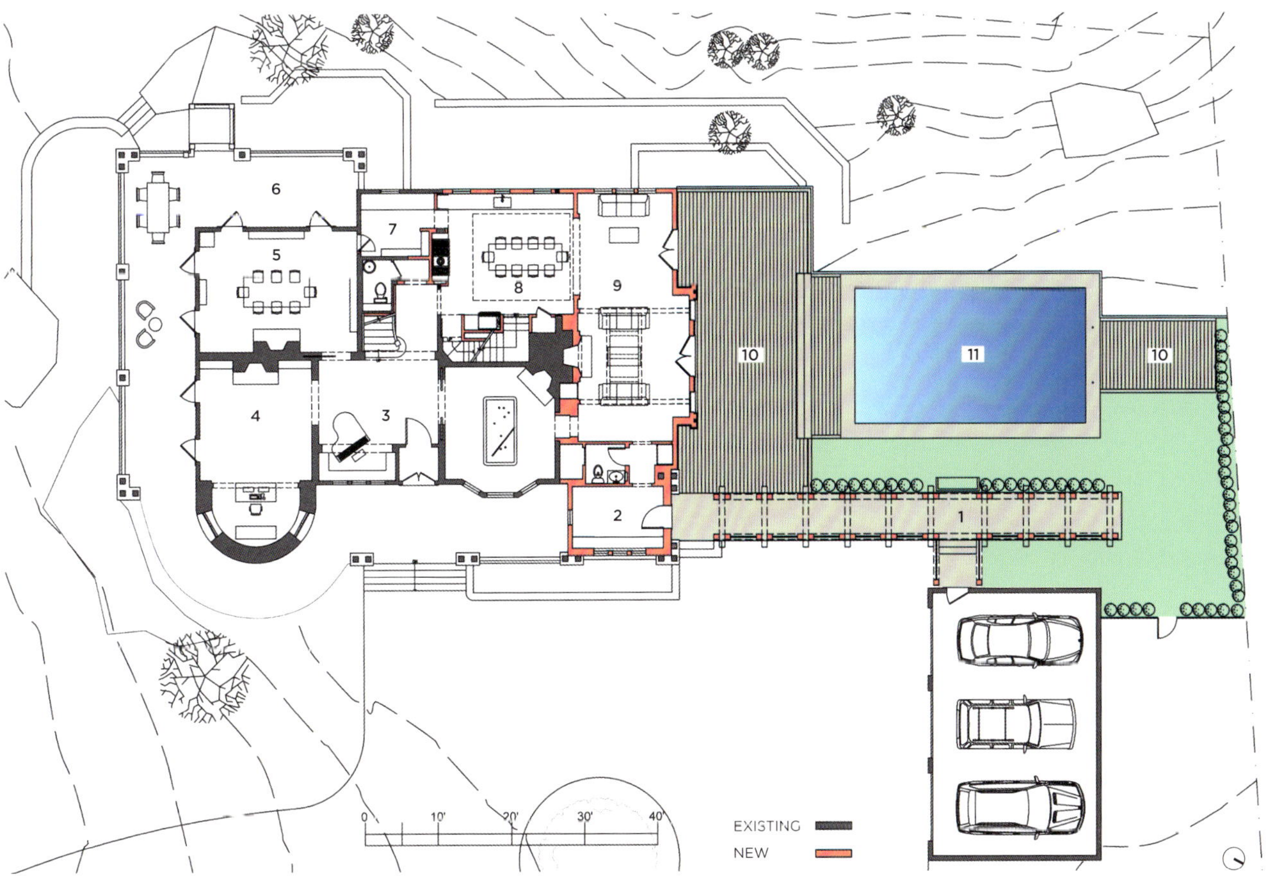

1. Breezeway
2. Mud room
3. Entry
4. Office
5. Library/dining area
6. Screen porch
7. Pantry
8. Kitchen
9. Family room
10. Deck
11. Pool

Ground level floor plan

seventy2architects

"Two minds, one vision. We merge passion with precision to bring architectural dreams to life."

Located an hour north of New York City, seventy2architects has had an office in downtown Danbury, Connecticut, since 2011. This husband-and-wife architect team shares a passion for design and innovation. With a harmonious blend of creativity and technical proficiency, a honed eye for detail, and a commitment to sustainability, they strive to create residences that complement the natural landscape and minimize environmental impact. Inspired by the region's lakes and rolling hills, their designs feature sleek lines, innovative materials, and expansive glass elements blurring indoor-outdoor boundaries. Collaborating closely with clients, they tailor each project to reflect individual tastes, ensuring a fusion of modern aesthetics and functional elegance. Maura and Emmanuel Juan have reshaped lakeside living in Connecticut through their dedication to architectural innovation.

Eine Stunde nördlich von New York City betreibt seventy2architects seit 2011 ein Büro in der Innenstadt von Danbury, Connecticut. Das Architektenteam, ein Ehepaar, teilt die Leidenschaft für Design und Innovation. Mit einer Kombination aus Kreativität, technischer Präzision, einem geschulten Auge fürs Detail und einem Engagement für Nachhaltigkeit entwerfen sie Wohnhäuser, die sich in die natürliche Landschaft einfügen und den ökologischen Fußabdruck minimieren. Inspiriert von den Seen und Hügeln der Region zeichnen sich ihre Entwürfe durch klare Linien, innovative Materialien und großflächige Glaselemente aus, die Innen- und Außenraum verschmelzen lassen. In enger Zusammenarbeit mit ihren Kunden passen sie jedes Projekt an individuelle Vorlieben an und schaffen so eine Symbiose aus modernem Design und Funktionalität. Maura und Emmanuel Juan haben das Wohnen am See in Connecticut neu definiert.

Situé à une heure au nord de New York, seventy2architects a un bureau au centre-ville de Danbury, dans le Connecticut, depuis 2011. Ce duo d'architectes, mari et femme, partage une passion pour le design et l'innovation. Grâce à un mélange harmonieux de créativité, maîtrise technique, sens du détail et engagement pour la durabilité, ils conçoivent des résidences qui complètent le paysage naturel en réduisant l'impact environnemental. Inspirés par les lacs et les collines de la région, leurs designs se distinguent par des lignes épurées, des matériaux innovants et de grandes surfaces vitrées, estompant les frontières entre intérieur et extérieur. En collaborant étroitement avec leurs clients, ils adaptent chaque projet aux goûts individuels, fusionnant esthétique moderne et élégance fonctionnelle. Maura et Emmanuel Juan ont redéfini la vie au bord des lacs dans le Connecticut grâce à leur dévouement à l'innovation architecturale.

Ubicada a una hora al norte de Nueva York, seventy2architects tiene su oficina en el centro de Danbury, Connecticut, desde 2011. Este dúo de arquitectos, un matrimonio, comparte una pasión por el diseño y la innovación. Con una combinación armoniosa de creatividad y destreza técnica, un agudo ojo para los detalles y un compromiso con la sostenibilidad, crean residencias que complementan el paisaje natural y minimizan el impacto ambiental. Inspirándose en los lagos y colinas onduladas de la región, sus diseños presentan líneas elegantes, materiales innovadores y amplios elementos de cristal que desdibujan los límites entre el interior y el exterior. Al colaborar estrechamente con sus clientes, personalizan cada proyecto para reflejar los gustos individuales, logrando una fusión de estética moderna y elegancia funcional. Maura y Emmanuel Juan han redefinido la vida junto al lago en Connecticut a través de su dedicación a la innovación arquitectónica.

seventy2architects | seventy2architects.com

IRON GREY HOUSE

SHERMAN LAKE HOUSE

IRON GREY HOUSE

Fairfield County, Connecticut, United States // Lot area: 9,310 sq ft; building area: 3,421 sq ft

This unique California-style house layout is celebrated in Fairfield County, Connecticut, and is embraced by a 150-foot expansive waterfront. The house, with its classic gable roof and sophisticated Iron Grey Artisan clapboard siding, exudes sophistication and modernity. As the sun sets, the large windows at the rear come live, casting a warm glow that transforms the house's aesthetic. These expansive windows frame breathtaking views of the shimmering lake from the interior and flood the rooms with natural light. The full-width rear deck extends gracefully along the water's edge, offering an idyllic setting for relaxing in the hot tub or enjoying meals with family and friends. From dawn till dusk, this home is where timeless design and natural beauty intertwine to create an unparalleled retreat.

Dieses einzigartige Haus im kalifornischen Stil wird in Fairfield County, Connecticut, gefeiert und erstreckt sich entlang eines 150 Fuß breiten Uferbereichs. Mit seinem klassischen Satteldach und der eleganten Iron Grey Artisan-Fassadenverkleidung strahlt das Haus sowohl Raffinesse als auch Modernität aus. Bei Sonnenuntergang erwecken die großen Fenster auf der Rückseite das Haus zum Leben und tauchen es in ein warmes Licht, das die Ästhetik des Hauses verwandelt. Diese großzügigen Fenster rahmen atemberaubende Ausblicke auf den funkelnden See ein und fluten die Räume mit natürlichem Licht. Die durchgehende Terrasse auf der Rückseite erstreckt sich anmutig entlang des Wassers und bietet einen idyllischen Rahmen, um im Whirlpool zu entspannen oder Mahlzeiten mit Familie und Freunden zu genießen. Von Sonnenaufgang bis Sonnenuntergang verschmelzen in diesem Zuhause zeitloses Design und natürliche Schönheit zu einem unvergleichlichen Rückzugsort.

West elevation

East elevation

Building section

Site plan

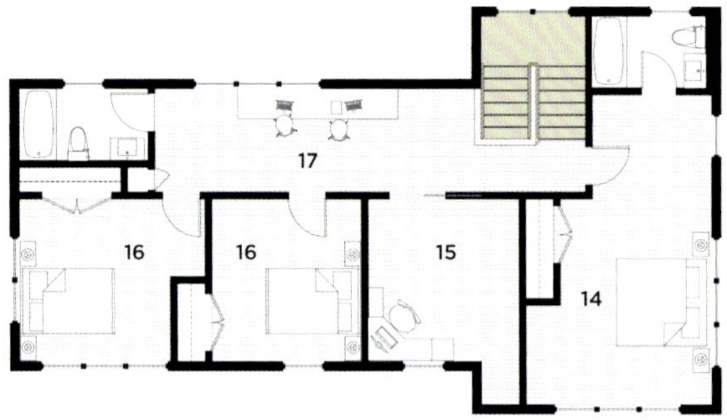

Second level floor plan

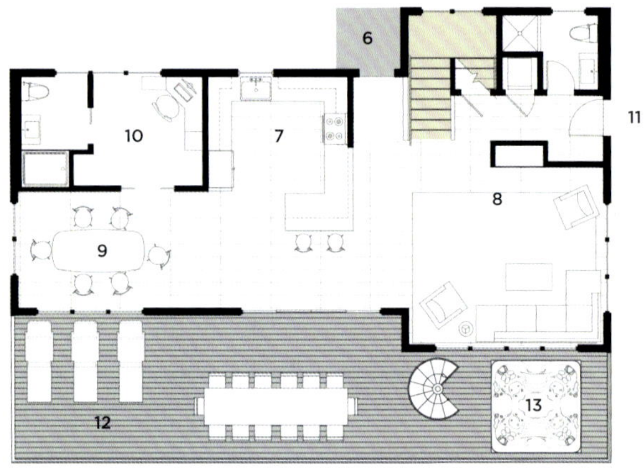

First level floor plan

Ce plan de maison unique de style californien est célébré dans le comté de Fairfield, Connecticut, et est entouré d'une vaste façade sur l'eau de 150 pieds. La maison, avec son toit à pignon classique et son revêtement en lames de bois Iron Grey Artisan sophistiqué, dégage sophistication et modernité. Au coucher du soleil, les grandes fenêtres à l'arrière prennent vie, diffusant une lueur chaleureuse qui transforme l'esthétique de la maison. Ces fenêtres généreuses offrent des vues époustouflantes sur le lac scintillant depuis l'intérieur et inondent les pièces de lumière naturelle. La terrasse arrière, qui s'étend sur toute la largeur de la maison, se prolonge élégamment le long du bord de l'eau, offrant un cadre idyllique pour se détendre dans le jacuzzi ou partager des repas en famille et entre amis. Du lever au coucher du soleil, cette maison est un lieu où le design intemporel et la beauté naturelle se mêlent pour créer un refuge inégalé.

Este diseño de casa único al estilo californiano es aclamado en el condado de Fairfield, Connecticut, y está rodeado por una amplia fachada frente al agua de 150 pies. La casa, con su techo a dos aguas clásico y su revestimiento de listones de madera Iron Grey Artisan sofisticado, emana sofisticación y modernidad. Al atardecer, las grandes ventanas en la parte trasera cobran vida, proyectando un resplandor cálido que transforma la estética de la casa. Estas amplias ventanas enmarcan vistas impresionantes del lago resplandeciente desde el interior y llenan las habitaciones de luz natural. La terraza trasera de toda la anchura se extiende elegantemente a lo largo del borde del agua, ofreciendo un entorno idílico para relajarse en el jacuzzi o disfrutar de comidas con familiares y amigos. Desde el amanecer hasta el anochecer, esta casa es un lugar donde el diseño atemporal y la belleza natural se entrelazan para crear un retiro incomparable.

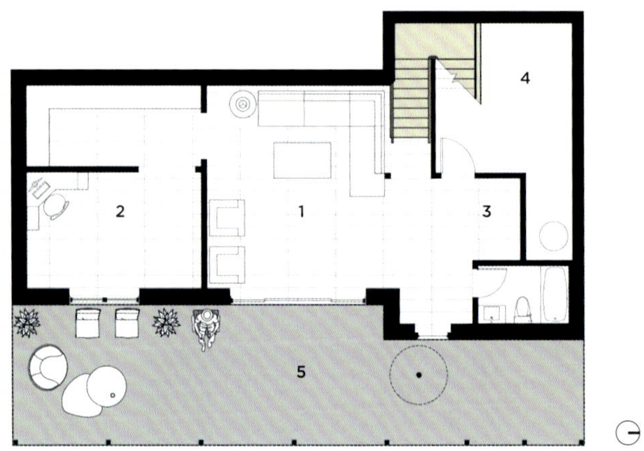

Lower level floor plan

1. Kids' playroom
2. Office
3. Exercise area
4. Mechanical room
5. Patio
6. Entry
7. Kitchen
8. Living area
9. Dining area
10. Office
11. Side entry
12. Deck
13. Hot tub
14. Primary bedroom
15. Office/den
16. Bedroom
17. Loft play area

SHERMAN LAKE HOUSE

Sherman, Connecticut, United States // Lot area: 66,788 sq ft; building area: 9,600 sq ft

Situated atop a gentle hill overlooking the serene expanse of a picturesque lake, this three-story contemporary house embodies the perfect fusion of modern design and natural beauty. Its thoughtful façade features white nickel gap siding, accentuated by vertical mahogany boards that add warmth, depth, and texture to the exterior. The lofty great room and kitchen area open onto a spacious rear terrace, providing an ideal setting for outdoor gatherings, dining, and relaxation amidst the beauty of the landscape. At the rear of the house, expansive windows offer uninterrupted views of the serene waters beyond, inviting the beauty of nature to become an integral part of everyday life. The Sherman Lake House harmoniously integrates with its surroundings, providing a haven of tranquility and luxury for its homeowners to immerse themselves in the beauty of nature.

Auf einem sanften Hügel gelegen, der über die ruhige Weite eines malerischen Sees blickt, verkörpert dieses dreigeschossige moderne Haus die perfekte Fusion aus zeitgemäßem Design und natürlicher Schönheit. Die durchdachte Fassade zeigt weiße Nickel-Gap-Verkleidung, die durch vertikale Mahagonibretter ergänzt wird, die Wärme, Tiefe und Textur verleihen. Der großzügige Wohn- und Küchenbereich öffnet sich zu einer geräumigen Terrasse im hinteren Bereich, die ideal für Outdoor-Geselligkeit, Mahlzeiten und Entspannung inmitten der Landschaft ist. Auf der Rückseite des Hauses bieten weitläufige Fenster ungehinderte Ausblicke auf das ruhige Wasser und laden die Schönheit der Natur ein, ein integraler Bestandteil des Alltags zu werden. Das Sherman Lake House integriert sich harmonisch in seine Umgebung und bietet den Bewohnern einen Rückzugsort der Ruhe und des Luxus, um sich in der Schönheit der Natur zu vertiefen.

Site plan

South elevation

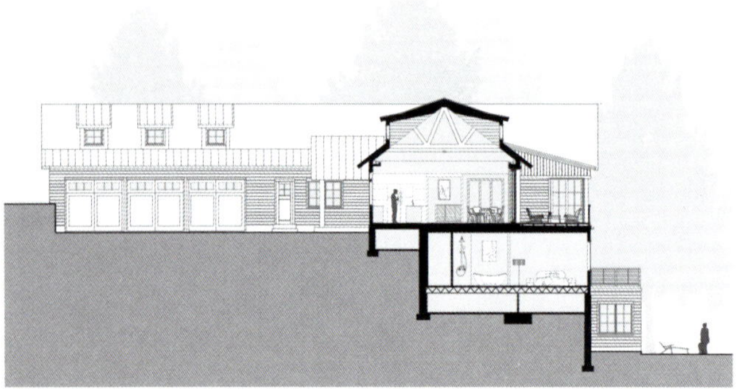

Building section

Située au sommet d'une colline douce surplombant l'étendue sereine d'un lac pittoresque, cette maison contemporaine de trois étages incarne la fusion parfaite entre design moderne et beauté naturelle. Sa façade soignée est ornée de revêtements en nickel blanc, accentués par des panneaux en acajou verticaux qui ajoutent chaleur, profondeur et texture à l'extérieur. Le grand salon lumineux et la cuisine s'ouvrent sur une terrasse arrière spacieuse, offrant un cadre idéal pour des rassemblements en extérieur, des repas et de la détente au milieu de la beauté du paysage. À l'arrière de la maison, de grandes fenêtres offrent des vues ininterrompues sur les eaux sereines au-delà, invitant la beauté de la nature à devenir une partie intégrante de la vie quotidienne. La Sherman Lake House s'intègre harmonieusement dans son environnement, offrant un havre de tranquillité et de luxe pour ses propriétaires afin qu'ils puissent se plonger dans la beauté de la nature.

Situada en la cima de una suave colina con vistas a la serena extensión de un lago pintoresco, esta casa contemporánea de tres pisos encarna la fusión perfecta entre el diseño moderno y la belleza natural. Su fachada cuidada presenta revestimientos de níquel blanco, acentuados por paneles verticales de caoba que añaden calidez, profundidad y textura al exterior. El amplio salón y la cocina se abren a una espaciosa terraza trasera, ofreciendo un entorno ideal para reuniones al aire libre, comidas y relajación en medio de la belleza del paisaje. En la parte trasera de la casa, amplias ventanas ofrecen vistas ininterrumpidas de las aguas serenas, invitando a la belleza de la naturaleza a convertirse en una parte integral de la vida cotidiana. La Sherman Lake House se integra armoniosamente con su entorno, proporcionando un refugio de tranquilidad y lujo para que sus propietarios se sumerjan en la belleza de la naturaleza.

Main level floor plan

Kids' level floor plan

Lake level floor plan

1. Den/play room
2. Exercise room
3. Wine room
4. Storage room
5. Mechanical closet
6. Elevator
7. Family room
8. Bedroom
9. Terrace/roof deck
10. Laundry room
11. Entry
12. Kitchen
13. Living area
14. Dining area
15. Covered terrace
16. Den/office
17. Primary bedroom
18. Primary bathroom
19. His closet
20. Her closet
21. Mud room
22. Storage/dog bath
23. Garage

PAVLIDES STUDIO

"We design functional and timeless spaces by blending innovation and elegance."

Pavlides Studio is a full-service residential design firm founded in 2003 by Stephanie Allen Pavlides and Lefteris Pavlides on the belief that good design has the power to transform lives. We craft spaces that reflect our clients' unique identities while thoughtfully planning for life's evolving needs. Through a consistent visual language, we tell each client's signature story, seamlessly integrating exterior and interior elements. Our collaborative approach, working with skilled craftspeople and fostering long-term relationships with clients and builders, allows us to address practical challenges with grace. In our intimate, small-office environment, the entire team is deeply involved in every design detail, ensuring balanced solutions tailored to each project. Rooted in architectural problem-solving, we honor history while embracing innovative ways of living in today's modern world.

Pavlides Studio ist ein umfassendes Wohn-Designbüro, das 2003 von Stephanie Allen Pavlides und Lefteris Pavlides gegründet wurde, mit der Überzeugung, dass gutes Design Leben verändern kann. Wir gestalten Räume, die die einzigartigen Identitäten unserer Kunden widerspiegeln und die sich entwickelnden Bedürfnisse des Lebens berücksichtigen. Durch eine konsistente visuelle Sprache erzählen wir die Geschichte jedes Kunden und integrieren nahtlos Außen- und Innenelemente. Unser kollaborativer Ansatz mit qualifizierten Handwerkern und langfristigen Beziehungen zu Kunden und Bauherren ermöglicht es uns, praktische Herausforderungen elegant zu meistern. In unserem kleinen Büro ist das gesamte Team in jedes Detail des Designs involviert, um ausgewogene Lösungen zu gewährleisten, die auf jedes Projekt zugeschnitten sind. Wir ehren die Geschichte und umarmen gleichzeitig innovative Lebensweisen in der modernen Welt.

Pavlides Studio est un cabinet de design résidentiel fondé en 2003 par Stephanie Allen Pavlides et Lefteris Pavlides, convaincu que le bon design peut transformer des vies. Nous créons des espaces reflétant l'identité unique de nos clients tout en anticipant leurs besoins évolutifs. Grâce à un langage visuel cohérent, nous intégrons harmonieusement les éléments extérieurs et intérieurs. Notre approche collaborative, impliquant des artisans qualifiés et favorisant des relations à long terme, nous permet de relever les défis pratiques avec élégance. Dans notre environnement de bureau intime, l'équipe s'investit dans chaque détail du design, assurant des solutions équilibrées pour chaque projet. Ancrés dans la résolution architecturale, nous honorons l'histoire tout en adoptant des modes de vie innovants dans le monde moderne.

Pavlides Studio es un estudio de diseño residencial fundado en 2003 por Stephanie Allen Pavlides y Lefteris Pavlides, con la creencia de que un buen diseño transforma vidas. Creamos espacios que reflejan las identidades únicas de nuestros clientes y planificamos sus necesidades evolutivas. Con un lenguaje visual coherente, contamos la historia distintiva de cada cliente, integrando elementos exteriores e interiores. Nuestro enfoque colaborativo, al trabajar con artesanos calificados y fomentar relaciones a largo plazo con clientes y constructores, nos permite abordar desafíos prácticos con destreza. En el entorno íntimo de nuestra oficina, todo el equipo se involucra en cada detalle del diseño, asegurando soluciones equilibradas adaptadas a cada proyecto. Enraizados en la resolución arquitectónica de problemas, honramos la historia mientras adoptamos formas innovadoras de vivir en el mundo moderno.

pavlidesstudio

pavlidesstudio.com

BERKSHIRES LEGACY HOME

FAMILY FARMHOUSE

BERKSHIRES LEGACY HOME

New Marlborough, Massachusetts, United States // Lot area: 9 acres; building area: 15,200 sq ft

This residence harmoniously melds intimate living with grand entertaining, seamlessly integrating with its lakeside setting. Floor-length windows in the foyer frame stunning views, establishing a design that blurs indoor-outdoor boundaries. A pocket door conceals the guest wing, while the cantilevered living room, perched on a peninsula, offers panoramic vistas through windows on three sides. Expansive sliding doors in the kitchen lead to a deck, complementing an oval dining table that seats 20 yet feels cozy for two. The main level features essential spaces, while guest accommodations and entertainment areas are tucked below and in the annex. A minimalist palette highlights nature, with wood-paneled ceilings and skylights flooding the interior with light. The walk-out green roof and wall-length sliding doors further dissolve the divide between indoors and out, creating a home that is both sanctuary and gathering space.

Diese Residenz verbindet intimes Wohnen mit großartiger Unterhaltung und integriert sich nahtlos in die Uferlandschaft. Bodentiefe Fenster im Foyer bieten atemberaubende Ausblicke und schaffen ein Design, das die Grenzen zwischen drinnen und draußen verwischt. Eine Schiebetür verbirgt den Gäste-Trakt, während das auskragende Wohnzimmer auf einer Halbinsel durch Fenster auf drei Seiten Panoramablicke bietet. Großzügige Schiebetüren in der Küche führen zu einer Terrasse, die einen ovalen Esstisch ergänzt, der Platz für 20 Personen bietet, sich jedoch gemütlich für zwei anfühlt. Die Hauptebene verfügt über wesentliche Räume, während die Gästeunterkünfte und Unterhaltungsbereiche im Untergeschoss und im Anbau untergebracht sind. Eine minimalistische Farbpalette hebt die Natur hervor, mit holzverkleideten Decken und Oberlichtern, die den Innenraum erhellen. Das begehbare Gründach und wandlange Schiebetüren lösen die Trennung zwischen drinnen und draußen auf und schaffen ein Zuhause, das Rückzugsort und Versammlungsraum ist.

Cette résidence harmonise un mode de vie intime avec de vastes possibilités d'accueil, s'intégrant parfaitement dans son cadre lacustre. Les fenêtres du sol au plafond dans le hall d'entrée offrent des vues imprenables, brouillant les frontières entre intérieur et extérieur. Une porte à galandage dissimule l'aile des invités, tandis que le salon en porte à faux, perché sur une péninsule, offre des panoramas à travers des fenêtres sur trois côtés. De grandes portes-fenêtres dans la cuisine mènent à une terrasse, complétant une table à manger ovale pour 20 personnes, tout en restant accueillante pour deux. Le niveau principal comprend les espaces essentiels, tandis que les chambres d'amis et les zones de divertissement sont en dessous et dans l'annexe. Une palette minimaliste met en valeur la nature, avec des plafonds lambrissés et des lucarnes inondant l'intérieur de lumière. Le toit vert accessible et les portes-fenêtres murales renforcent l'union entre l'intérieur et l'extérieur, créant un foyer qui est à la fois un sanctuaire et un lieu de rassemblement.

Esta residencia armoniza un estilo de vida íntimo con amplias posibilidades de acogida, integrándose perfectamente en su entorno lacustre. Las ventanas de suelo a techo en el vestíbulo ofrecen vistas impresionantes, difuminando los límites entre el interior y el exterior. Una puerta corrediza oculta el ala de huéspedes, mientras que la sala de estar en voladizo, situada en una península, ofrece panorámicas a través de ventanas en tres lados. Grandes puertas de cristal en la cocina conducen a una terraza, complementando una mesa ovalada para 20 personas, que también resulta acogedora para dos. El nivel principal incluye los espacios esenciales, mientras que las habitaciones para huéspedes y las áreas de entretenimiento se encuentran abajo y en el anexo. Una paleta minimalista resalta la naturaleza, con techos de madera y tragaluces que inundan el interior de luz. El techo verde accesible y las puertas acristaladas de pared a pared refuerzan la conexión entre el interior y el exterior, creando un hogar que es tanto un santuario como un lugar de encuentro.

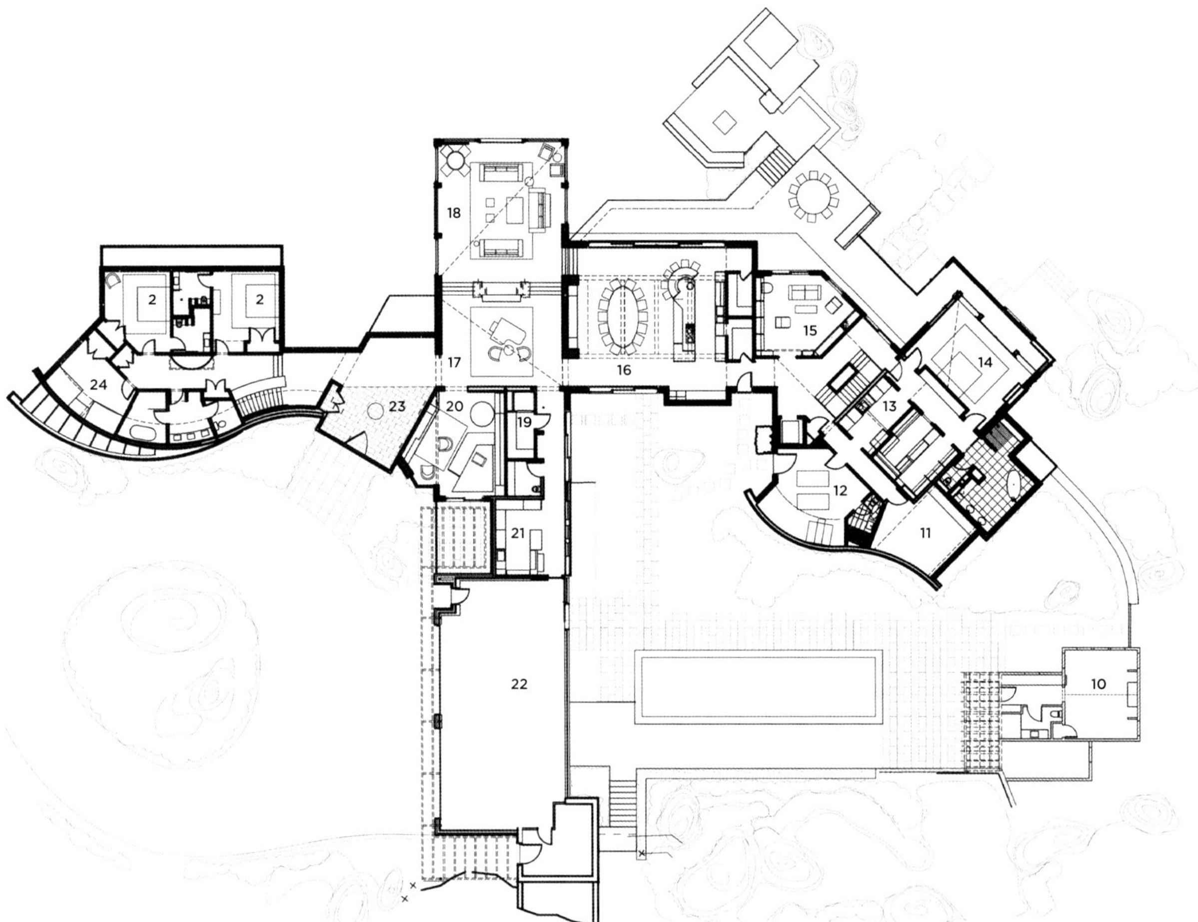

Main level floor plan

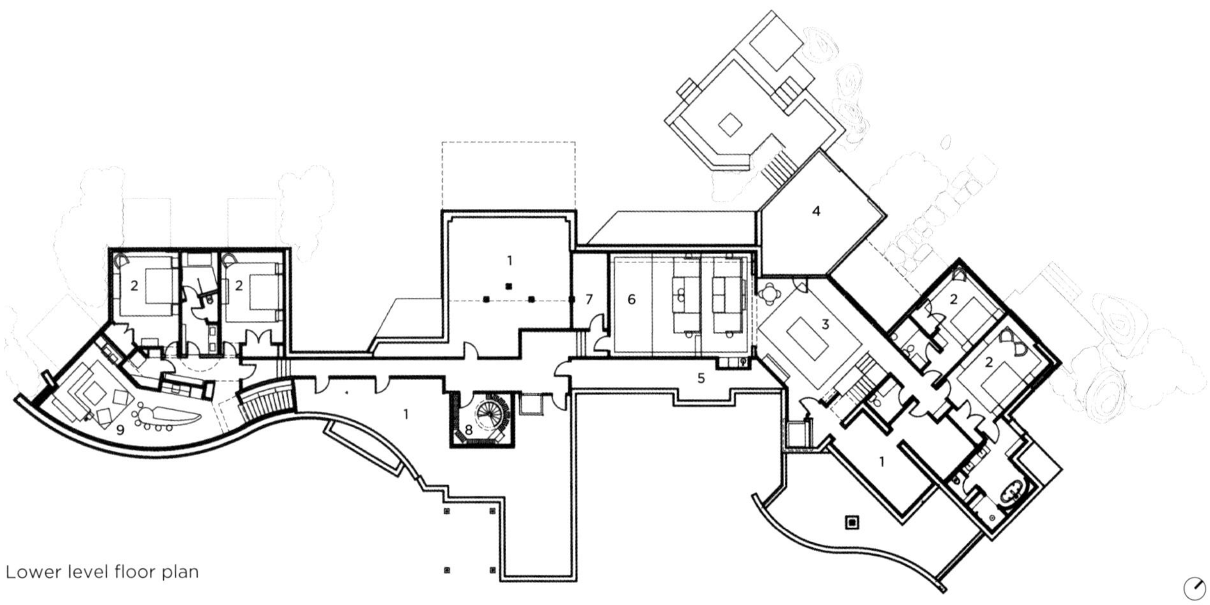

Lower level floor plan

1. Mechanical room
2. Guest bedroom
3. Billiard room
4. Outdoor storage room
5. Equipment
6. Media room
7. Storage
8. Wine cellar
9. Rumpus room
10. Pool house
11. Music room
12. Exercise room
13. Laundry room
14. Primary bedroom
15. Library
16. Kitchen
17. Piano room
18. Living area
19. Utility room
20. Office
21. Mudroom
22. garage
23. Entry
24. Bunk room

FAMILY FARMHOUSE

Tiverton, Rohode Island, United States // Lot area: 59,953 sq ft; building area: 5,748 sq ft

Our renovation and addition to a New England farmhouse embrace vibrant summers while ensuring year-round enjoyment. The barn-inspired addition houses a garage, gardening shed, and airy family room that opens to a patio, seamlessly connecting indoors and out. Above, a serene primary retreat offers privacy. Positioned to preserve mature trees and meadow views, the addition feels timeless. We honored the original proportions while creating views that link interior spaces with nature. Playful dormers and windows continue past renovations. The relocated kitchen improves patio access, encouraging family gatherings. Fir beams, reclaimed materials, and a central fireplace with a cantilevered concrete hearth balance history and modernity. Thoughtful finishes complete this country home, designed for family enjoyment and contemporary living, where memories are made and cherished.

Unsere Renovierung und der Anbau an ein New England Bauernhaus nehmen die lebendigen Sommer auf und sorgen für ganzjährigen Genuss. Der von Scheunen inspirierte Anbau beherbergt eine Garage, einen Gartenraum und ein luftiges Familienzimmer, das sich zu einer Terrasse öffnet und so drinnen und draußen nahtlos verbindet. Oben bietet ein ruhiger Hauptbereich Privatsphäre. Der Anbau ist so positioniert, dass er reife Bäume und Wiesenblicke bewahrt und zeitlos wirkt. Wir haben die ursprünglichen Proportionen geehrt und gleichzeitig Ausblicke geschaffen, die die Innenräume mit der Natur verbinden. Verspielte Gauben und Fenster setzen die früheren Renovierungen fort. Die verlegte Küche verbessert den Zugang zur Terrasse und fördert Familienzusammenkünfte. Fichtenbalken, recycelte Materialien und ein zentraler Kamin mit einem vorgehängten Betonsims bringen Geschichte und Modernität ins Gleichgewicht. Durchdachte Oberflächen vervollständigen dieses Landhaus, das für familiären Genuss und modernes Wohnen entworfen wurde, wo Erinnerungen geschaffen und geschätzt werden.

Notre rénovation et l'extension d'une ferme du New England capturent les étés vibrants tout en assurant un plaisir toute l'année. L'extension inspirée des granges comprend un garage, un abri de jardin et un salon aéré ouvrant sur une terrasse qui relient harmonieusement intérieur et extérieur. À l'étage, un paisible espace principal offre de l'intimité. Positionnée pour préserver les arbres matures et les vues sur les prairies, l'extension dégage une sensation intemporelle. Nous avons respecté les proportions originales tout en créant des perspectives qui unissent les espaces intérieurs à la nature. Des lucarnes et des fenêtres prolongent les rénovations antérieures. La cuisine déplacée améliore l'accès à la terrasse, favorisant les réunions familiales. Des poutres en sapin, des matériaux récupérés et une cheminée centrale avec un manteau en béton en porte-à-faux équilibrent histoire et modernité. Des finitions réfléchies complètent cette maison de campagne, conçue pour le plaisir familial et la vie contemporaine, où des souvenirs sont créés et chéris.

Nuestra renovación y la ampliación de una granja de Nueva Inglaterra capturan veranos vibrantes mientras aseguran un disfrute durante todo el año. La ampliación inspirada en graneros alberga un garaje, un cobertizo de jardinería y una sala de estar luminosa que se abre a un patio, conectando sin esfuerzo el interior con el exterior. Arriba, un sereno espacio principal ofrece privacidad. Situada para preservar árboles maduros y vistas a los prados, la ampliación tiene un aire atemporal. Honramos las proporciones originales mientras creamos vistas que vinculan los espacios interiores con la naturaleza. Las buhardillas y ventanas continúan las renovaciones anteriores. La cocina fue reubicada para mejora el acceso al patio y fomentar reuniones familiares. Vigas de abeto, materiales recuperados y una chimenea central con un lar de hormigón en voladizo equilibran historia y modernidad. Detalles bien pensados completan este hogar rural, diseñado para el disfrute familiar y la vida contemporánea, donde se crean y atesoran recuerdos.

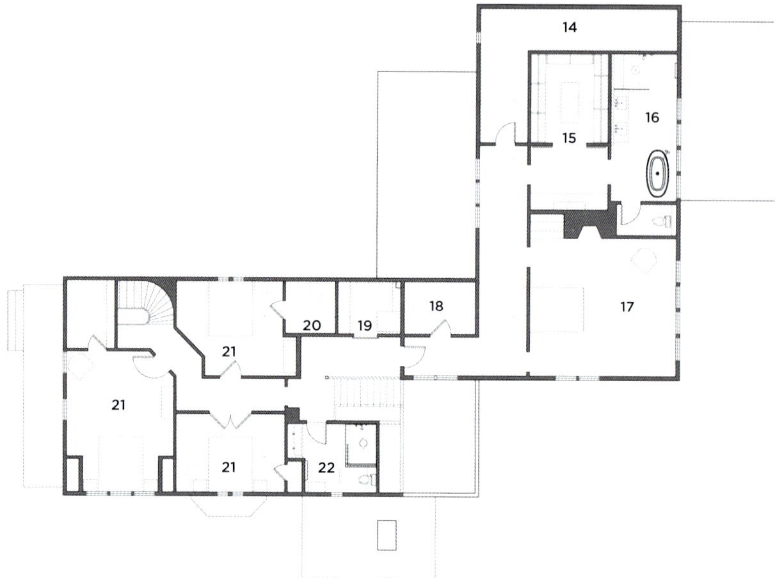

Second level floor plan

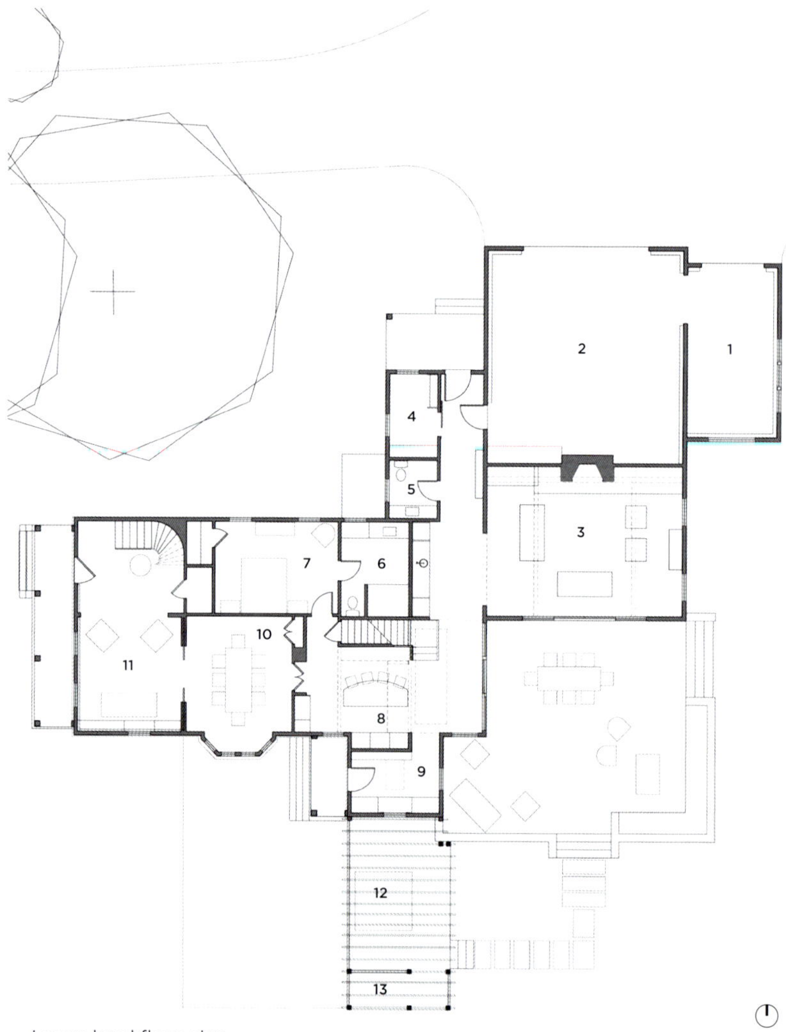

Lower level floor plan

1. Shed
2. Garage
3. Family "barn" room
4. Mudroom
5. Powder room
6. Guest bathroom
7. Guest bedroom
8. Kitchen
9. Pantry
10. Dining room
11. Living room
12. Hot tub
13. Outdoor shower
14. Storage room
15. Primary Closet
16. Primary bathroom
17. Primary bedroom
18. Cedar closet
19. Laundry room
20. Walk-in closet
21. Bedroom
22. Bathroom

GALE GOFF ARCHITECT

"A well designed home is more than shelter, but the architect's understanding of place, light and shadow."

Gale Goff has worked for forty years developing her distinctive style of residential architecture that reflects a sense of place, light and shadow, blurring indoors to outdoors, and addressing environmental conditions. Gale graduated from the Rhode Island School of Design Department of Architecture and after her position as design associate at Estes/Twombly Architects in Newport, RI, she opened her architecture firm in Little Compton, RI. Gale Goff Architect is located in a farming community along the southeast coast of New England where stone walls and rolling fields descend to the Atlantic coastline. She is informed and influenced by the land, the environment, and the vernacular tradition of the built form. Gale Goff has won awards from the RI AIA, Custom Home, and the Doris Duke Foundation for her award-winning and published projects. Her work has been featured in the latest book "New View, Twenty Magnificent Homes by Northeast Architects".

Gale Goff entwickelt seit vierzig Jahren ihren unverwechselbaren Stil der Wohnarchitektur, der ein Gefühl für den Ort, Licht und Schatten sowie die Verschmelzung von Innen- und Außenräumen widerspiegelt und die Umweltbedingungen des Standorts berücksichtigt. Nach ihrem Abschluss am Rhode Island School of Design und ihrer Tätigkeit bei Estes/Twombly Architects in Newport, RI, eröffnete sie ihr Architekturbüro in Little Compton, RI. Gale Goff Architect befindet sich in einer landwirtschaftlichen Gemeinde an der Südostküste Neuenglands, wo Steinmauern und sanfte Felder zum Atlantik hinabsteigen. Sie lässt sich von der Landschaft, der Umwelt und der örtlichen Bauformtradition inspirieren. Während ihrer Karriere entwarf sie zahlreiche preisgekrönte Projekte und erhielt Auszeichnungen von der RI AIA, Custom Home und der Doris Duke Foundation. Ihre Arbeiten wurden in mehreren Büchern vorgestellt, zuletzt in „New View, Twenty Magnificent Homes by Northeast Architects".

Gale Goff développe depuis quarante ans son style distinctif d'architecture résidentielle, qui reflète un sens du lieu, de la lumière et de l'ombre, brouillant les frontières entre l'intérieur et l'extérieur et prenant en compte les conditions environnementales. Diplômée du Département d'Architecture de la Rhode Island School of Design, elle a été associée en design chez Estes/Twombly Architects à Newport, RI, avant d'ouvrir son cabinet à Little Compton, RI. Gale Goff Architect est situé dans une communauté agricole de la côte sud-est de la Nouvelle-Angleterre, où des murs de pierre et des champs descendent vers l'Atlantique. Elle s'inspire de la terre, de l'environnement et de la tradition vernaculaire. Gale Goff a remporté des prix de la RI AIA, Custom Home, et de la Fondation Doris Duke pour ses projets primés et publiés. Son travail a été présenté dans le dernier livre « New View, Twenty Magnificent Homes by Northeast Architects ».

Gale Goff ha desarrollado durante cuarenta años su estilo distintivo de arquitectura residencial, que refleja un sentido del lugar, la luz y la sombra, difuminando las fronteras entre el interior y el exterior, y teniendo en cuenta las condiciones ambientales. Graduada del Departamento de Arquitectura de la Rhode Island School of Design, fue asociada en diseño en Estes/Twombly Architects antes de abrir su propio despacho en Little Compton, RI. Gale Goff Architect está ubicado en una comunidad agrícola de la costa sureste de Nueva Inglaterra, donde los muros de piedra y los campos descienden hacia el Atlántico. Se inspira en la tierra, el entorno y la tradición vernácula. Gale Goff ha ganado premios de la RI AIA, Custom Home y la Fundación Doris Duke por sus proyectos premiados y publicados. Su trabajo ha sido presentado en el libro «New View, Twenty Magnificent Homes by Northeast Architects».

galegoffarchitect | galegoff.com

TRANQUILITY BASE

TAPPENS BEACH HOUSE

TRANQUILITY BASE

Little Compton, Rhode Island, United States // Lot area: 3.2 acres; building area: 3,300 sq ft

Our clients sought to maximize their property's stunning feature: a sloping meadow leading to a coastal inlet. The house comprises distinct volumes that enhance its dramatic setting and adapt to seasonal needs. Each volume serves a unique purpose, with the living area and bedrooms on one level, connected by flat roofs for weather protection. The roofline features a chimney and an observation tower for exceptional views and stargazing. The design allows the volumes to function independently or together. The main and guest bedroom wings ensure privacy, facilitating summer enjoyment without disturbances, and can be closed off in winter for a more manageable living space. The central gathering area has an open plan, with a kitchen flowing into a screened porch for indoor-outdoor living. Large sliding glass doors open to a terrace, connecting the interior with the meadow. Unique features, like a blackened steel fireplace and a cedar log outdoor shower, elegantly utilize local materials. The house accommodates various needs while harmonizing with its surroundings.

Unsere Kunden wollten das beeindruckende Merkmal ihres Grundstücks maximieren: eine abfallende Wiese zu einer Küstenbucht. Das Haus besteht aus verschiedenen Volumina, die die dramatische Lage betonen und sich an saisonale Bedürfnisse anpassen. Wohnbereich und Schlafzimmer befinden sich auf einer Ebene und sind durch Flachdächer geschützt. Die Dachlinie umfasst einen Kamin und einen Aussichtsturm für außergewöhnliche Ausblicke. Die Volumina können unabhängig oder gemeinsam funktionieren. Haupt- und Gästewing bieten Privatsphäre, erleichtern den Sommergenuss und können im Winter abgetrennt werden. Der zentrale Versammlungsbereich ist offen gestaltet, mit einer Küche, die in eine verglaste Veranda übergeht. Große Schiebetüren öffnen sich zur Terrasse und verbinden das Innere mit der Wiese. Merkmale wie ein schwarzer Stahlkamin und eine Außendusche aus Zedernholz nutzen lokal Materialien. Das Haus erfüllt verschiedene Bedürfnisse und harmoniert mit seiner Umgebung.

Nos clients ont souhaité maximiser l'atout majeur de leur propriété : une prairie en pente menant à une crique côtière. La maison se compose de volumes distincts qui mettent en valeur son cadre et s'adaptent aux besoins saisonniers. Chaque volume a un but unique, avec le salon et les chambres sur un même niveau, reliés par des toits plats. La ligne de toit comprend une cheminée et une tour d'observation offrant des vues exceptionnelles. Le design permet aux volumes de fonctionner indépendamment ou ensemble. Les ailes principales et d'amis garantissent l'intimité, facilitant le plaisir estival sans perturbations, et peuvent être fermées en hiver. L'espace central est ouvert, avec une cuisine qui s'ouvre sur une véranda. De grandes portes-fenêtres coulissantes mènent à une terrasse, reliant l'intérieur à la prairie. Des éléments comme une cheminée en acier noirci et une douche extérieure en rondins de cèdre utilisent des matériaux locaux. La maison répond à divers besoins tout en s'harmonisant avec son environnement.

Nuestros clientes buscaron maximizar la característica principal de su propiedad: un prado en pendiente que conduce a una ensenada costera. La casa se compone de volúmenes distintos que resaltan su entorno y se adaptan a las necesidades estacionales. Cada volumen tiene un propósito único, con la sala de estar y los dormitorios en un mismo nivel, conectados por techos planos. La línea del techo incluye una chimenea y una torre de observación que ofrecen vistas excepcionales. El diseño permite que los volúmenes funcionen de manera independiente o conjunta. Las alas principal y de invitados garantizan la privacidad, facilitando el disfrute estival sin perturbaciones, y pueden cerrarse en invierno. El espacio central es abierto, con una cocina que se conecta a una veranda. Grandes puertas corredizas de cristal dan acceso a una terraza, uniendo el interior con el prado. Elementos como una chimenea de acero ennegrecido y una ducha exterior de troncos de cedro emplean materiales locales. La casa satisface diversas necesidades mientras se armoniza con su entorno.

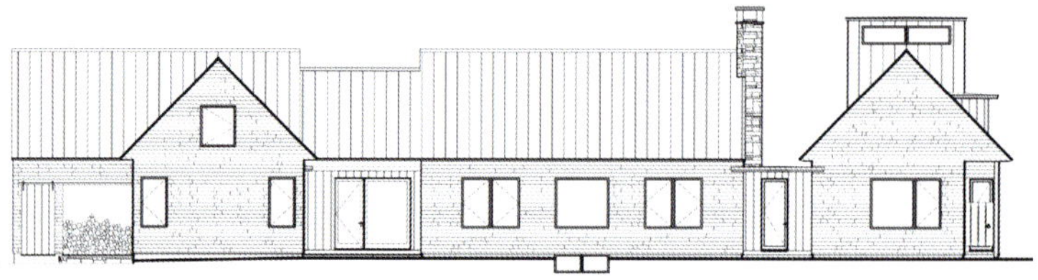

North elevation

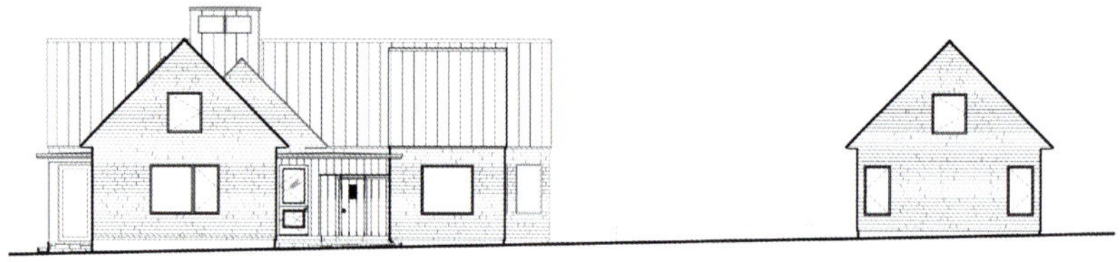

East elevation

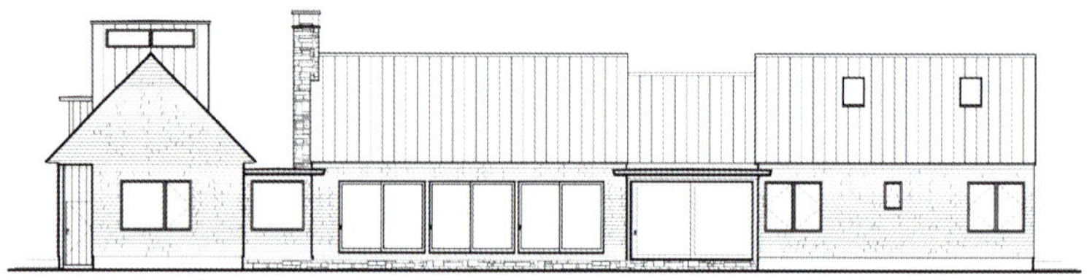

South elevation

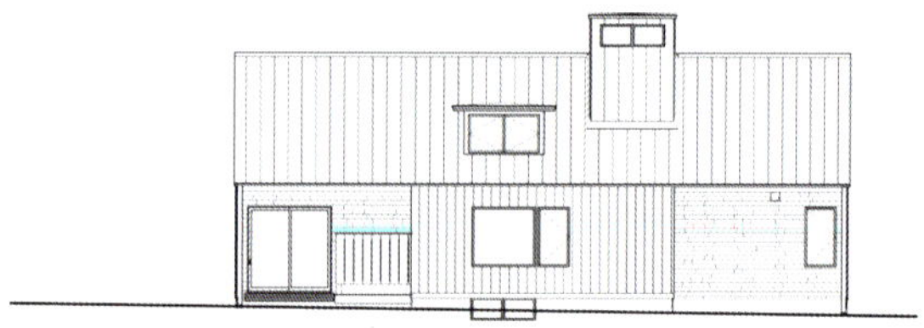

West elevation

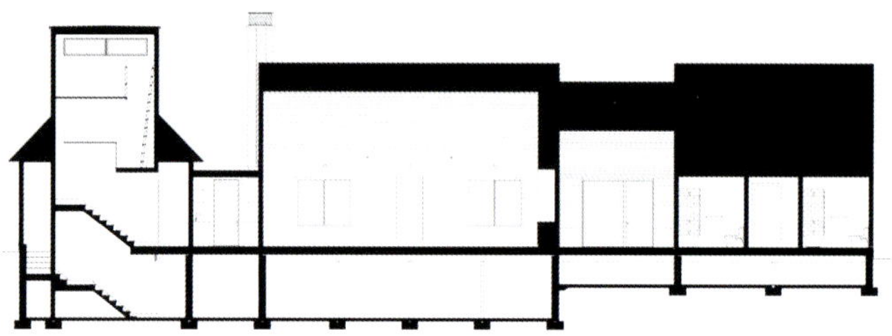

Longitudinal section

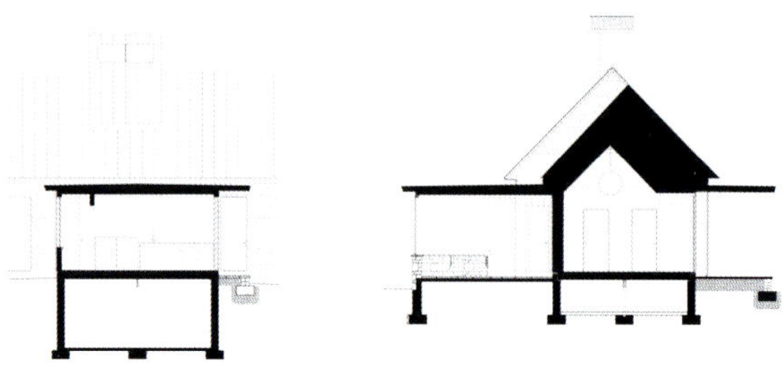

Cross Sections

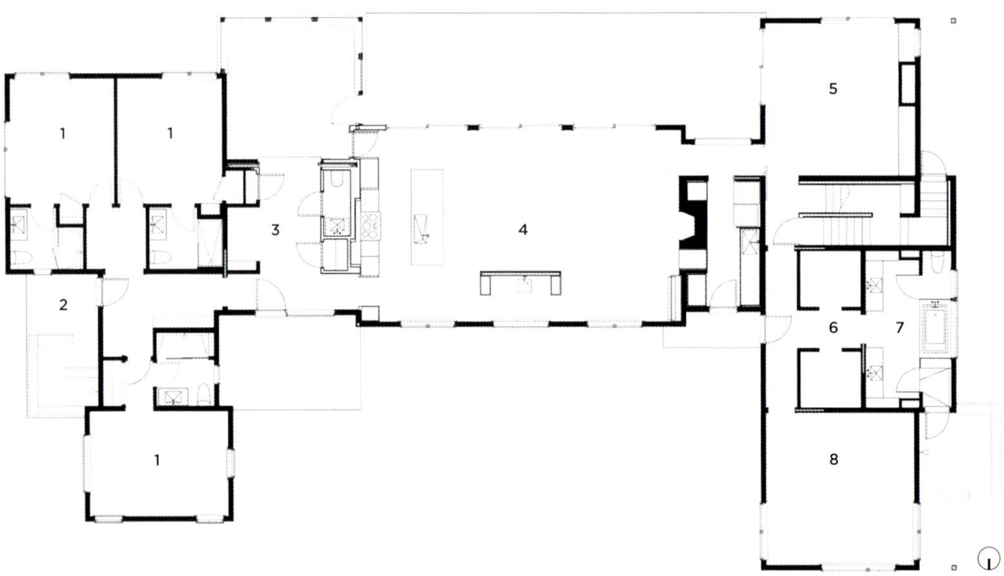

Floor plan

1. Guest room
2. Side entry
3. Front hall
4. Great room
5. Den/study
6. Primary closets
7. Primary bathroom
8. Primary bedroom

TAPPENS BEACH HOUSE

Little Compton, Rhode Island, United States // Lot area: 16,000 sq ft; building area: 1,600 sq ft

On a small sandy lot with strict zoning limits, the project addressed both horizontal and vertical challenges. The clients wanted a four-bedroom, three-bath home with space for entertaining and ocean-view decks. Despite the required ten-foot elevation in a high-risk flood zone, height restrictions were met. Built on reinforced pilings, the home avoids a stilted look with flow-through slats forming deck railings. Slender stainless steel posts support layered decks and roofs, balancing mass and verticality. The exterior features Eastern white shingles and Alaskan Yellow Cedar slats, with large windows providing views and deck access from every room. Inside, exposed fir beams elevate the living room ceiling, with built-in benches flanking the stuccoed fireplace. The open-plan kitchen and dining area connect directly to the exterior decks, and a pass-through window serves the outdoor dining area, seamlessly blending indoor and outdoor living.

Auf einem kleinen Sandgrundstück mit strengen Bebauungsvorschriften stellte das Projekt sowohl horizontale als auch vertikale Herausforderungen dar. Die Bauherren wünschten sich ein Haus mit vier Schlafzimmern, drei Bädern, Platz für Unterhaltung und eine Terrasse mit Meerblick. Trotz der zehn Fuß Höhe in der Hochwasserschutzzone wurden die Höhenvorgaben eingehalten. Das auf Pfählen errichtete Haus wirkt durch durchgehende Lamellen am Terrassengeländer weniger gestelzt. Schlanke Edelstahlpfosten tragen die übereinanderliegenden Decks und Dächer, was ein Gleichgewicht zwischen Masse und Vertikalität schafft. Weiße Ostschindeln und Latten aus Alaskan Yellow Cedar verkleiden das Haus, während große Fenster von jedem Zimmer aus den Blick und Zugang zur Terrasse bieten. Innen heben freiliegende Tannenbalken die Wohnzimmerdecke an, und eingebaute Bänke flankieren den Kamin. Die offene Küche und der Essbereich sind direkt mit den Außenterrassen verbunden, wobei ein Durchgangsfenster das Essen im Freien bedient und den Übergang zwischen Innen- und Außenbereichen nahtlos gestaltet.

Sur un petit terrain sablonneux avec des contraintes de zonage strictes, ce projet a relevé des défis horizontaux et verticaux. Les clients souhaitaient une maison de quatre chambres et trois salles de bains, avec des espaces pour recevoir et des terrasses surplombant l'océan. Bien que la maison doive être surélevée de dix pieds dans une zone inondable, les restrictions de hauteur ont été respectées. Construite sur des pieux renforcés, elle évite l'apparence sur pilotis grâce à des garde-corps ajourés. Des poteaux en acier inoxydable soutiennent les terrasses, équilibrant verticalité et masse. L'extérieur associe bardeaux blancs et lattes de cèdre jaune d'Alaska, avec de grandes fenêtres offrant des vues et un accès à la terrasse depuis chaque pièce. À l'intérieur, des poutres apparentes surélèvent le plafond du salon, et des bancs intégrés flanquent la cheminée en stuc. La cuisine ouverte et la salle à manger se connectent aux terrasses, avec une fenêtre passe-plat facilitant les repas en extérieur, fusionnant harmonieusement l'intérieur et l'extérieur.

En un pequeño terreno arenoso con una estricta normativa de zonificación, este proyecto enfrentó desafíos horizontales y verticales. Los clientes deseaban una casa de cuatro dormitorios y tres baños, con espacio para entretenimiento y terrazas con vistas al océano. A pesar de la elevación requerida de tres metros en una zona de alto riesgo de inundación, se respetaron las restricciones de altura. Construida sobre pilotes reforzados, la casa evita parecer elevada gracias a las lamas que forman las barandillas. Delgados postes de acero inoxidable sostienen las cubiertas y techos en capas, equilibrando masa y verticalidad. El exterior combina tejas blancas y listones de cedro amarillo de Alaska, con grandes ventanales que ofrecen vistas y acceso a la terraza desde todas las habitaciones. En el interior, vigas de abeto elevan el techo del salón, con bancos empotrados flanqueando la chimenea estucada. La cocina abierta y el comedor se conectan directamente con las terrazas, y una ventana de paso sirve al comedor exterior, integrando la vida interior y exterior sin interrupciones.

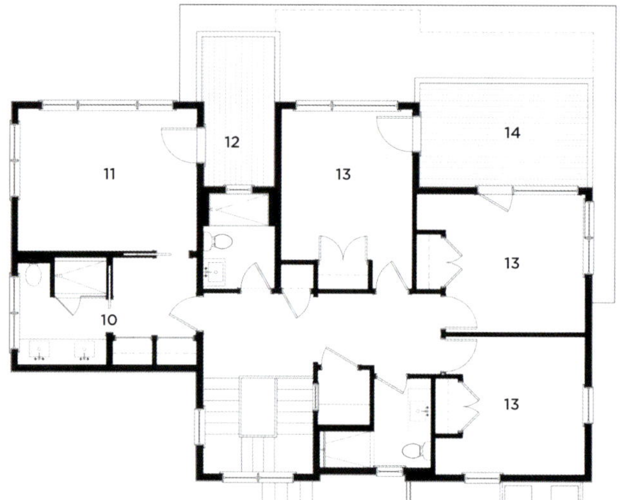

Upper floor plan

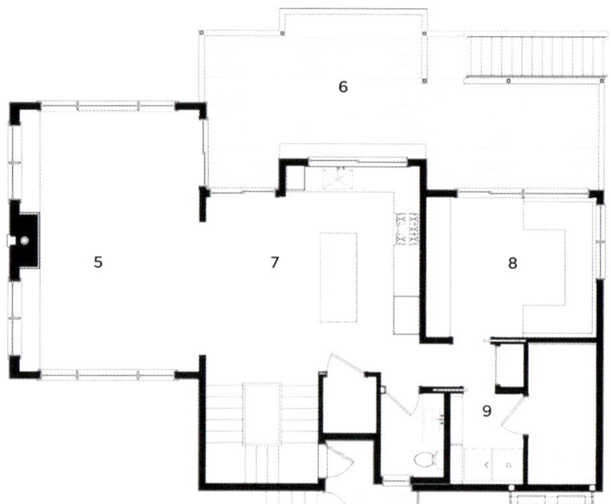

Main level floor plan

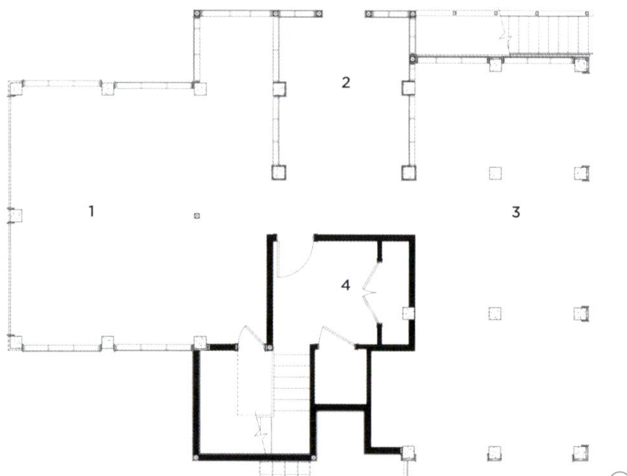

Ground level floor plan

1. Garage
2. Street entry
3. Recreation area
4. Formal entry
5. Living area
6. Entertaining deck
7. Kitchen and dining area
8. Den
9. Laundry room
10. Primary wardrobe and bathroom
11. Primary bedroom
12. Primary deck
13. Bedroom
14. Shared deck

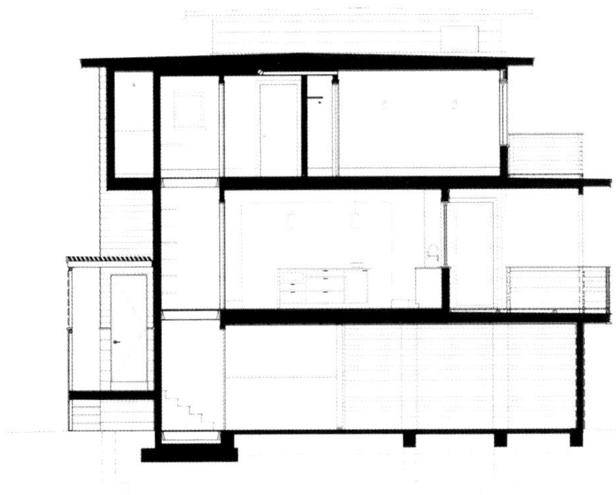

Section through staircase

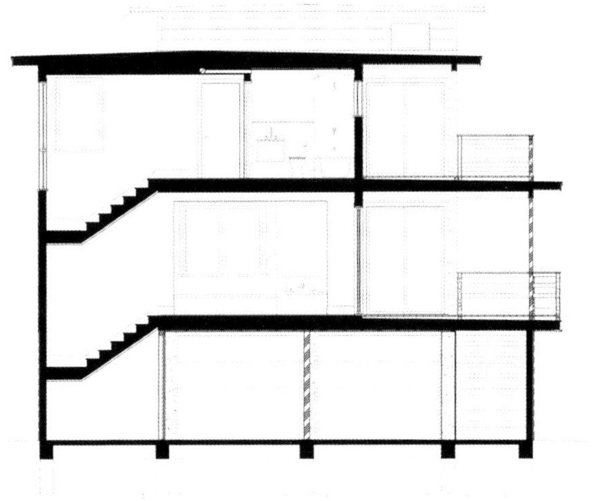

East-west section

East elevation

South elevation

West elevation

North elevation

LESSONS in CHEMISTRY
Bonnie Garmus

PRIESTLEY + ASSOCIATES ARCHITECTURE

"We understand that building or renovating a home is one of the most personal things you can do."

Priestley + Associates Architecture's mission is to create a lasting foundation for daily life, starting with building a relationship with clients. Trust is established by responding to location, context, and aspirations. Exceptional design reflects individual identity. The process involves listening and understanding unique needs, resulting in tailored plans. The best projects result from collaboration between clients, architects, contractors, and consultants, working toward a shared vision. The role of the designer is to guide clients through the process, asking what is most important and how they live. Client aspirations are central to design efforts, ensuring the vision endures long after completion. The work is not bound by style or trends but focuses on what makes clients happiest at home, combining creativity and expertise with a genuine curiosity about their desires.

Die Mission von Priestley + Associates Architecture ist, eine dauerhafte Grundlage für das tägliche Leben zu schaffen, beginnend mit einer Beziehung zu den Kunden. Vertrauen wird durch das Eingehen auf Standort, Kontext und Wünsche aufgebaut. Herausragendes Design spiegelt die individuelle Identität wider. Der Prozess umfasst das Zuhören und Verstehen einzigartiger Bedürfnisse, was zu maßgeschneiderten Plänen führt. Die besten Projekte entstehen aus der Zusammenarbeit zwischen Kunden, Architekten, Auftragnehmern und Beratern, die auf eine gemeinsame Vision hinarbeiten. Die Rolle des Designers ist es, die Kunden zu führen und ihre wichtigsten Bedürfnisse zu erfragen. Kundenwünsche stehen im Mittelpunkt, um sicherzustellen, dass die Vision nach Abschluss des Projekts Bestand hat. Die Arbeit konzentriert sich darauf, was die Kunden glücklich macht, indem Kreativität und Fachwissen mit echter Neugier kombiniert werden.

La mission de Priestley + Associates Architecture est de créer une fondation durable pour la vie quotidienne, en établissant une relation avec les clients. La confiance se construit en répondant à la localisation, au contexte et aux aspirations. Un design exceptionnel reflète l'identité individuelle. Le processus implique d'écouter et de comprendre les besoins uniques, aboutissant à des plans sur mesure. Les meilleurs projets résultent de la collaboration entre clients, architectes, entrepreneurs et consultants, travaillant vers une vision commune. Le designer guide les clients à travers le processus, en s'interrogeant sur ce qui est important et comment ils vivent. Les aspirations des clients sont au cœur des efforts de conception, garantissant que la vision perdure après l'achèvement. Le travail n'est pas lié à un style ou à des tendances, mais se concentre sur ce qui rend les clients heureux chez eux, en combinant créativité et expertise avec une véritable curiosité pour leurs désirs.

La misión de Priestley + Associates Architecture es crear una base duradera para la vida diaria, comenzando con una relación con los clientes. La confianza se establece respondiendo a la ubicación, el contexto y las aspiraciones. Un diseño excepcional refleja la identidad individual. El proceso implica escuchar y comprender las necesidades únicas, resultando en planes personalizados. Los mejores proyectos surgen de la colaboración entre clientes, arquitectos, contratistas y colaboradores, trabajando hacia una visión compartida. El diseñador guía a los clientes, preguntando qué es lo más importante y cómo viven. Las aspiraciones de los clientes son clave en el diseño, asegurando que la visión perdure después de la finalización. El trabajo no se limita a estilos o tendencias, sino que se enfoca en lo que hace felices a los clientes en casa, combinando creatividad y experiencia con genuina curiosidad por sus deseos.

priestleyplus | priestleyarchitecture.com

MOUNTAIN ESCAPE

VILLAGE CONTEMPORARY

MOUNTAIN ESCAPE

Northport, Maine, United States // Lot area: 5 acres; building area 2,994 sq ft

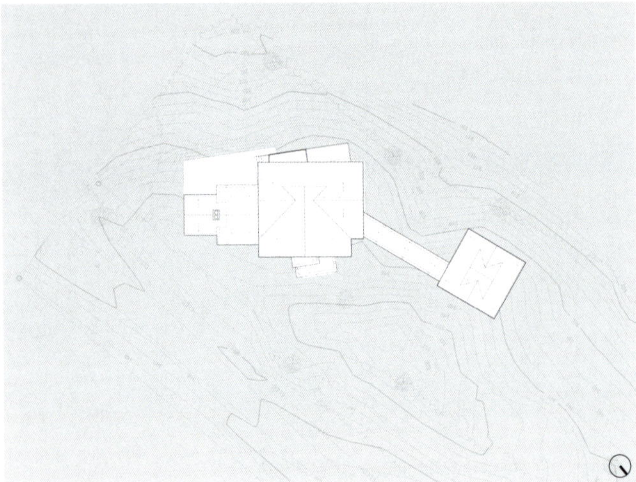

Site plan

A couple, describing themselves as "two plus dogs," envisioned a home blending modern and traditional elements with a spacious kitchen for cooking and hosting. They chose a coastal site with a sliver of buildable level terrain between a steep slope and a prominent ledge. Terraces, decks, and balconies capture breathtaking views, while the entrance welcomes visitors. Inside, guests are greeted with views of the dining and living room fireplace and a glimpse of the kitchen, creating an intriguing layout. The design optimizes natural light and visual connections, with the expansive kitchen island central to socializing and cooking. Traditional and modern elements blend seamlessly: classically proportioned windows have lean muntin layouts; exterior casings are replaced with crisp shingle returns; eaves have a knife-edge finish; and friezes and cornices are abstracted into sleek, taut bands.

Ein Ehepaar, das sich selbst als „zwei plus Hund" beschreibt, stellte sich ein Haus vor, das moderne und traditionelle Elemente mit einem geräumigen Platz zum Kochen und zur Bewirtung von Gästen verbindet. Sie wählten ein Küstengrundstück mit einem schmalen Streifen bebaubaren Landes zwischen einem steilen Hang und einem markanten Überhang. Terrassen, Decks und Balkone bieten atemberaubende Ausblicke, während der Eingang die Besucher willkommen heißt. Im Inneren werden die Gäste mit Blicken auf das Esszimmer, den Kamin im Wohnzimmer und die Küche begrüßt, wodurch ein faszinierendes Design entsteht, das das natürliche Licht und die visuellen Verbindungen optimiert, wobei die große Insel das Zentrum der Geselligkeit bildet. Traditionelle und moderne Elemente verschmelzen mühelos miteinander: klassisch proportionierte Fenster sind mit schlanken Pfosten versehen, die Außenverkleidung wurde durch klare Kacheln ersetzt, die Traufe ist mit einer Randleiste versehen, und Friese und Gesimse sind zu schlanken, engen Bändern abstrahiert.

Un couple, qui se décrit comme « deux plus des chiens », a imaginé une maison qui combine des éléments modernes et traditionnels avec un endroit spacieux pour cuisiner et recevoir des invités. Ils ont choisi un site côtier avec une petite bande de terrain constructible entre une pente raide et un surplomb proéminent. Les terrasses, les ponts et les balcons offrent des vues à couper le souffle, tandis que l'entrée accueille les visiteurs. À l'intérieur, les invités sont accueillis avec des vues sur la salle à manger, la cheminée du salon et la cuisine, créant un design intrigant qui optimise la lumière naturelle et les connexions visuelles, avec l'île expansive comme centre de socialisation. Les éléments traditionnels et modernes se mélangent sans effort : les fenêtres aux proportions classiques sont dotées de minces meneaux ; le revêtement extérieur est remplacé par des retours de tuiles croustillantes ; les avant-toits sont finis par une bordure; les frises et les corniches sont abstraites et deviennent des bandes étroites et épurées.

Una pareja, que se describe a sí misma como «dos más perros», imaginó una casa que combina elementos modernos y tradicionales con un espacioso lugar para cocinar y recibir invitados. Eligieron un sitio costero con una pequeña franja de terreno edificable entre una pendiente pronunciada y un saliente prominente. Terrazas, cubiertas y balcones capturan vistas impresionantes, mientras la entrada da la bienvenida a los visitantes. En el interior, los invitados son recibidos con vistas al comedor, la chimenea de la sala de estar y la cocina, creando un diseño intrigante que optimiza la luz natural y las conexiones visuales, con la amplia isla como centro de socialización. Los elementos tradicionales y modernos se mezclan sin esfuerzo: las ventanas de proporciones clásicas tienen disposiciones de montantes delgados; los revestimientos exteriores se reemplazan con retornos de tejas nítidos; los aleros tienen un acabado de filo; y los frisos y cornisas se abstraen en bandas elegantes y ajustadas.

North elevation

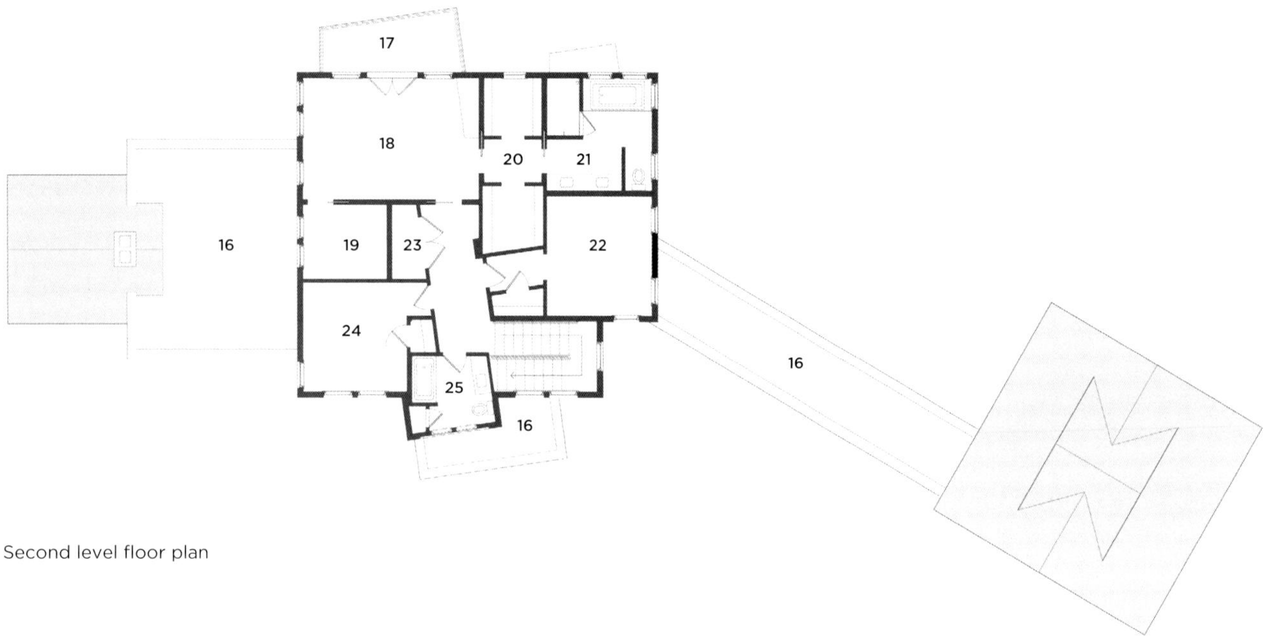

Second level floor plan

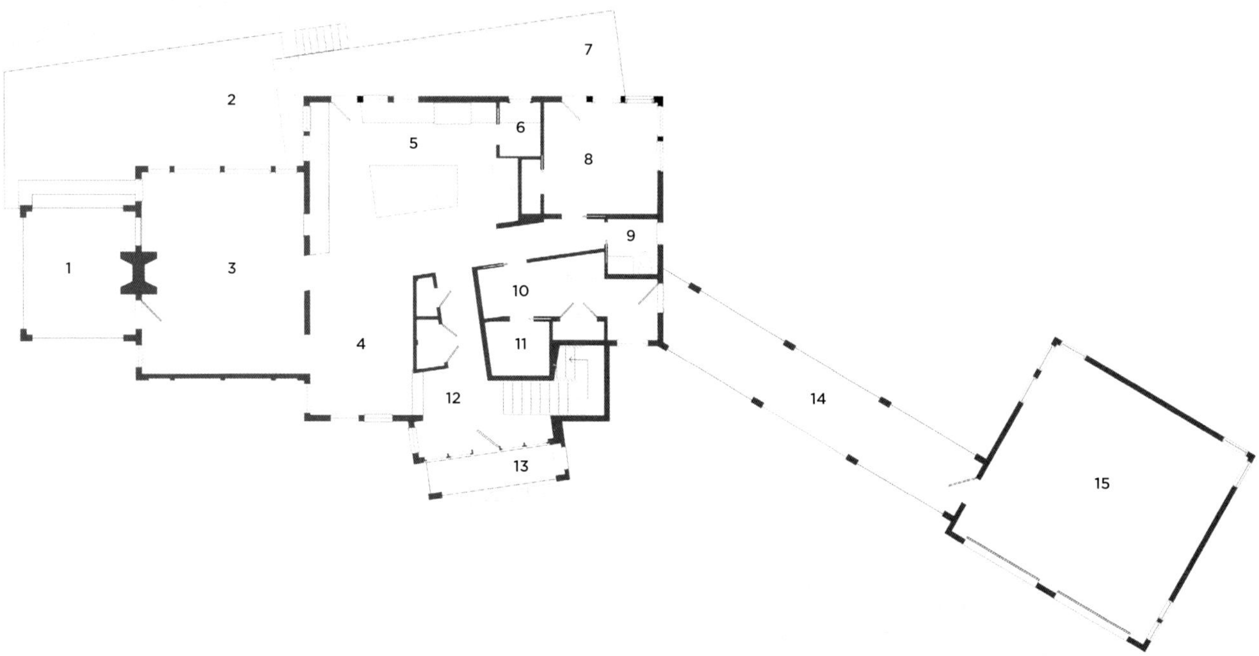

Ground level floor plan

1. Covered porch
2. Terrace
3. Living area
4. Dining area
5. Kitchen
6. Pantry
7. Deck
8. Office
9. Lavatory
10. Boot room
11. Wine
12. Entry hall
13. Entry porch
14. Breezeway
15. Garage
16. Green roof
17. Balcony
18. Primary bedroom
19. Exercise room
20. Dressing room
21. Primary bathroom
22. Bedroom
23. Laundry room
24. Bathroom

VILLAGE CONTEMPORARY

Rockport, Maine, United States // Lot area: 0.1 acre; building area: 1,344 sq ft

This compact residence in Rockport Village seamlessly reflects the art collector owner's minimalist aesthetic, with an exterior that pairs knife-edge eaves and simple massing, offering a refined interpretation of the area's historical architecture. The restrained palette — white-on-white finishes, charcoal gray roofing, stainless steel accents, and cable railings — introduces a contemporary flair that harmonizes with the neighborhood. Inside, vertical flat boards, detailed with precise gaps, extend from walls to cabinets, bathroom vanities, and even the scored white surfaces of the shower. A frameless slab of tempered glass encloses the second-floor stairwell, while ash floors, washed in translucent white, unify the space. The deliberate omission of baseboards, casings, molding, and trim contributes to a serene backdrop, allowing the furnishings and artwork to take center stage.

Diese kompakte Residenz im Rockport Village wurde entworfen, um den sauberen, minimalistischen Stil des Kunstsammlers zu reflektieren. Das Äußere zeichnet sich durch scharfe Dachüberstände und eine einfache Formgebung aus, mit einem vertrauten, aber raffinierten Design, das den historischen Kontext der Gegend aufgreift. Die strenge Palette aus Weiß-auf-Weiß-Oberflächen, dunkelgrauen Dächern, Akzenten aus Edelstahl und Seilgeländern fügt sich gut in die Nachbarschaft ein. Das gesamte Innere ist mit vertikalen Flachbrettern verkleidet, die mit gleichmäßig präzisen Abständen versehen sind und sich auf alle Schränke, Waschtische und sogar die gefräste weiße Duschverkleidung aus festem Material erstrecken. Eine rahmenlose Scheibe aus gehärtetem Glas schützt das Treppenhaus im zweiten Stock. Alle Böden sind mit Eschenholzdielen belegt, die mit durchscheinendem Weiß gewaschen wurden, was ein einheitliches Erscheinungsbild im gesamten Raum schafft. Das Fehlen von Sockelleisten, Verkleidungen, Zierleisten und Leisten schafft eine ruhige Kulisse für Möbel und Kunstwerke.

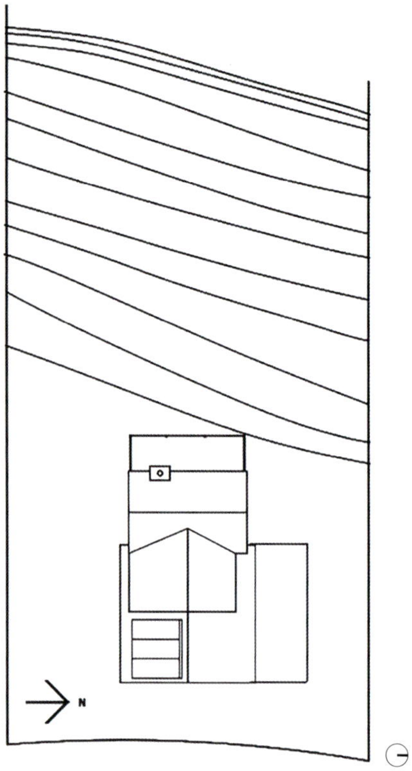

Site plan

Cette résidence compacte à Rockport Village a été conçue pour refléter le style propre et minimaliste du propriétaire collectionneur d'art. L'extérieur présente des avant-toits tranchants et une masse simple, avec un design familier mais raffiné qui embrasse le contexte historique de la région. La palette austère de finitions blanc sur blanc, de toiture gris charbon, d'accents en acier inoxydable et de garde-corps en câble ajoute une touche contemporaine qui s'intègre bien dans le quartier. Tout l'intérieur est habillé de planches plates verticales détaillées avec des espacements constamment précis, s'étendant à tous les placards, à la vanité de la salle de bains et même au revêtement de douche en surface solide blanche. Une dalle sans cadre en verre trempé protège la cage d'escalier du deuxième étage. Les sols sont tous recouverts de planches de frêne lavées en blanc translucide, créant une apparence cohérente dans tout l'espace. L'absence de plinthes, d'encadrements, de moulures et de garnitures crée un fond calme pour les meubles et les œuvres d'art.

Esta residencia compacta en Rockport Village fue diseñada para reflejar el estilo limpio y minimalista del propietario, un coleccionista de arte. El exterior presenta aleros de filo y una masa simple, con un diseño familiar pero refinado que abraza el contexto histórico de la zona. La austera paleta de acabados blanco sobre blanco, techos gris carbón, acentos de acero inoxidable y barandillas de cable añade un toque contemporáneo que se integra bien con el vecindario. Todo el interior está revestido con tablas planas verticales detalladas con espacios consistentemente precisos, que se extienden a todos los armarios, el tocador del baño e incluso el revestimiento de la ducha de superficie sólida blanca. Una losa sin marco de vidrio templado protege la escalera del segundo piso. Los suelos están cubiertos con tablas de fresno lavadas en blanco translúcido, creando un aspecto uniforme en todo el espacio. La ausencia de zócalos, molduras, cornisas y molduras crea un fondo tranquilo para muebles y obras de arte.

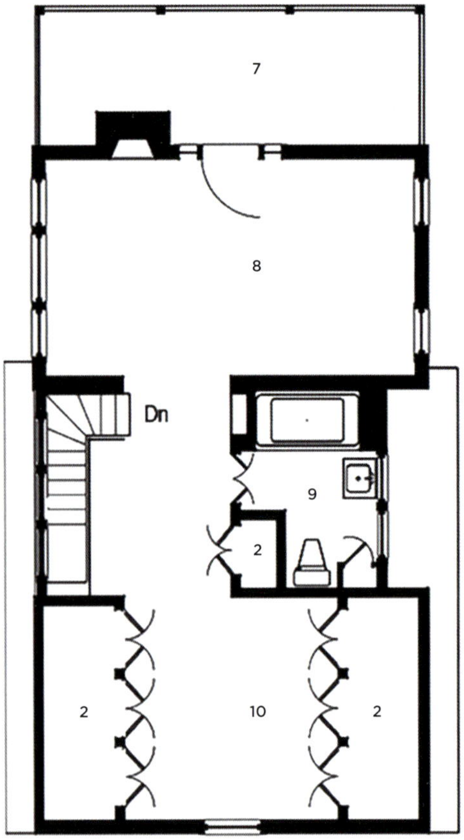

Second level floor plan

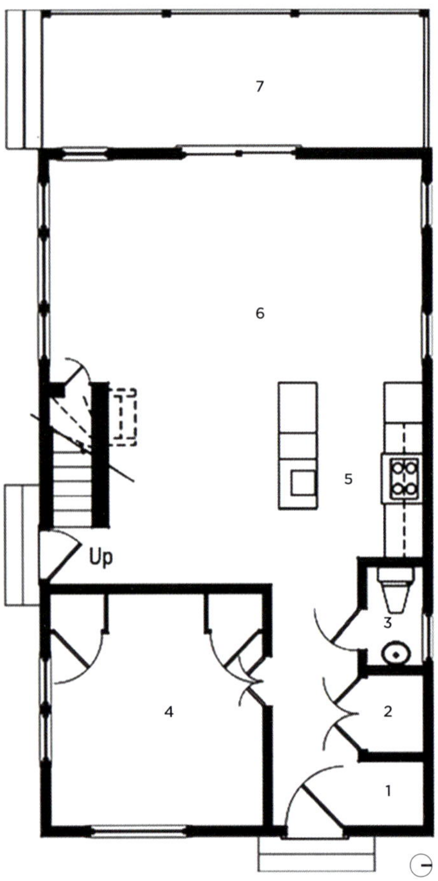

Ground level floor plan

1. Entry
2. Closet
3. Water closet
4. Office/guest room
5. Kitchen
6. Dining area
7. Porch
8. Sitting area
9. Primary bathroom
10. Primary bedroom

REVERSE ARCHITECTURE

"Sustainable thinking and inspirational design for the modern world."

Reverse Architecture, founded in 2007 by Carl Solander in Cambridge, Massachusetts, specializes in modern sustainable design for multifamily, commercial, academic, public buildings, residences, and custom interiors. The firm manages new construction, renovations, adaptive reuse, and bespoke fabrications, known for its "total design" approach. Offering services such as architectural and interior design, passive house certification, energy-efficient retrofits, furniture and landscape design, and energy modeling, the firm ensures high-quality, integrated solutions. Emphasizing thorough analysis and experimentation, their design philosophy considers client needs, site requirements, cultural and ecological aspects, material characteristics, and transformative technologies. Inspired by reverse engineering, they prioritize sustainability and innovation, earning several awards for design excellence.

Reverse Architecture, 2007 von Carl Solander in Cambridge, Massachusetts gegründet, fokussiert sich auf nachhaltiges, modernes Design für Mehrfamilienhäuser, gewerbliche, akademische und öffentliche Gebäude sowie maßgeschneiderte Innenräume. Das Büro betreut Neubauten, Renovierungen und adaptive Wiederverwendungen, bekannt für seinen „Total Design"-Ansatz. Es bietet Architektur- und Innendesign, Passivhaus-Zertifizierung, energieeffiziente Sanierungen, Möbel- und Landschaftsgestaltung sowie Energieberechnungen an. Ihre Designphilosophie basiert auf Analyse und Experimenten, berücksichtigt Kundenbedürfnisse, Standortanforderungen, kulturelle und ökologische Aspekte sowie transformative Technologien. Inspiriert von Reverse Engineering, setzen sie auf Nachhaltigkeit und Innovation und haben mehrere Auszeichnungen für ihre Designs erhalten.

Reverse Architecture, fondée en 2007 par Carl Solander à Cambridge, Massachusetts, se spécialise dans le design durable et moderne pour bâtiments multifamiliaux, commerciaux, académiques, publics, résidences et intérieurs sur mesure. Le cabinet gère les nouvelles constructions, rénovations, réutilisation adaptative et fabrications sur mesure, avec une approche de « design total ». Il propose des services d'architecture, design intérieur, certification de maisons passives, rénovations écoénergétiques, design de mobilier et de paysage, ainsi que modélisation énergétique. Leur philosophie repose sur une analyse approfondie et l'expérimentation, tenant compte des besoins des clients, des exigences du site, et des aspects culturels, écologiques, des matériaux et des technologies innovantes. Inspiré par le génie inverse, le cabinet privilégie la durabilité et l'innovation, ayant reçu plusieurs prix pour l'excellence de ses designs.

Reverse Architecture, fundada en 2007 por Carl Solander en Cambridge, Massachusetts, se especializa en diseño sostenible moderno para edificios multifamiliares, comerciales, académicos, públicos, residencias e interiores personalizados. La firma gestiona nuevas construcciones, renovaciones, reutilización adaptativa y fabricaciones a medida, conocida por su enfoque de «diseño total». Ofreciendo servicios como diseño arquitectónico e interior, certificación de casas pasivas, reformas energéticamente eficientes, diseño de muebles y paisajes, y modelado energético, la firma asegura soluciones integradas de alta calidad. Al enfatizar un análisis y experimentación exhaustivos, su filosofía de diseño considera las necesidades del cliente, los requisitos del sitio, los aspectos culturales y ecológicos, las características de los materiales y las tecnologías transformadoras. Inspirados por la ingeniería inversa, priorizan la sostenibilidad y la innovación, ganando varios premios por excelencia en diseño.

reversearchitecture

reversearchitecture.com

WAYLAND RESIDENCE

CAMBRIDGE TOWNHOUSE

WAYLAND RESIDENCE

Wayland, Massachusetts, United States // Lot area: 85,250 sq ft; building area: 1,655 sq ft

This modest midcentury home originally embodied a minimalistic and economical approach to modernism. The renovation introduces aspirational modernism with spacious, sunlit, adaptable living areas focused on sustainability, featuring passive house design elements like foam-insulated windows, composite z-girt cladding, and exterior wall and roof insulation. The new addition creates two wood-clad courtyards and features a hinged butterfly roof with soaring ceilings, contrasting with the salvaged portions of the house, which are now ancillary spaces. In the kitchen, a built-in maple table seamlessly integrates with the island, expanding the compact dining area to accommodate guests. Though located in the suburbs, the home enjoys wooded surroundings, offering views of trees and dappled light through clerestory windows. The Wayland Residence highlights sustainability by reclaiming the house and preserving the site, making conservation a central design element.

Dieses bescheidene Haus aus der Mitte des Jahrhunderts verkörperte ursprünglich einen minimalistischen und wirtschaftlichen Ansatz des Modernismus. Die Renovierung bringt ihm einen ehrgeizigeren Modernismus mit geräumigen, sonnigen, anpassungsfähigen Wohnbereichen, die alle um Nachhaltigkeit zentriert sind. In Anlehnung an das Passivhaus-Design reduziert die Renovierung Wärmebrücken durch schaumisolierte Fenster, Verbund-Z-Gurt-Verkleidung und Außenisolierung für Wände und Dach. Der neue Anbau schafft zwei holzverkleidete Innenhöfe und verfügt über ein klappbares Schmetterlingsdach mit hohen Decken, das im Kontrast zu den wiederverwendeten Teilen des Hauses steht, die nun Nebenräume sind. Trotz seiner Lage in einem Vorort bietet das dicht bewaldete Grundstück Ausblicke auf die umliegenden Bäume und getupftes Licht durch Oberlichter. Die Wayland-Residenz betont Nachhaltigkeit als Ressourcenschonung. Das Haus selbst ist zurückgewonnen, das Gelände erhalten, was den Naturschutz zu einem zentralen Gestaltungselement macht.

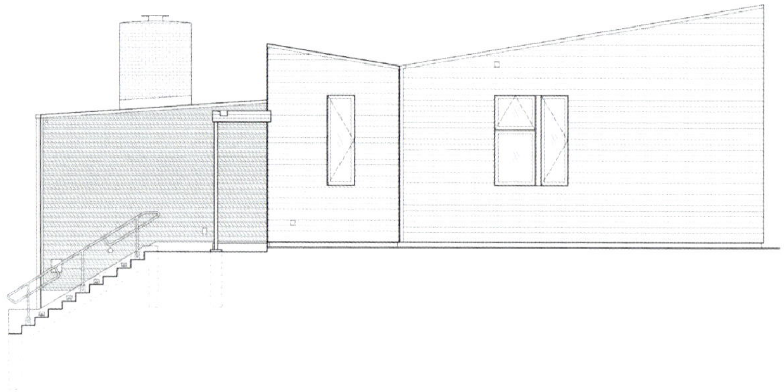

North elevation

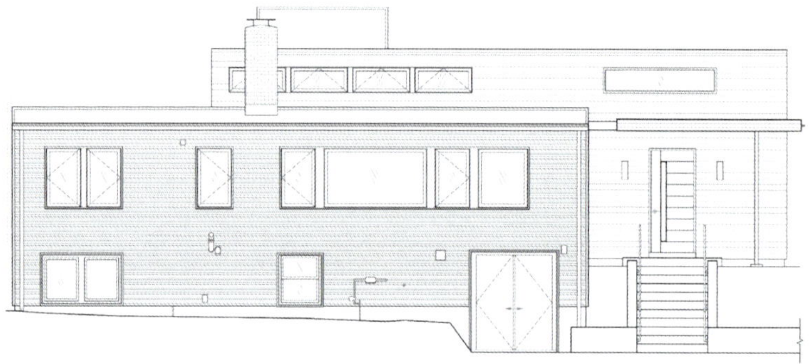

East elevation

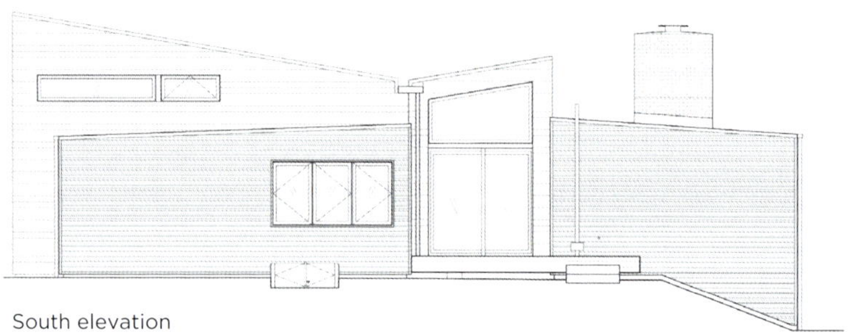

South elevation

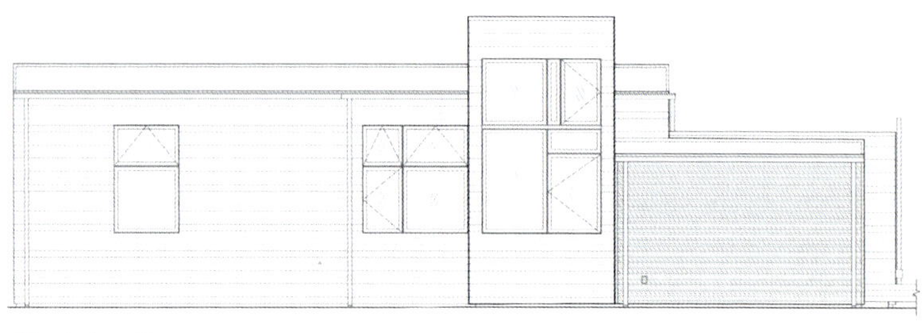

West elevation

Cette modeste maison de l'époque moderne incarnait à l'origine une approche minimaliste et économique du modernisme. La rénovation lui apporte un modernisme plus ambitieux, avec des espaces de vie spacieux, ensoleillés et adaptables, tous centrés sur la durabilité. En respectant la conception de maison passive, la rénovation réduit les ponts thermiques grâce à des fenêtres isolées en mousse, un bardage composite z-girt et une isolation extérieure pour les murs et le toit. La nouvelle extension crée deux cours en bois et dispose d'un toit papillon à charnières avec des plafonds élevés, contrastant avec les parties récupérées de la maison, qui sont maintenant des espaces auxiliaires. Malgré son emplacement en banlieue, le site densément boisé offre des vues sur les arbres environnants et une lumière tamisée à travers des fenêtres en claire-voie. La résidence Wayland met l'accent sur la durabilité en tant que conservation des ressources. La maison elle-même est récupérée, le site préservé, faisant de la conservation un élément central du design.

Esta modesta casa de mediados de siglo originalmente encarnaba un enfoque minimalista y económico del modernismo. La renovación le aporta un estilo más aspiracional, con áreas de estar amplias, soleadas y adaptables, todas centradas en la sostenibilidad. Adhiriéndose al diseño de casa pasiva, la renovación reduce los puentes térmicos con ventanas de espuma aislada, revestimiento compuesto z-girt y aislamiento exterior para paredes y techo. La nueva adición crea dos patios revestidos de madera y cuenta con un techo de mariposa con bisagras y techos altos, que contrastan con las partes recuperadas de la casa, que ahora son espacios auxiliares. A pesar de su ubicación suburbana, el terreno densamente arbolado ofrece vistas de los árboles circundantes y luz moteada a través de claraboyas. La residencia Wayland enfatiza la ecología como conservación de recursos. La casa en sí está recuperada, el lugar preservado, haciendo de la conservación un elemento central del diseño.

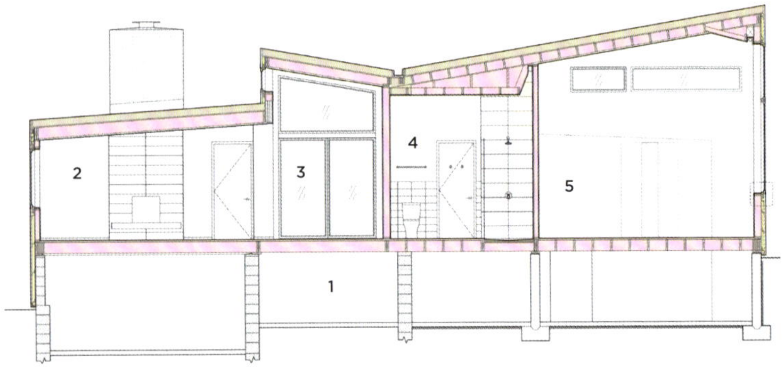

East-West section

1. Basement
2. Living area
3. Kitchen
4. Primary bathroom
5. Primary bedroom

Insulation types

- Mineral wool
- Cellulose
- Polyiso rigid foam board
- Type IX EPS rigid foam

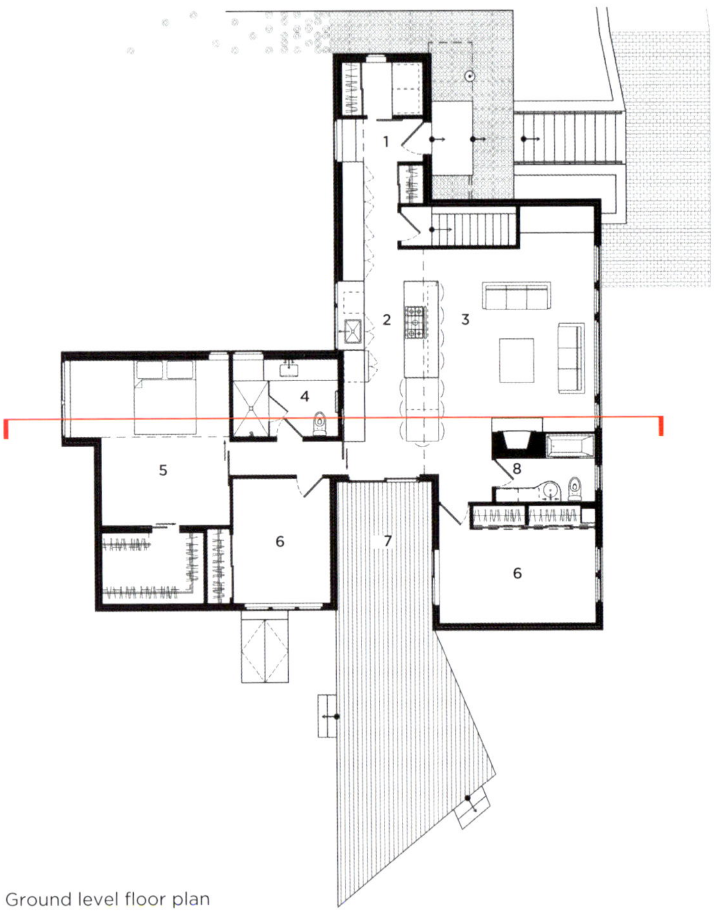

Ground level floor plan

1. Entry
2. Kitchen
3. Living area
4. Primary bathroom
5. Primary bedroom
6. Bedroom
7. Deck
8. Guest bathroom

CAMBRIDGE TOWNHOUSE

Cambridge, Massachusetts, United States // Lot area: 1,658 sq ft; building area: 1,885 sq ft

A row of four modern townhouses, built in 1977, originally featured distinct bright color infill panels and trim. Over time, many of the panels deteriorated, which risked altering the block's character. The end unit's renovation restores and enhances the façade by adding a front deck screen, a green glass guardrail at the master suite balcony, and a five-panel folding door system. The 24-foot square footprint of the townhouse promotes urban density and adaptability. The main floor is opened for entertaining, with the five-panel door extending the living room onto the front deck. An exterior stair provides direct patio access from a convertible playroom or in-law suite. A new steel and glass stair admits light from above, creating openness and connectivity as a focal point. Preserving and upgrading existing buildings conserves materials and contributes to local cultural heritage. The small footprint and adaptable layout encourage urban density, reducing rural development.

Eine Reihe von vier modernen Stadthäusern, die 1977 erbaut wurden, verfügte ursprünglich über helle Füllungspaneele und Zierleisten. Mit der Zeit verschlechterten sich viele Paneele, was den Charakter des Blocks gefährdete. Die Renovierung der Endeinheit stellt die Fassade wieder her und verbessert sie durch eine Frontdeckblende, ein grünes Glasgeländer am Balkon der Hauptsuite und ein Falttürsystem. Die 7,3 x 7,3 Meter Grundfläche des Hauses fördert urbane Dichte und Flexibilität. Das Hauptgeschoss ist offen, wobei die Falttür das Wohnzimmer auf das Deck erweitert. Eine Außentreppe bietet Zugang zum Patio von einem wandelbaren Spielzimmer oder einer Schwiegerelternsuite. Eine neue Stahl- und Glastreppe bringt Licht von oben ein und schafft Offenheit als zentralen Punkt. Die Aufwertung bestehender Gebäude schont Materialien und trägt zum kulturellen Erbe bei. Die kompakte Grundfläche und das flexible Layout fördern städtische Dichte und mindern die ländliche Entwicklung.

Une rangée de quatre maisons de ville modernes, construites en 1977, comportait à l'origine des panneaux et garnitures de couleurs vives. Avec le temps, plusieurs se sont détériorés, menaçant le caractère du quartier. La rénovation de l'unité d'extrémité restaure et améliore la façade avec un écran de terrasse avant, un garde-corps en verre vert au balcon principal et un système de porte pliante à cinq panneaux. La superficie de 7,3 sur 7,3 mètres favorise la densité urbaine et l'adaptabilité. Le rez-de-chaussée, ouvert pour recevoir, voit le salon prolongé sur la terrasse avant par la porte à cinq panneaux. Un escalier extérieur permet l'accès direct au patio depuis une salle de jeux convertible ou une suite pour invités. Un nouvel escalier en acier et en verre laisse entrer la lumière d'en haut, créant ouverture et connectivité comme point central. La préservation et la modernisation des bâtiments conservent les matériaux et enrichissent le patrimoine culturel local. La petite empreinte et le design adaptable favorisent la densité urbaine tout en réduisant le développement rural.

Una hilera de cuatro casas adosadas modernas, construidas en 1977, tenía inicialmente paneles y molduras de colores brillantes. Con el tiempo, muchos paneles se deterioraron, afectando el carácter del barrio. La renovación de la casa en la esquina restaura y mejora la fachada con una pantalla en la terraza delantera, una barandilla de cristal verde en el balcón del dormitorio principal y un sistema de puertas plegables de cinco paneles. La huella de 7,3 por 7,3 metros fomenta la densidad urbana y la adaptabilidad. La planta principal, abierta para el entretenimiento, extiende la sala hacia la terraza. Una escalera exterior da acceso directo al patio desde una sala de juegos convertible o una suite para suegros. Una nueva escalera de acero y cristal deja pasar la luz zenital, expandiendo y conectando el espacio. Preservar y modernizar edificios existentes conserva materiales y enriquece el patrimonio cultural local. La huella compacta y el diseño adaptable fomentan la densidad urbana y reducen el desarrollo rural.

EXISTING

PROPOSED

North elevation

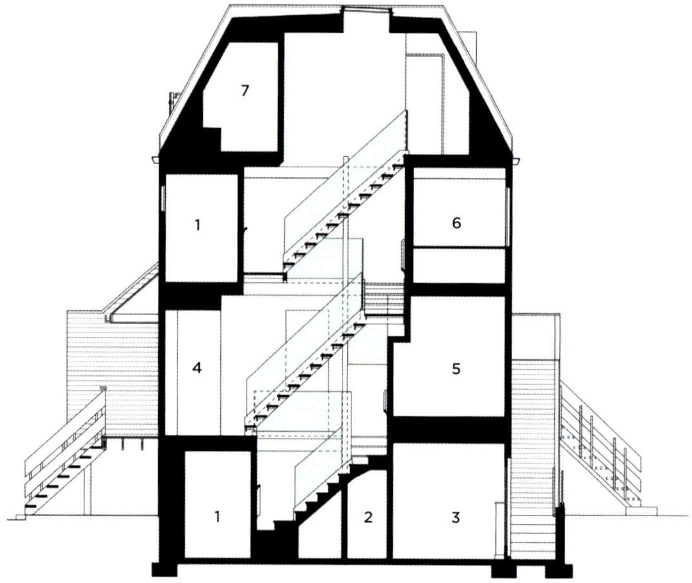

North-South section

1. Bathroom
2. Closet
3. Playroom
4. Entry
5. Kitchen
6. Study
7. Primary shower

Proposed south elevation

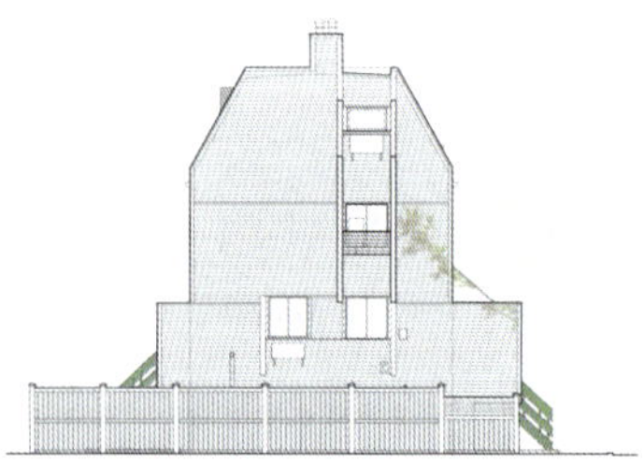

EXISTING

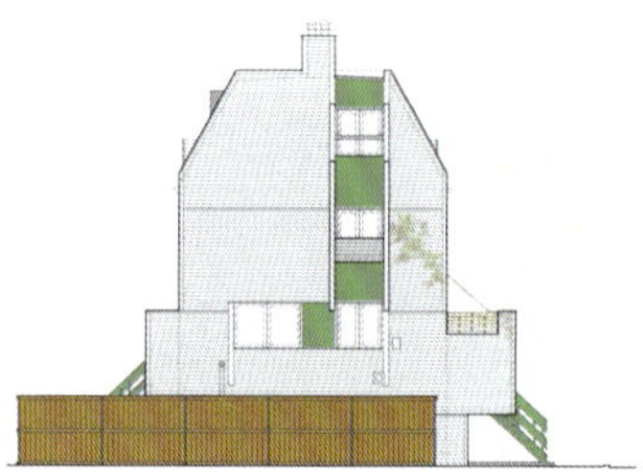

PROPOSED

West elevation

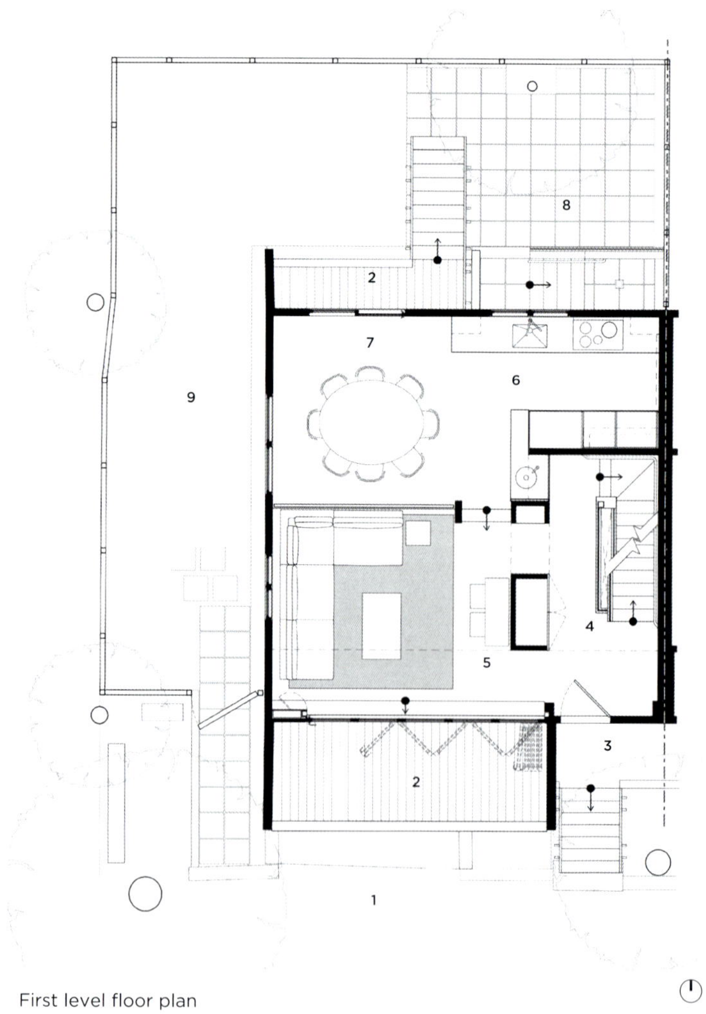

First level floor plan

1. Sidewalk
2. Deck
3. Porch
4. Entry
5. Living area
6. Kitchen
7. Dining area
8. Patio
9. Yard

ALAN CHRIST ARCHITECTS

"Buildings are the threads that quietly shape our actions, weaving the social fabric of our society."

In their residential work, Alan Christ Architects endeavors to create beautiful, sustainable homes that grow out of a careful study of their context. The firm believes that design excellence can be achieved by carefully considering spatial organization, urban context, architectural detailing, and environmental impact, and all of their projects are based on this fundamental premise. ACA's work brings a sensitive and modern approach to renovating older homes, balancing careful attention to their original detailing with a more aggressively modern approach to bringing space and light to the interior spaces. The firm emphasizes that each project is a collaboration with the client, ensuring that the finished product is tailored to their specific needs. This collaboration is supported by research into new technologies and materials, as well as a commitment to sustainable urbanism.

Alan Christ Architects strebt danach, schöne, nachhaltige Häuser zu schaffen, die aus einer sorgfältigen Untersuchung ihres Kontextes entstehen. Das Büro glaubt, dass gestalterische Exzellenz durch die durchdachte Betrachtung von Raumorganisation, städtischem Umfeld, architektonischen Details und Umweltverträglichkeit erreicht wird. Alle Projekte basieren auf diesem Grundsatz. ACA bringt einen sensiblen, modernen Ansatz in die Renovierung älterer Häuser, indem sie die ursprünglichen Details bewahren und gleichzeitig moderne Raum- und Lichtkonzepte umsetzen. Jedes Projekt ist eine Zusammenarbeit mit den Kunden und wird auf deren spezifische Bedürfnisse zugeschnitten. Diese Kooperation wird durch Forschung zu neuen Technologien und Materialien sowie dem Engagement für nachhaltigen Urbanismus unterstützt.

Dans leurs projets résidentiels, Alan Christ Architects s'efforce de créer des maisons belles et durables, issues d'une étude approfondie de leur contexte. Le cabinet est convaincu que l'excellence en design peut être atteinte en prenant soigneusement en compte l'organisation spatiale, le contexte urbain, les détails architecturaux et l'impact environnemental, et tous leurs projets reposent sur ce principe fondamental. Le travail d'ACA adopte une approche sensible et moderne pour la rénovation de maisons anciennes, alliant une attention particulière aux détails d'origine à une approche plus audacieusement moderne pour apporter lumière et espace aux intérieurs. Le cabinet souligne que chaque projet est une collaboration avec le client, garantissant que le produit final est adapté à leurs besoins spécifiques. Cette collaboration est soutenue par la recherche sur les nouvelles technologies et matériaux, ainsi que par un engagement en faveur de l'urbanisme durable.

En su trabajo residencial, Alan Christ Architects se esfuerza por crear hogares hermosos y sostenibles que surgen de un estudio cuidadoso de su contexto. La firma cree que la excelencia en el diseño se puede lograr mediante la consideración meticulosa de la organización espacial, el contexto urbano, los detalles arquitectónicos y el impacto ambiental, y todos sus proyectos se basan en este principio fundamental. El trabajo de ACA aporta un enfoque sensible y moderno a la renovación de casas antiguas, equilibrando una atención cuidadosa a los detalles originales con un enfoque más moderno para aportar luz y espacio a los interiores. La firma enfatiza que cada proyecto es una colaboración con el cliente, asegurando que el producto final se ajuste a sus necesidades específicas. Esta colaboración se apoya en la investigación de nuevas tecnologías y materiales, así como en un compromiso con el urbanismo sostenible.

ac-architects.net

TAYLOR STREET RESIDENCE

LAWRENCE ROAD RESIDENCE

TAYLOR STREET RESIDENCE

Boston, Massachusetts, United States // Lot area: 2,245 sq ft; building area: 4,200 sq ft

ACA served as the architect of record in collaboration with SAS Design-Build for this 4,200 square-foot residence located in Boston's South End. The project involved restoring the facade of an existing rowhouse dating back to 1899 while renovating the interior space and adding a substantial extension to the south side. The resulting dwelling presents two distinct yet harmonious structures, with the existing house acting as a screen for the modern interior within. The southern addition continues this theme with wood sun shading, offering privacy while preserving views of the adjacent park. The interior boasts a modern aesthetic, blending old and new elements in light, open, and layered spaces. A void space between the old and new structures extends the full height of the house, marking the boundary between the original footprint and the addition. Materials such as glass, steel, and wood are left exposed, celebrating the construction process and creating a visually dynamic composition throughout the home.

ACA war der verantwortliche Architekt in Zusammenarbeit mit SAS Design-Build für diese 4.200 Quadratfuß große Residenz im South End von Boston. Das Projekt umfasste die Restaurierung der Fassade eines Reihenhauses aus dem Jahr 1899 sowie die Renovierung des Innenraums und eine Erweiterung auf der Südseite. Das Gebäude besteht aus zwei harmonischen Strukturen, wobei das bestehende Haus als Sichtschutz für das moderne Innere fungiert. Der südliche Anbau setzt dieses Thema mit Holz-Sonnenschutz fort, der Privatsphäre bietet und den Blick auf den angrenzenden Park bewahrt. Der Innenraum vereint alte und neue Elemente in hellen, offenen Räumen. Ein Luftraum zwischen den Strukturen erstreckt sich über die gesamte Höhe des Hauses und markiert die Grenze zwischen dem ursprünglichen Grundriss und dem Anbau. Materialien wie Glas, Stahl und Holz bleiben sichtbar und feiern den Bauprozess, wodurch eine dynamische Komposition im gesamten Haus entsteht.

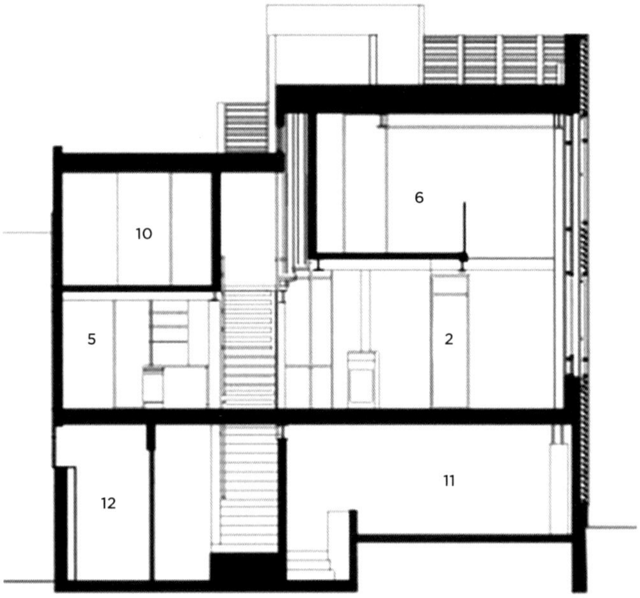

Section AA

ACA a agi en tant qu'architecte de référence en collaboration avec SAS Design-Build pour cette résidence de 4 200 pieds carrés située dans le South End de Boston. Le projet a consisté à restaurer la façade d'un ancien immeuble de rangée datant de 1899 tout en rénovant l'espace intérieur et en ajoutant une extension substantielle sur le côté sud. La maison résultante présente deux structures distinctes mais harmonieuses, l'ancienne maison servant d'écran pour l'intérieur moderne. L'ajout sud poursuit ce thème avec un pare-soleil en bois, offrant de l'intimité tout en préservant les vues sur le parc adjacent. L'intérieur affiche une esthétique moderne, mêlant des éléments anciens et nouveaux dans des espaces lumineux, ouverts et en couches. Un vide entre les anciennes et nouvelles structures s'étend sur toute la hauteur de la maison, marquant la limite entre l'emprise originale et l'extension. Des matériaux tels que le verre, l'acier et le bois restent exposés, célébrant le processus de construction et créant une composition visuellement dynamique dans toute la maison.

ACA actuó como el arquitecto responsable en colaboración con SAS Design-Build para esta residencia de 4,200 pies cuadrados en el South End de Boston. El proyecto incluyó la restauración de la fachada de un antiguo edificio en fila de 1899, la renovación del interior y la adición de una extensión en el lado sur. La vivienda presenta dos estructuras distintas pero armoniosas, con la casa existente sirviendo de pantalla para el interior moderno. La adición del sur continúa este tema con protección solar de madera, ofreciendo privacidad y preservando las vistas del parque adyacente. El interior cuenta con una estética moderna, combinando elementos antiguos y nuevos en espacios luminosos y abiertos. Un vacío entre las estructuras antigua y nueva se extiende por toda la altura de la casa, marcando el límite entre la huella original y la adición. Materiales como vidrio, acero y madera se dejan expuestos, celebrando el proceso de construcción y creando una composición visualmente dinámica en toda la casa.

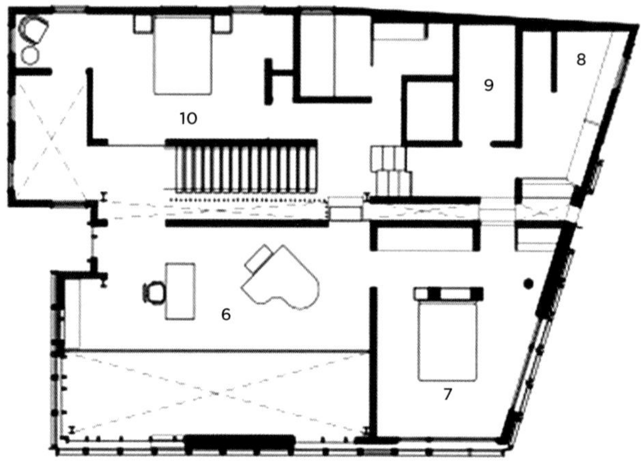

Upper level floor plan

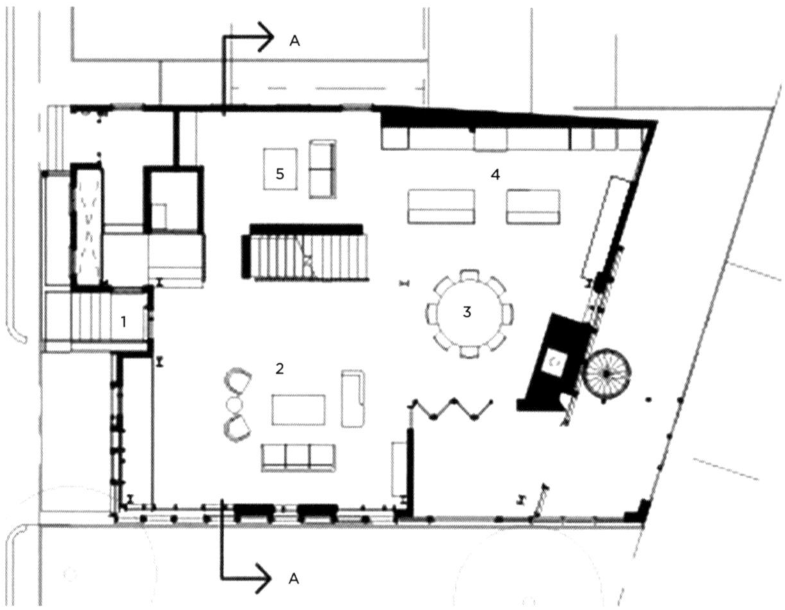

Entry level floor plan

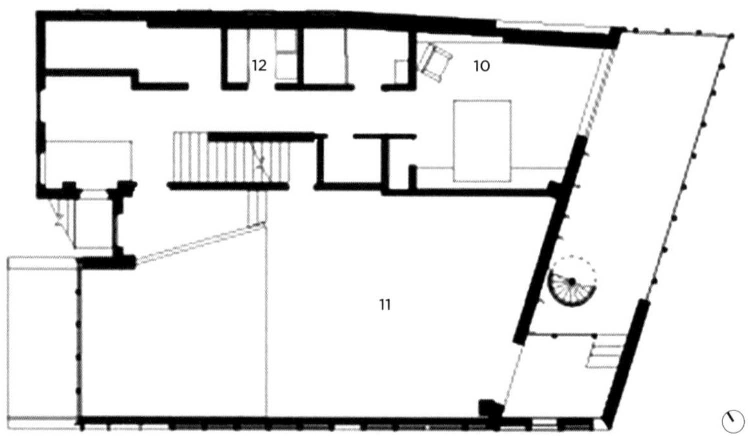

Lower level floor plan

1. Entry
2. Living area
3. Dining area
4. Kitchen
5. Den
6. Loft
7. Primary bedroom
8. Primary bathroom
9. Primary closet
10. Guest room
11. Garage
12. Laundry room

LAWRENCE ROAD RESIDENCE

Brookline, Massachusetts, United States // Lot area: 5,155 sq ft; building area: 5,091 sq ft

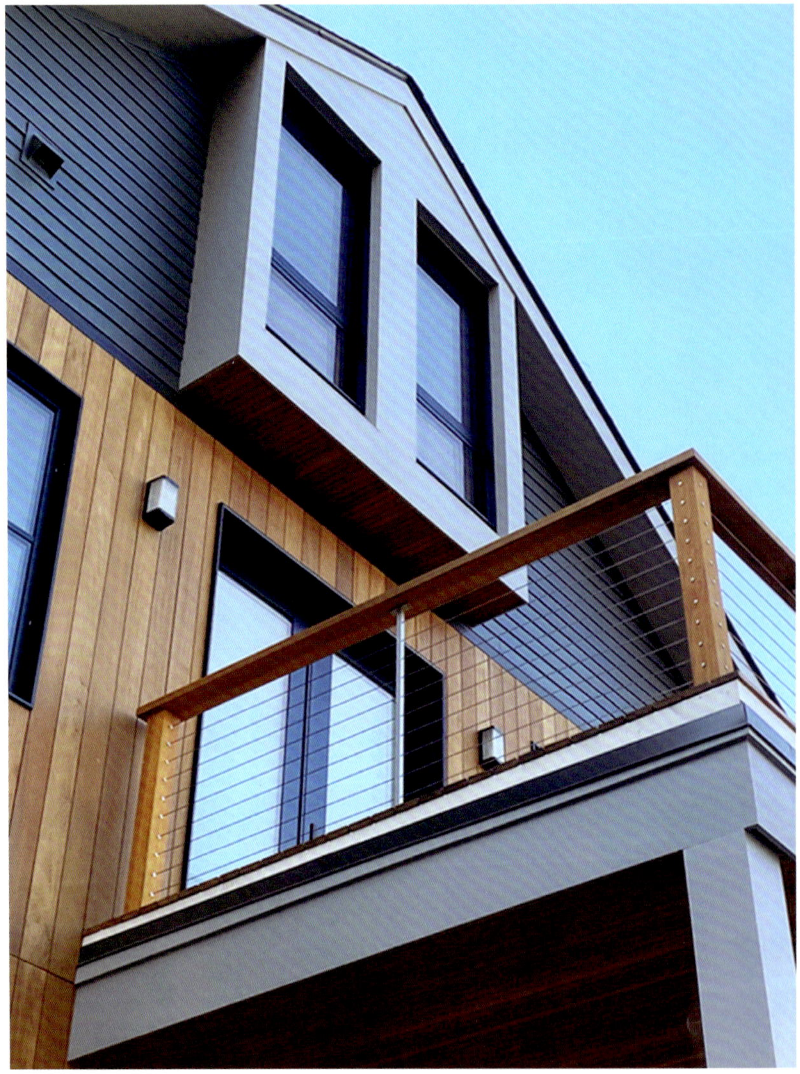

The project consisted of converting a two-family building constructed in 1905 into a single-family home, while also implementing a comprehensive energy-efficient upgrade to improve its overall performance. The primary focus of the design was to create a unified living and dining area on the first floor that takes advantage of the adjacent park views. The exterior features a modern aesthetic achieved through a combination of clear finish garapa wood cladding and gray clapboard, which offers a warm welcome to the entry and porch areas. The interior design has an extensive use of millwork that creates intimate seating and display areas. Energy efficiency is a top priority, and this has been achieved through the use of exterior insulation, triple-glazed windows, an electric heat pump system, an induction cooktop, low-flow plumbing fixtures, and rooftop photovoltaic panels.

Das Projekt bestand darin, ein 1905 erbautes Zweifamilienhaus in ein Einfamilienhaus umzuwandeln und gleichzeitig ein umfassendes energieeffizientes Upgrade umzusetzen, um die Gesamtleistung zu verbessern. Der Schwerpunkt des Designs lag darauf, im Erdgeschoss einen einheitlichen Wohn- und Essbereich zu schaffen, der die angrenzenden Parkblicke nutzt. Die Fassade weist eine moderne Ästhetik auf, die durch eine Kombination aus klar lackierter Garapa-Holzverkleidung und grauen Holzschindeln erreicht wird und einen einladenden Empfang für den Eingangs- und Verandabereich bietet. Das Innendesign nutzt umfangreich Tischlerarbeiten, die intime Sitz- und Ausstellungsbereiche schaffen. Energieeffizienz hat höchste Priorität und wurde durch den Einsatz von Außendämmung, dreifach verglasten Fenstern, einem elektrischen Wärmepumpensystem, einem Induktionskochfeld, wassersparenden Armaturen und Photovoltaikanlagen auf dem Dach erreicht.

Le projet consistait à convertir un bâtiment bifamilial construit en 1905 en une maison unifamiliale, tout en mettant en œuvre une mise à niveau énergétique complète pour améliorer sa performance globale. L'accent principal du design était de créer un espace de vie et de salle à manger unifié au premier étage, tirant parti des vues sur le parc adjacent. L'extérieur présente une esthétique moderne réalisée grâce à une combinaison de revêtement en bois de garapa à finition claire et de bardeaux gris, offrant un accueil chaleureux aux zones d'entrée et de porche. Le design intérieur utilise largement des travaux de menuiserie, créant des espaces de sièges et d'exposition intimes. L'efficacité énergétique est une priorité majeure, atteinte grâce à l'utilisation d'une isolation extérieure, de fenêtres à triple vitrage, d'un système de pompe à chaleur électrique, d'une plaque de cuisson à induction, de robinetteries à faible débit et de panneaux photovoltaïques sur le toit.

El proyecto consistió en convertir un edificio bifamiliar construido en 1905 en una casa unifamiliar, al mismo tiempo que se implementó una mejora energética integral para mejorar su rendimiento general. El enfoque principal del diseño fue crear un área de estar y comedor unificada en el primer piso que aproveche las vistas del parque adyacente. El exterior presenta una estética moderna lograda mediante una combinación de revestimiento de madera de garapa con acabado claro y tablones de madera grises, que ofrecen una cálida bienvenida a las áreas de entrada y porche. El diseño interior utiliza ampliamente trabajos de carpintería que crean áreas de asientos y exhibición íntimas. La eficiencia energética es una prioridad, y se ha logrado a través del uso de aislamiento exterior, ventanas de triple acristalamiento, un sistema de bomba de calor eléctrica, una placa de inducción, griferías de bajo flujo y paneles fotovoltaicos en el techo.

WILLIAM WEGMAN

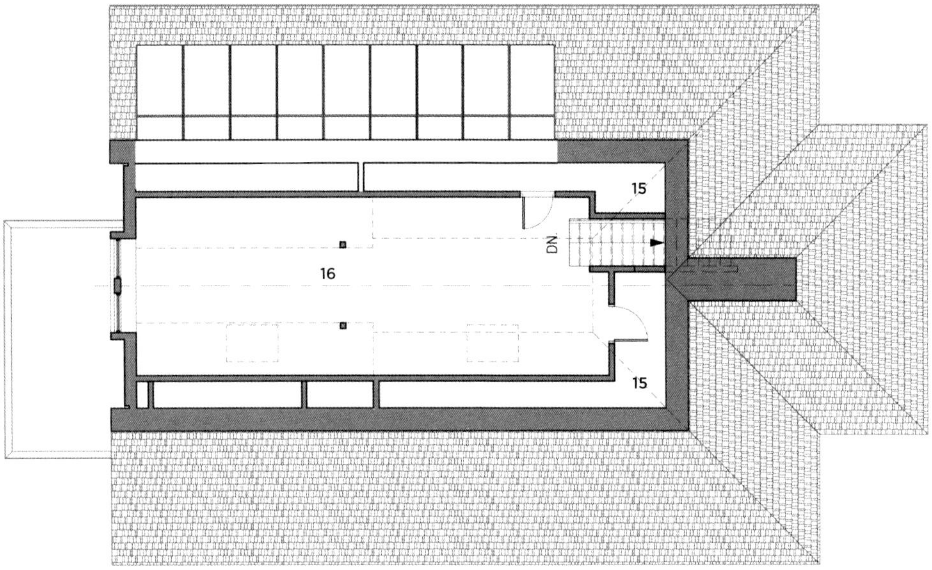

Third level floor plan

Second level floor plan

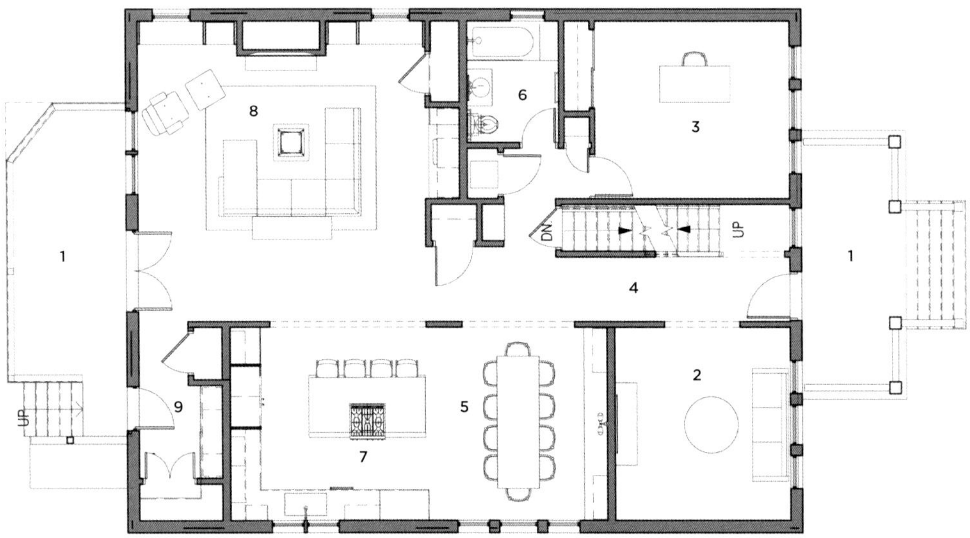

Entry level floor plan

1. Porch
2. Den
3. Study
4. Hall
5. Dining area
6. Bathroom
7. Kitchen
8. Living area
9. Mud room
10. Bedroom
11. Laundry room
12. Primary closet
13. Primary bedroom
14. Primary bathroom
15. Mechanical space
16. Loft

NICHOLSON CERETTI ARCHITECTURE

"Our work blends sustainability, modernity, and local traditions to create a strong sense of place."

NICHOLSON CERETTI ARCHITECTURE was founded by architect, musician, and visual artist Glen Nicholson. The firm is based on Canada's East Coast and is known for its commitment to environmental design, sustainability, and local context. Glen's work, rooted in Critical Regionalism, blends global design with the region's cultural and environmental heritage. Established in 2019, the firm quickly gained recognition for its thoughtful balance of modern design and functionality, creating timeless and sustainable spaces that harmonize with their urban surroundings and foster a strong sense of place. Glen's creative background as a founding member of the award-winning band In-Flight Safety further enriches his vision of architecture as a dynamic, creative force capable of shaping and elevating the human experience.

Nicholson Ceretti Architecture wurde von dem Architekten, Musiker und bildenden Künstler Glen Nicholson gegründet. Das Büro mit Sitz an der kanadischen Ostküste ist bekannt für sein Engagement für Umweltdesign, Nachhaltigkeit und den lokalen Kontext. Glens Arbeit, die auf dem Critical Regionalism basiert, verbindet globales Design mit dem kulturellen und ökologischen Erbe der Region. Das 2019 gegründete Büro erlangte schnell Anerkennung für sein durchdachtes Gleichgewicht zwischen modernem Design und Funktionalität, das zeitlose und nachhaltige Räume schafft, die mit ihrer städtischen Umgebung harmonieren und ein starkes Gefühl für den Ort vermitteln. Glens kreativer Hintergrund als Gründungsmitglied der preisgekrönten Band In-Flight Safety bereichert seine Vision von Architektur als einer dynamischen, kreativen Kraft, die in der Lage ist, die menschliche Erfahrung zu formen und zu verbessern.

Nicholson Ceretti Architecture a été fondée par l'architecte, musicien et artiste visuel Glen Nicholson. L'agence est basée sur la côte Est du Canada et est reconnue pour son engagement en faveur du design environnemental, de la durabilité et du contexte local. Le travail de Glen, ancré dans le régionalisme critique, combine un design global avec l'héritage culturel et environnemental de la région. Fondée en 2019, l'agence a rapidement gagné en notoriété grâce à son équilibre réfléchi entre design moderne et fonctionnalité, créant des espaces intemporels et durables qui s'harmonisent avec leur environnement urbain et favorisent un fort sentiment d'appartenance. Le parcours créatif de Glen, en tant que membre fondateur du groupe primé In-Flight Safety, enrichit sa vision de l'architecture en tant que force créative dynamique, capable de façonner et d'élever l'expérience humaine.

Nicholson Ceretti Architecture fue fundada por el arquitecto, músico y artista visual Glen Nicholson. El estudio tiene su sede en la costa este de Canadá y es conocido por su compromiso con el diseño medioambiental, la sostenibilidad y el contexto local. El trabajo de Glen, arraigado en el Regionalismo Crítico, mezcla el diseño global con el patrimonio cultural y ambiental de la región. Fundada en 2019, la firma ganó rápidamente reconocimiento por su reflexivo equilibrio entre diseño moderno y funcionalidad, creando espacios atemporales y sostenibles que armonizan con su entorno urbano y fomentan un fuerte sentido del lugar. Los antecedentes creativos de Glen como miembro fundador de la galardonada banda In-Flight Safety enriquecen aún más su visión de la arquitectura como una fuerza dinámica y creativa capaz de dar forma y elevar la experiencia humana.

glen__nicholson

nicholsonceretti.com

NORWOOD

SEAFORTH ARCADE

NORWOOD

Halifax, Nova Scotia, Canada // Lot area: 5,406 sq ft; building area: 3,700 sq ft

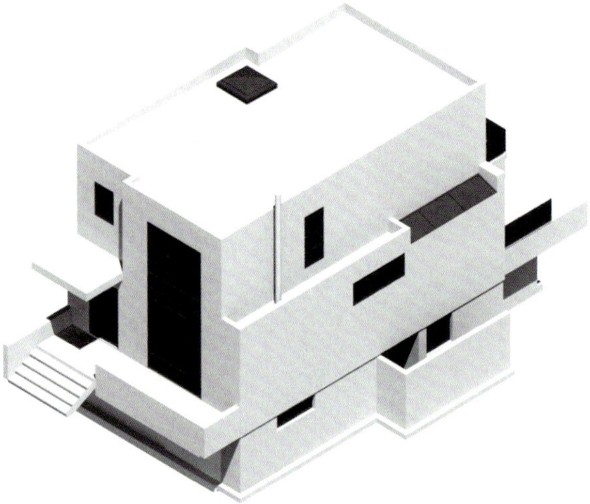

Axonometric view

Located in West End Halifax, this project transforms an unsalvageable home into a modern build that honors its predecessor. The design merges local tradition with contemporary living, featuring expansive glazed openings and durable cedar shingles, recalling the region's vernacular architecture and anchoring the home in its coastal context. Salvaged cast iron radiators link the home to its past, while maple flooring and walnut accents add warmth and complement the home's clean lines. A vertical core organizes three levels, balancing public and private spaces. The open ground floor fosters family interaction, seamlessly connecting indoor and outdoor areas. Natural light plays a key role, with filtered sunlight and an operable skylight enhancing energy efficiency. This home thoughtfully blends modern design with local tradition, responding to the region's heritage and family life demands.

Dieses Projekt im West End von Halifax verwandelt ein baufälliges Haus in ein modernes Gebäude, das seinen Vorgänger ehrt. Das Design verbindet lokale Tradition mit zeitgenössischem Wohnen, mit großzügigen Glasöffnungen und langlebigen Zedernschindeln, die an die traditionelle Architektur der Region erinnern und das Haus in seinem Küstenkontext verankern. Gerettete gusseiserne Heizkörper verbinden das Haus mit seiner Vergangenheit, während Ahornböden und Akzente aus Walnussholz für Wärme sorgen. Ein vertikaler Kern gliedert die drei Ebenen und schafft ein Gleichgewicht zwischen öffentlichen und privaten Räumen. Das offene Erdgeschoss fördert die Interaktion mit der Familie und verbindet nahtlos Innen- und Außenbereiche. Natürliches Licht spielt eine wichtige Rolle: Gefiltertes Sonnenlicht und ein bedienbares Oberlicht verbessern die Energieeffizienz. Dieses Haus verbindet auf durchdachte Weise modernes Design mit lokaler Tradition und reagiert auf das Erbe der Region und die Anforderungen des Familienlebens.

Situé dans le quartier de West End Halifax, ce projet transforme une maison irrécupérable en une construction moderne qui rend hommage à son prédécesseur. Le design fusionne tradition locale et vie contemporaine, avec de larges ouvertures vitrées et des bardeaux de cèdre durables, évoquant l'architecture vernaculaire de la région et ancrant la maison dans son contexte côtier. Des radiateurs en fonte récupérés relient la maison à son passé, tandis que le parquet en érable et les accents de noyer apportent de la chaleur. Un noyau vertical organise trois niveaux, équilibrant les espaces publics et privés. Le rez-de-chaussée ouvert favorise l'interaction familiale, reliant harmonieusement les espaces intérieurs et extérieurs. La lumière naturelle joue un rôle clé, avec une lumière tamisée et un puits de lumière ouvrable qui améliorent l'efficacité énergétique. Cette maison combine intelligemment design moderne et tradition locale, répondant à l'héritage de la région et aux exigences de la vie familiale.

Situado en el West End de Halifax, este proyecto transforma una casa insalvable en una construcción moderna que rinde homenaje a su predecesora. El diseño fusiona la tradición local con la vida contemporánea, presentando amplias aberturas acristaladas y duraderas tejas de cedro, que recuerdan la arquitectura vernácula de la región y anclan la casa en su contexto costero. Los radiadores de hierro fundido recuperados conectan la casa con su pasado, mientras que el suelo de arce y los detalles de nogal añaden calidez. Un núcleo vertical organiza los tres niveles, equilibrando los espacios públicos y privados. La planta baja abierta fomenta la interacción familiar, conectando a la perfección las zonas interiores y exteriores. La luz natural desempeña un papel clave, con luz solar filtrada y una claraboya que mejora la eficiencia energética. Esta casa combina cuidadosamente el diseño moderno con la tradición local, respondiendo al patrimonio de la región y a las exigencias de la vida familiar.

Site plan

North elevation

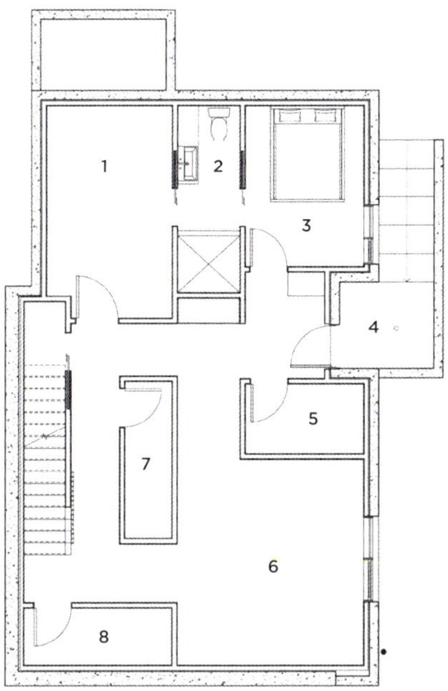

Basement level floor plan

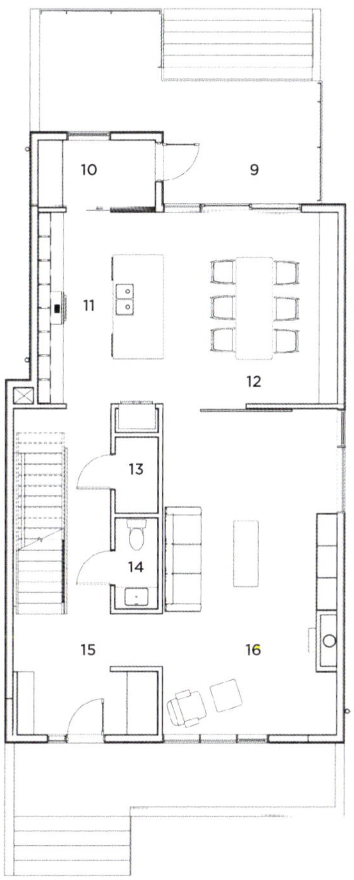

First level floor plan

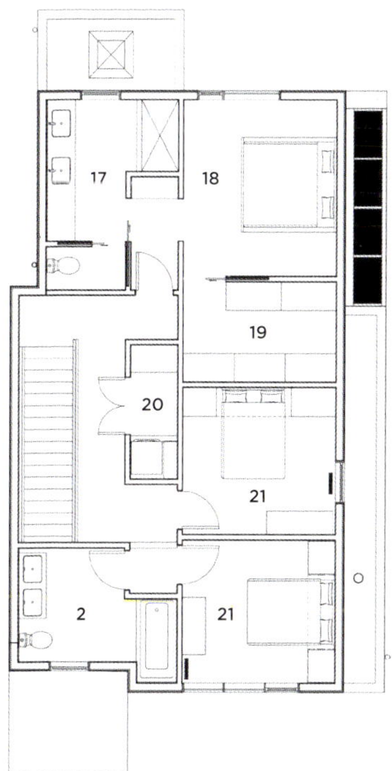

Second level floor plan

1. Fitness/gym
2. Bathroom
3. Guest bedroom
4. Basement entry
5. Storage/hockey closet
6. Sitting area
7. Wine cellar
8. Mechanical room
9. Outdoor living
10. Back entry/mudroom
11. Kitchen
12. Dining area
13. Pantry
14. Powder room
15. Entry fower
16. Living area
17. Primary bathroom
18. Primary bedroom
19. Walk-in closet
20. Laundry room
21. Bedroom

SEAFORTH ARCADE

Halifax, Nova Scotia, Canada // Lot area: 3,473 sq ft; building area: 2,605 sq ft

Seaforth Arcade blends traditional architecture with a passion for vintage pinball. Its gabled roof and entry bump-out reflect the area's vernacular style, while black siding, cedar-clad stairs, and large windows add playful contrast. A black standing-seam roof ensures durability and elegance. Inside, a white oak-wrapped core anchors the space, with rift oak paneling discreetly hiding closets and a powder room. The laminated oak stair guardrail connects each level, while the basement repurposes an old foundation for the arcade. The minimalist kitchen, with oak paneling and black fixtures, enhances the indoor-outdoor flow. Skylights illuminate the stairwell, while sloped ceilings mirror the gabled exterior. In the primary bedroom, black fixtures contrast with oak millwork. Seaforth Arcade elegantly merges tradition and modern passion, creating a minimalist home that honors Halifax's heritage.

Seaforth Arcade kombiniert traditionelle Architektur mit einer Leidenschaft für Flipperautomaten. Das Giebeldach und der Eingangsvorsprung greifen den regionalen Baustil auf, während die schwarze Fassade, die mit Zedernholz verkleidete Treppe und große Fenster einen modernen Kontrast setzen. Das Stehfalzdach in Schwarz verleiht dem Haus Beständigkeit und Eleganz. Innen verankert ein mit weißer Eiche verkleideter Kern den Raum, wobei die Verkleidung aus gerissener Eiche diskret Schränke und eine Nasszelle verbirgt. Ein Treppengeländer aus laminiertem Eichenholz verbindet die verschiedenen Etagen. Das Untergeschoss nutzt ein altes Fundament für die Arcade. Die minimalistische Küche, mit Eichenverkleidung und schwarzen Akzenten, betont die Verbindung zwischen Innen und Außen. Oberlichter erhellen das Treppenhaus, während schräge Decken die Giebelform des Hauses widerspiegeln. Im Hauptschlafzimmer bilden schwarze Armaturen einen markanten Kontrast zu den Eichenholzausführungen. Seaforth Arcade verbindet elegant Tradition und moderne Leidenschaft und schafft ein minimalistisches Zuhause, das das Erbe von Halifax ehrt.

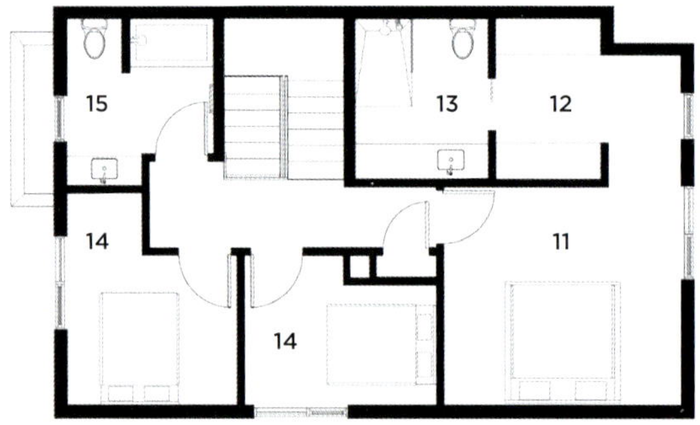

Second level floor plan

First level floor plan

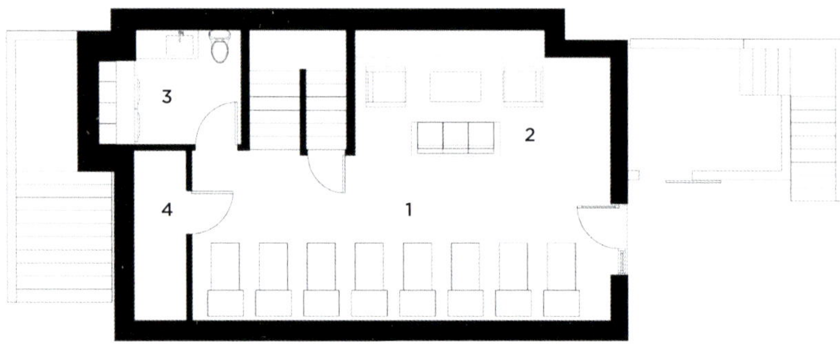

Basement level floor plan

1. Pinball arcade
2. Sitting area
3. Bathroom/ laundry room
4. Storage/ mechanical room
5. Entry fower
6. Livin area
7. Powder room
8. Kitchen
9. Dining area
10. Rear deck
11. Primary bedroom
12. Walk-in closet
13. Primary bathroom
14. Bedroom
15. Bathroom

6368

Seaforth Arcade combine une architecture traditionnelle avec une passion pour les flippers vintage. Son toit à pignon et son renfoncement d'entrée reflètent le style vernaculaire de la région, tandis que le revêtement noir, les escaliers en cèdre et les grandes fenêtres apportent un contraste moderne. Un toit à joint debout noir allie durabilité et élégance. À l'intérieur, un noyau enveloppé de chêne blanc structure l'espace, cachant habilement des placards et une salle d'eau. La rampe d'escalier en chêne stratifié relie chaque niveau, et le sous-sol réutilise une ancienne fondation pour abriter l'arcade. La cuisine minimaliste, avec ses panneaux de chêne et ses accessoires noirs, améliore la fluidité entre l'intérieur et l'extérieur. Des puits de lumière illuminent la cage d'escalier, et les plafonds inclinés reflètent l'extérieur à pignon. Les accessoires noirs de la chambre principale contrastent avec le travail de menuiserie en chêne. Seaforth Arcade fusionne admirablement tradition et passion moderne, créant une maison minimaliste qui honore l'héritage d'Halifax.

Seaforth Arcade combina la arquitectura tradicional con la pasión por el pinball vintage. Su tejado a dos aguas y el saliente de la entrada reflejan el estilo vernáculo de la zona, mientras que el revestimiento negro, las escaleras revestidas de cedro y los grandes ventanales añaden un contraste moderno. El tejado negro con juntas alzadas garantiza la durabilidad y la elegancia. En el interior, un núcleo revestido de roble blanco con paneles de roble rift ocultan discretamente armarios y un tocador. La barandilla de roble laminado de la escalera conecta cada nivel, mientras que el sótano reutiliza unos antiguos cimientos para la sala de pinball. La cocina minimalista, con paneles de roble y accesorios negros, realza el vínculo interior-exterior. Las claraboyas iluminan el hueco de la escalera y los techos inclinados reflejan el exterior a dos aguas. Los apliques negros del dormitorio principal contrastan con la carpintería de roble. Seaforth Arcade fusiona a la perfección tradición y pasión moderna, creando una casa minimalista que honra el patrimonio de Halifax.

NORDAIS ARCHITECTURE

"How to better inhabit the land and nurture the richness of landscapes."

Nordais is an architecture studio based in the Acadian Peninsula, New Brunswick, Canada, founded in 2019 by Marika Drolet-Ferguson and Mathieu Boucher-Côté. Guided by values of simplicity, craftsmanship, and sustainability, Nordais views each project as a way to enhance quality of life and enrich landscapes. The team is driven by creating comfortable spaces where people and communities can recognize themselves and thrive. Nordais sees construction as an opportunity to reflect on our use of the planet's resources, positioning architecture as a key to fostering a responsible attitude towards our environment. The studio has received awards such as the Lieutenant Governor Award of Excellence in Architecture of New Brunswick and the Atlantic Architectural Design Excellence Award. Additionally, it has showcased its work in exhibitions and installations in Canada, Italy, Iceland, and Sweden.

Nordais ist ein Architekturbüro auf der Akadischen Halbinsel in New Brunswick, Kanada, das 2019 von Marika Drolet-Ferguson und Mathieu Boucher-Côté gegründet wurde. Geleitet von den Werten Einfachheit, Handwerkskunst und Nachhaltigkeit sieht Nordais jedes Projekt als Chance, die Lebensqualität zu verbessern und Landschaften zu bereichern. Das Team schafft komfortable Räume, in denen Menschen und Gemeinschaften sich wiedererkennen und gedeihen können. Architektur ist für Nordais der Schlüssel, eine verantwortungsvolle Haltung gegenüber unserer Umwelt zu fördern. Das Studio hat Auszeichnungen wie den Lieutenant Governor Award of Excellence in Architecture von New Brunswick und den Atlantic Architectural Design Excellence Award erhalten und seine Arbeiten in Kanada, Italien, Island und Schweden präsentiert.

Nordais est un studio d'architecture basé dans la Péninsule acadienne, au Nouveau-Brunswick, Canada, fondé en 2019 par Marika Drolet-Ferguson et Mathieu Boucher-Côté. Guidé par des valeurs de simplicité, savoir-faire et durabilité, Nordais voit chaque projet comme une occasion d'améliorer la qualité de vie et d'enrichir les paysages. L'équipe crée des espaces confortables où les gens et les communautés peuvent se reconnaître et prospérer. Nordais perçoit la construction comme une réflexion sur l'utilisation des ressources de la planète, positionnant l'architecture comme un élément clé pour encourager une attitude responsable envers l'environnement. Le studio a reçu des prix comme le Prix d'excellence en architecture du lieutenant-gouverneur du Nouveau-Brunswick et le Prix d'excellence en design architectural de l'Atlantique, et a exposé ses travaux au Canada, en Italie, en Islande et en Suède.

Nordais es un estudio de arquitectura con sede en la Península Acadiana, en Nuevo Brunswick, Canadá, fundado en 2019 por Marika Drolet-Ferguson y Mathieu Boucher-Côté. Guiado por valores de simplicidad, artesanía y sostenibilidad, Nordais ve cada proyecto como una oportunidad para mejorar la calidad de vida y enriquecer los paisajes. El equipo se impulsa creando espacios cómodos donde las personas y las comunidades puedan reconocerse y prosperar. Nordais ve la construcción como una oportunidad para reflexionar sobre nuestro uso de los recursos del planeta, posicionando la arquitectura como clave para fomentar una actitud responsable hacia nuestro entorno. El estudio ha recibido premios como el Premio a la Excelencia en Arquitectura del Teniente Gobernador de New Brunswick y el Premio a la Excelencia en Diseño Arquitectónico del Atlántico. Además, ha exhibido su trabajo en exposiciones e instalaciones en Canadá, Italia, Islandia y Suecia.

nordais_architecture nordais.com

MAISON DU BOCAGE

SOMMARHUS

MAISON DU BOCAGE

Sainte Anne du Bocage, New Brunswick, Canada // Lot area: 4.6 acres; building area: 880 sq ft (main floor)

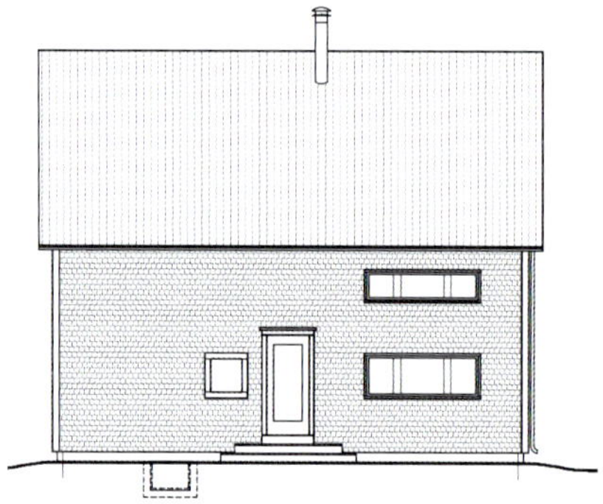

North elevation

East elevation

The rehabilitation of the oldest house in the Caraquet region, estimated to be two hundred years old, beautifully blends past Acadian craftsmanship with modern design. The project aimed to highlight the quality of the spaces and materials, demonstrating how architecture can preserve and promote local culture, heritage, and skills in rural settings. The house's new insulation layer allows the H-Bent-type structure to be visible from the inside. The spaces are designed for the client's contemporary lifestyle while showcasing intricate hand-crafted structural details and wide boards that reflect the region's nineteenth-century trees. Community collaboration, including the wood miller and the lead carpenter — a former wooden boat builder—, was crucial in preserving this heritage building. These efforts allow the project to narrate the Acadian identity of the past while integrating it into modern existence.

Die Sanierung des ältesten Hauses in der Region Caraquet, das auf zweihundert Jahre geschätzt wird, verbindet auf wunderschöne Weise die akadische Handwerkskunst der Vergangenheit mit modernem Design. Das Projekt zielte darauf ab, die Qualität der Räume und Materialien hervorzuheben und zu zeigen, wie Architektur die lokale Kultur, das Erbe und die Fähigkeiten in ländlichen Umgebungen bewahren und fördern kann. Die neue Dämmschicht des Hauses ermöglicht es, dass die H-Bent-Struktur von innen sichtbar ist. Die Räume sind für den zeitgenössischen Lebensstil des Kunden konzipiert und zeigen gleichzeitig aufwendige handgefertigte Strukturelemente und breite Bretter, die die Bäume der Region aus dem 19. Jahrhundert widerspiegeln. Die Zusammenarbeit mit der Gemeinde, einschließlich des Holzarbeiters und des leitenden Zimmermanns — ein ehemaliger Holzbootbauer — war entscheidend für den Erhalt dieses denkmalgeschützten Gebäudes. Diese Bemühungen ermöglichen es dem Projekt, die akadische Identität der Vergangenheit zu erzählen und sie in die moderne Existenz zu integrieren.

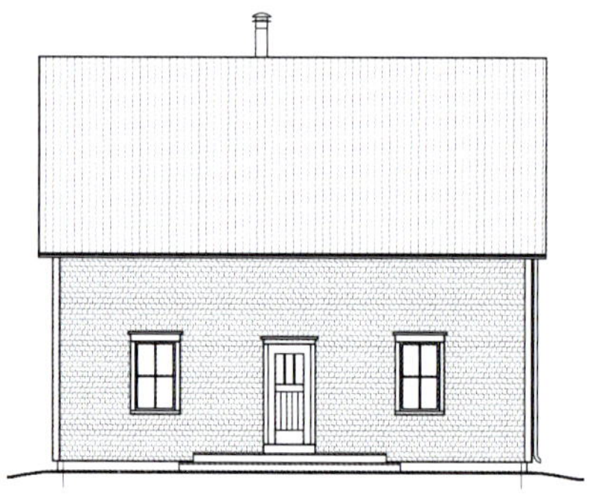

South elevation

West elevation

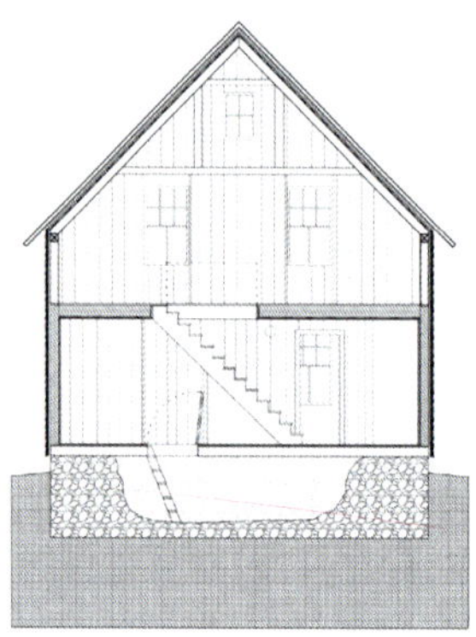

Building section (existing)

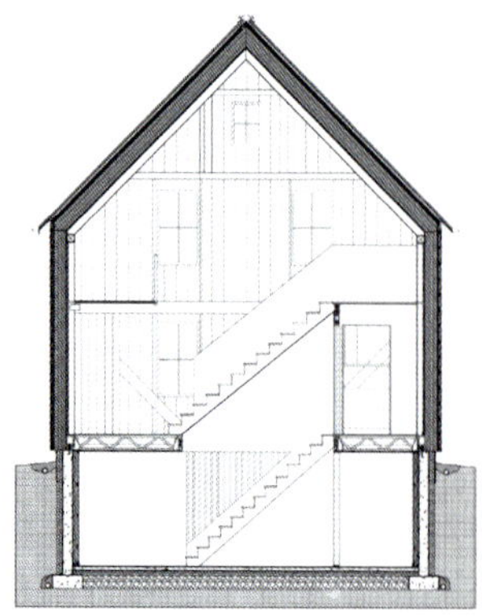

Building section (proposed)

La réhabilitation de la plus ancienne maison de la région de Caraquet, estimée à 200 ans, mêle magnifiquement l'artisanat acadien du passé au design moderne. Le projet visait à mettre en valeur la qualité des espaces et des matériaux, démontrant comment l'architecture peut préserver et promouvoir la culture locale, le patrimoine et les compétences dans les milieux ruraux. La nouvelle couche d'isolation de la maison permet de rendre la structure de type H-Bent visible de l'intérieur. Les espaces sont conçus pour le style de vie contemporain du client tout en mettant en valeur des détails structurels complexes faits à la main et des planches larges qui reflètent les arbres du XIXe siècle de la région. La collaboration communautaire, incluant le meunier de bois et le charpentier principal — un ancien constructeur de bateaux en bois — a été cruciale pour préserver ce bâtiment patrimonial. Ces efforts permettent au projet de raconter l'identité acadienne du passé tout en l'intégrant à l'existence moderne.

La rehabilitación de la casa más antigua de la región de Caraquet, estimada en 200 años de antigüedad, mezcla hermosamente la artesanía Acadiana del pasado con el diseño moderno. El proyecto tenía como objetivo destacar la calidad de los espacios y materiales, demostrando cómo la arquitectura puede preservar y promover la cultura, el patrimonio y las habilidades locales en entornos rurales. La nueva capa de aislamiento de la vivienda permite que la estructura tipo H-Bent sea visible desde el interior. Los espacios están diseñados para el estilo de vida contemporáneo del cliente mientras muestran intrincados detalles estructurales hechos a mano y tablas anchas que recuerdan los árboles del siglo XIX de la región. La colaboración comunitaria, que incluyó al molinero y al carpintero principal —un ex constructor de barcos de madera—, fue crucial para preservar este edificio patrimonial. Estos esfuerzos permiten que el proyecto narre la antigua identidad Acadiana mientras la integra en la existencia moderna.

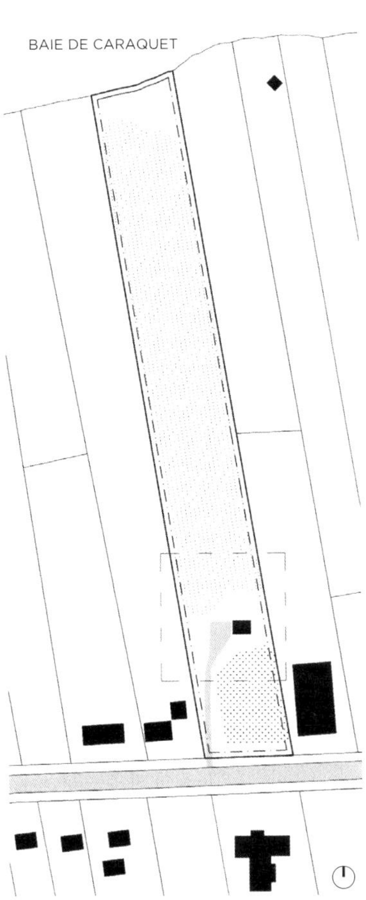

Site plan

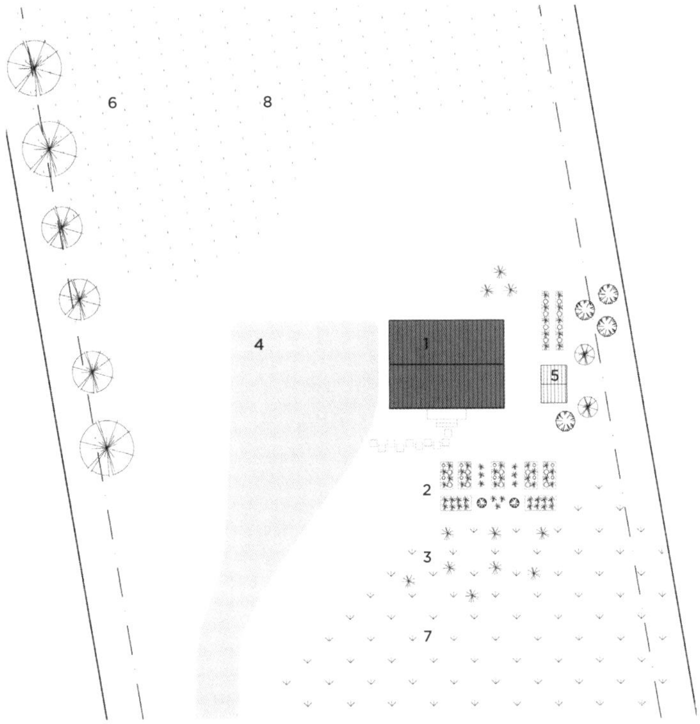

Site plan (close up)

1. Maison du Bocage
2. Garden
3. Orchard
4. Parking
5. Chicken coop
6. Wild blueberries
7. Wild flowers
8. Tall grasses

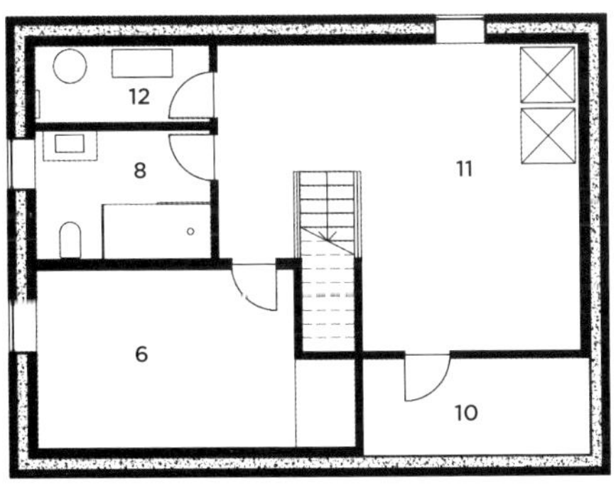

Basement level floor plan

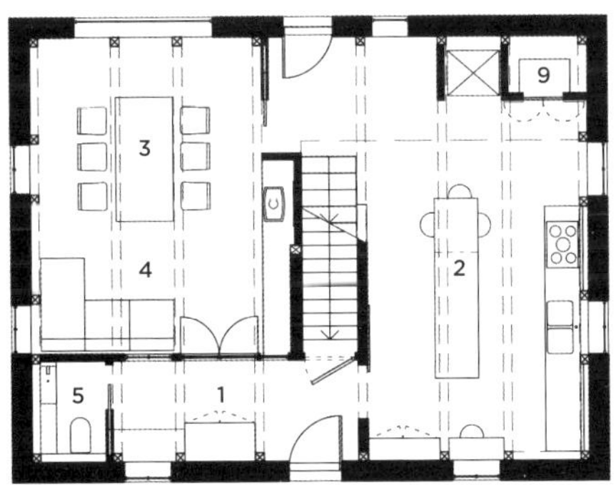

Main level floor plan

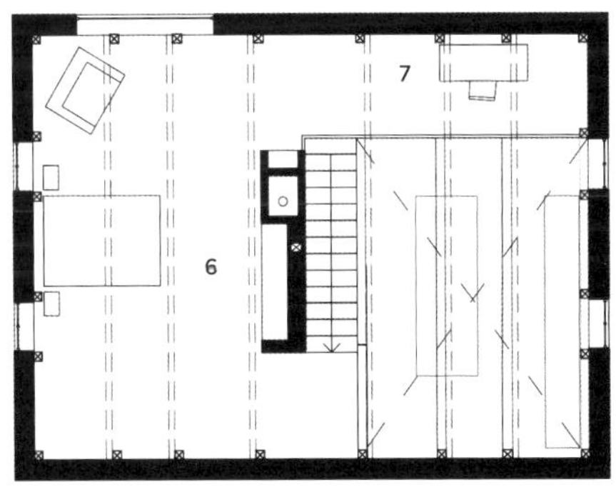

Second level floor plan

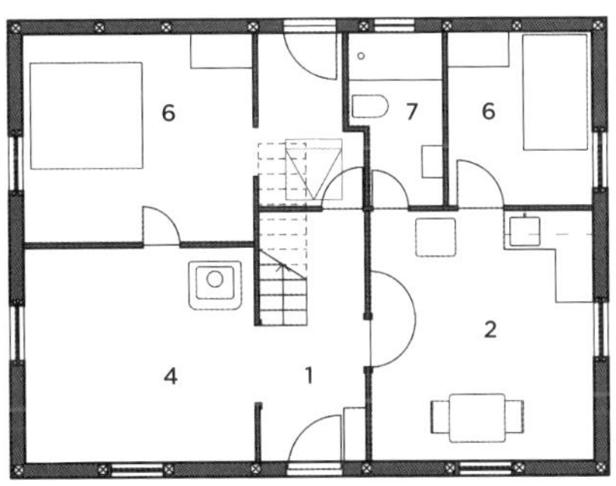

Main level floor plan (existing)

1. Entrance
2. Kitchen
3. Dining area
4. Living area
5. Water closet
6. Bedroom
7. Office
8. Bathroom
9. Pantry
10. Cold room
11. Storage/laundry
12. Mechanical room

SOMMARHUS

Tracadie, New Brunswick, Canada // Lot area: 2 acres; building area: 1,160 sq ft existing house + 600 sq ft extension

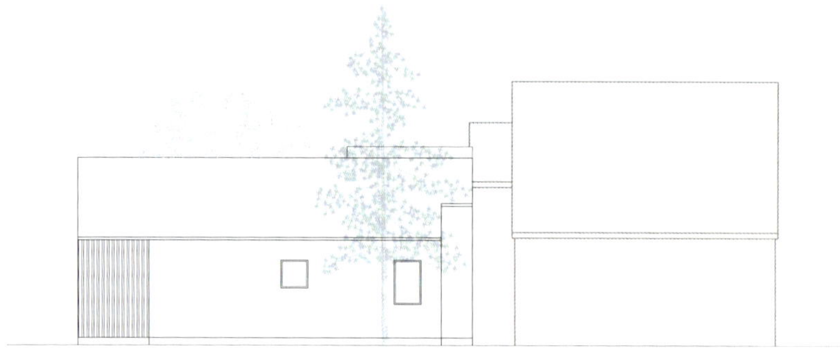

North elevation

This 600-square-foot extension has transformed an existing house into a solar-powered, multi-generational home where two families coexist, each with their own private spaces. Various sustainable elements were integrated into the design, including strategically placed windows for passive solar energy, a layout promoting cross-ventilation, and concrete flooring for thermal gain. The foliage of an existing Linden tree provides summer shade on the south-facing façade. Wood was the preferred material for the framework, interior and exterior finishes, and built-in furniture. The project also features salvaged planks from a 125-year-old barn used in the ceiling, and incorporates recycled and renewable materials, including hemp batting and wood-fiber panels for insulation. The insulation level was increased to keep the house warm in winter and cool in summer, aiming to reduce energy consumption.

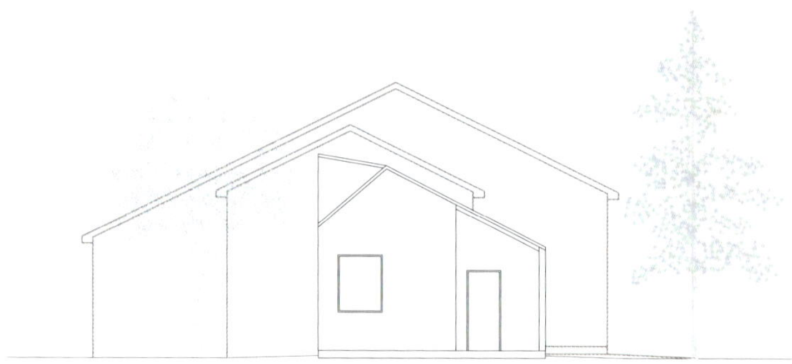

East elevation

Diese 55 Quadratmeter große Erweiterung hat ein bestehendes Haus in ein solarbetriebenes Mehrgenerationenhaus verwandelt, in dem zwei Familien koexistieren, jede mit ihren eigenen privaten Bereichen. Mehrere nachhaltige Elemente wurden in den Entwurf integriert, darunter strategisch platzierte Fenster zur Nutzung passiver Solarenergie, ein Design, das die Querlüftung fördert, und Betonböden für Wärmegewinne. Das Laub einer bestehenden Linde spendet der nach Süden ausgerichteten Fassade im Sommer Schatten. Holz war das bevorzugte Material für die Struktur, die Innen- und Außenverkleidung und die Einbaumöbel. Das Projekt umfasst auch wiederverwendete Bretter einer 125 Jahre alten Scheune, die für das Dach verwendet wurden, sowie recycelte und erneuerbare Materialien, einschließlich Hanfpolster und Holzfaserplatten für die Isolierung, die erhöht wurde, um das Haus im Winter warm und im Sommer kühl zu halten, mit dem Ziel, den Energieverbrauch zu senken.

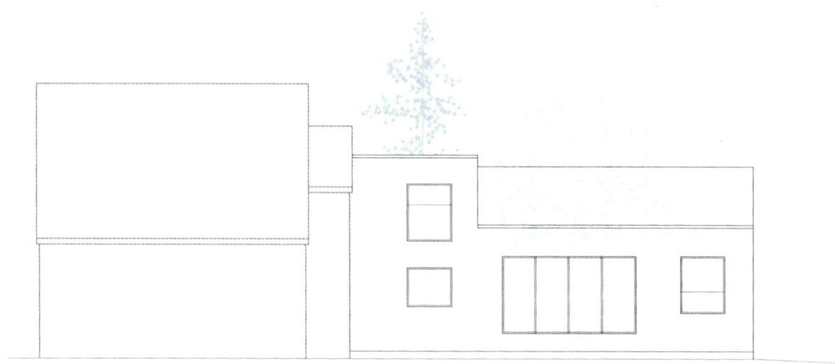

South elevation

Cette extension de 55 mètres carrés a transformé une maison existante en une maison intergénérationnelle alimentée par l'énergie solaire, où deux familles coexistent, chacune avec ses propres espaces privés. Plusieurs éléments durables ont été intégrés dans la conception, notamment des fenêtres stratégiquement placées pour exploiter l'énergie solaire passive, une conception qui favorise la ventilation transversale et des sols en béton pour le gain thermique. Le feuillage d'un tilleul existant fournit de l'ombre en été sur la façade orientée au sud. Le bois a été le matériau privilégié pour la structure, les finitions intérieures et extérieures et le mobilier intégré. Le projet comprend également des planches récupérées d'une grange vieille de 125 ans, utilisées pour le toit, et incorpore des matériaux recyclés et renouvelables, y compris un rembourrage en chanvre et des panneaux en fibre de bois pour l'isolation qui a été augmentée afin de garder la maison chaude en hiver et fraîche en été, dans le but de réduire la consommation d'énergie.

Esta extensión de 55 metros cuadrados ha transformado una casa existente en un hogar intergeneracional alimentado por energía solar, donde coexisten dos familias, cada una con sus propios espacios privados. Se integraron varios elementos sostenibles en el diseño, incluyendo ventanas colocadas estratégicamente para aprovechar la energía solar pasiva, un diseño que promueve la ventilación cruzada, y suelos de hormigón para el aprovechamiento térmico. El follaje de un árbol de tilo existente proporciona sombra en verano en la fachada orientada al sur. La madera fue el material preferido para la estructura, los acabados interiores y exteriores, y los muebles empotrados. El proyecto también cuenta con tablas recuperadas de un granero de 125 años de antigüedad utilizadas en el techo, e incorpora materiales reciclados y renovables, incluyendo acolchados de cáñamo y paneles de fibra de madera para un aislamiento que se incrementó para mantener la casa cálida en invierno y fresca en verano, con el objetivo de reducir el consumo de energía.

Site plan

1. Existing house
2. Addition: Sommarhus
3. Linden tree
4. Solar panels
5. Shed
6. Garden
7. Greenhouse
8. Bees
9. River

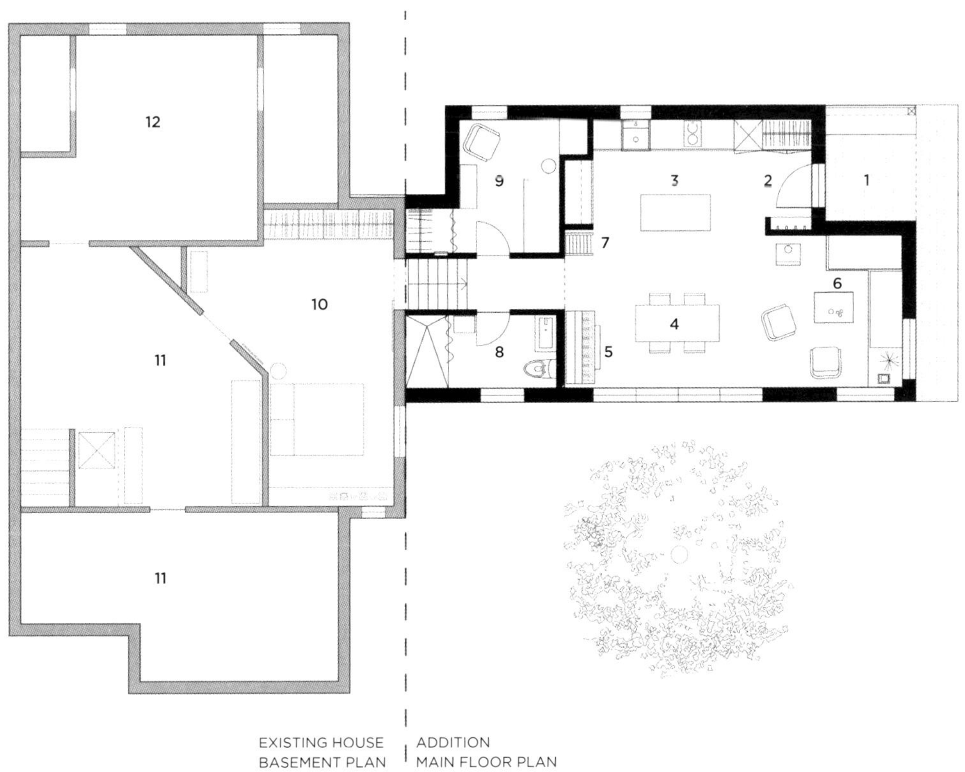

Floor plan

1. Covered entrance
2. Entrance
3. Kitchen
4. Dining area
5. Piano
6. Living area
7. Mezzanine access
8. Bathroom
9. Bedroom
10. Storage
11. Multipurpose room

QUINZHEE ARCHITECTURE

"No matter the project, our only prerequisite is to design differently and have fun."

Founded in 2013, Quinzhee promotes everyday architecture, focusing on urbanity and sustainability. In 2019, Guillaume Fafard, Quinzhee's founder, received the first *Prix de la Relève en Architecture* for the quality of his practice and for making architecture accessible. Initially working solo, Guillaume is now joined by partner Catherine Parent and a team of ten, all committed to a fresh approach. Quinzhee responds to the challenges of climate change by proposing gentle urban densification through typologies that optimize living space while providing access to outdoor spaces that promote housing for urban families. The firm also takes pleasure in designing experiential cottages in natural, but no less complex, contexts. Their "Passive House" certification underlines their commitment to sustainable development by integrating ecological strategies such as building energy performance and minimum environmental impact.

Quinzhee, 2013 gegründet, fördert Alltagsarchitektur mit Fokus auf Urbanität und Nachhaltigkeit. 2019 erhielt Gründer Guillaume Fafard den *Prix de la Relève en Architecture* für die Qualität und Zugänglichkeit seiner Arbeit. Anfangs allein, wird er heute von Catherine Parent und einem zehnköpfigen Team unterstützt, das eine innovative Herangehensweise verfolgt. Quinzhee begegnet den Herausforderungen des Klimawandels mit sanfter urbaner Verdichtung durch Typologien, die den Wohnraum optimieren und gleichzeitig Außenbereiche schaffen, was städtischen Familien den Zugang zu Wohnraum erleichtert. Zudem entwirft das Büro experimentelle Chalets in komplexen, natürlichen Umgebungen. Ihre „Passive House"-Zertifizierung bekräftigt das Engagement für Nachhaltigkeit durch Energieeffizienz und einen minimalen Fußabdruck.

Fondée en 2013, Quinzhee promouvoit l'architecture quotidienne en valorisant l'urbanité et la durabilité. En 2019, Guillaume Fafard, fondateur de Quinzhee, a reçu le Prix de la Relève en Architecture pour la qualité de sa pratique et l'accessibilité de l'architecture. D'abord seul, Guillaume est aujourd'hui soutenu par Catherine Parent et une équipe de dix, tous engagés dans une approche innovante. Quinzhee répond aux défis des changements climatiques en proposant une densification urbaine douce par des typologies optimisant l'aire habitable tout en donnant accès à des espaces extérieurs qui favorisent l'accès à des logements aux familles urbaines. La firme s'amuse également à concevoir des chalets expérientiels dans des contextes naturels, mais non moins complexes. Leur certification « Passive House » souligne leur engagement envers le développement durable en intégrant des stratégies écologiques telles que la performance énergétique des bâtiments et l'empreinte minimale.

Fundada en 2013, Quinzhee promueve la arquitectura cotidiana valorando la urbanidad y la sostenibilidad. En 2019, Guillaume Fafard, fundador de Quinzhee, recibió el *Prix de la Relève en Architecture* por la calidad de su práctica y por promover una arquitectura accesible. Primero en solitario, Guillaume ahora cuenta con el apoyo de Catherine Parent y un equipo de diez personas, todos comprometidos con un enfoque innovador. Quinzhee aborda los desafíos del cambio climático proponiendo una densificación urbana suave mediante tipologías que optimizan el espacio habitable y ofrecen acceso a áreas exteriores, facilitando así la disponibilidad de viviendas para familias urbanas. No menos complejos son los diseños del estudio para chalets concebidos para enriquecer la experiecia en la naturaleza. Su certificación «Passive House» subralla su compromiso con el desarrollo sostenible, integrando estrategias ecológicas como el rendimiento energético de los edificios y una huella ambiental mínima.

quinzhee_architecture — quinzhee.ca

LES FRÈRES TINO

CHEZ LÉON

LES FRÈRES TINO

Orford, Québec, Canada // Lot area: 24,252 sq ft; building area: 3,046 sq ft

Cross section 1

Les Frères Tino embraces nature and mountain activities with a design of three volumes: two chalets and a central service area, connected by a canopy for sheltered access. Cedar shingles and pine siding harmonize with the wooded surroundings. Each chalet is independent, suitable for family rentals or larger groups of up to sixteen guests. Although oriented differently, both units have similar layouts for a consistent experience. The first floor includes mudroom entrances for sports gear and minimalist bedrooms. Upstairs, bright living spaces with cathedral ceilings provide expansive views of Mont Orford. Both chalets share access to an outdoor terrace with a spa atop the central volume. The design aims for a minimalist yet memorable interior, welcoming mountain sports enthusiasts and nature seekers alike.

Les Frères Tino ist ein Projekt, das die Natur und die Aktivitäten in den Bergen in den Mittelpunkt stellt und aus drei Teilen besteht: zwei Chalets und ein zentraler Servicebereich, der durch ein Vordach für einen geschützten Zugang verbunden ist. Zedernholzschindeln und Kiefernholzverkleidung harmonieren mit der waldreichen Umgebung. Jedes Chalet ist unabhängig und eignet sich für die Vermietung an Familien oder größere Gruppen von bis zu sechzehn Personen. Obwohl beide Einheiten unterschiedlich ausgerichtet sind, haben sie einen ähnlichen Grundriss, um ein einheitliches Erlebnis zu bieten. In der ersten Etage gibt es einen Eingangsbereich für die Sportausrüstung und minimalistische Schlafzimmer. Im Obergeschoss befinden sich helle Wohnräume mit kathedralen Decken, von denen man einen weiten Blick auf den Mont Orford hat. Beide Chalets haben Zugang zu einer Außenterrasse mit einem Whirlpool in der Mitte des Gebäudes. Das Design zielt auf ein minimalistisches, aber einprägsames Interieur ab, das Bergsportler und Naturliebhaber gleichermaßen willkommen heißt.

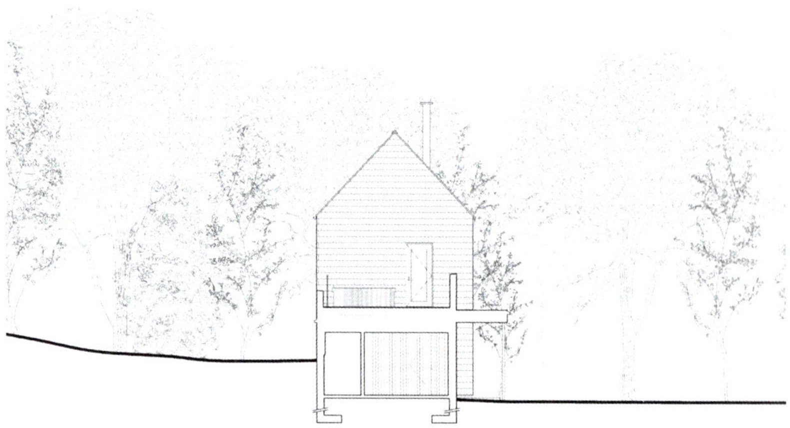

Cross section 2

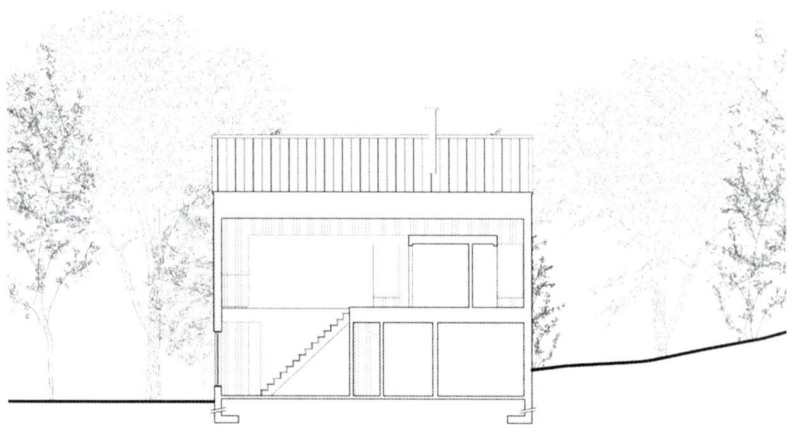

Longitudinal section

Les Frères Tino embrassent la nature et les activités de montagne grâce à un design en trois volumes : deux chalets et une zone de service centrale, reliés par une canopée pour un accès abrité. Les bardeaux de cèdre et les revêtements en pin se fondent harmonieusement dans le cadre boisé. Chaque chalet est indépendant, adapté aux familles ou à des groupes plus importants allant jusqu'à seize personnes. Bien que orientés différemment, les deux unités ont des dispositions similaires pour une expérience cohérente. Le premier étage comprend des entrées-mudrooms pour l'équipement de sport et des chambres minimalistes. À l'étage, les espaces de vie lumineux avec plafonds cathédrale offrent des vues panoramiques sur le Mont Orford. Les deux chalets partagent une terrasse extérieure avec un spa surplombant le volume central. Le design vise un intérieur minimaliste mais mémorable, accueillant les amateurs de sports de montagne et les amoureux de la nature.

Les Frères Tino abraza la naturaleza y las actividades de montaña con un diseño de tres volúmenes: dos chalés y un área de servicio central, conectados por una marquesina para un acceso protegido. Las tejas de cedro y el revestimiento de pino armonizan con el entorno boscoso. Cada chalé es independiente, adecuado para alquileres familiares o grupos más grandes de hasta dieciséis huéspedes. Aunque están orientados de forma diferente, los dos chalés tienen una distribución similar. En la primera planta hay entradas para el equipo deportivo y dormitorios minimalistas. Arriba, las luminosas salas de estar con techos altos ofrecen amplias vistas de Mont Orford. Ambos chalés comparten el acceso a una terraza exterior con un spa sobre el volumen central. El diseño busca un interior minimalista pero memorable, que dé la bienvenida tanto a los entusiastas de los deportes de montaña como a los amantes de la naturaleza.

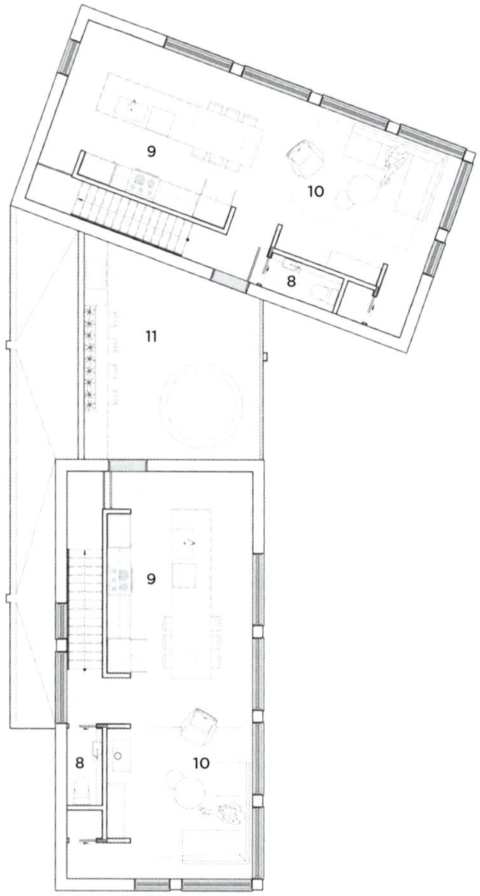

Upper level floor plan

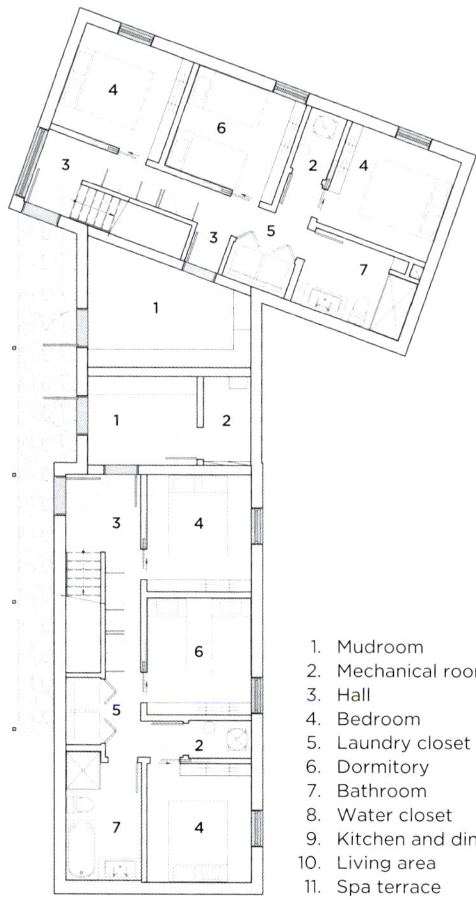

1. Mudroom
2. Mechanical room
3. Hall
4. Bedroom
5. Laundry closet
6. Dormitory
7. Bathroom
8. Water closet
9. Kitchen and dining area
10. Living area
11. Spa terrace

Lower level floor plan

CHEZ LÉON

Fief du Massif, Charlevoix, Québec, Canada // Lot area: 54,028 sq ft; building area: 1,675 sq ft

Situated on a wooded slope, this residence is elevated on stilts to reach the treetops and capture river views, minimizing its ground footprint. The sheltered area below provides a space to enjoy the outdoors in any weather while allowing nature to reclaim the land. A concrete monolith intersects the main volume, and inside, a mudroom, laundry room, and bathroom offer a welcoming retreat after skiing or biking. The upper floor features a staircase and hall that transition from the open gathering areas to the private bedrooms. Clad in cedar matching the exterior, these circulation spaces frame views of the mountains and river. The open living areas blend seamlessly with the surroundings, while the rear spa terrace offers privacy. Glass doors near the kitchen open to a screened room, perfect for quiet contemplation amidst the mountain's sounds and scents.

Dieses an einem bewaldeten Hang gelegene Wohnhaus steht auf Stelzen, um die Baumkronen zu erreichen und den Blick auf den Fluss einzufangen, wobei die Grundfläche minimiert wird. Der geschützte Bereich darunter bietet einen Raum, in dem man sich bei jedem Wetter im Freien aufhalten kann, während sich die Natur das Land zurückerobern kann. Ein Betonmonolith durchschneidet das Hauptvolumen, und im Inneren bieten eine Waschküche, ein Waschraum und ein Badezimmer einen einladenden Rückzugsort nach dem Skifahren oder Radfahren. Im Obergeschoss gibt es eine Treppe und einen Flur, die von den offenen Versammlungsräumen zu den privaten Schlafzimmern führen. Diese mit Zedernholz verkleideten Räume, die zur Außenfassade passen, geben den Blick auf die Berge und den Fluss frei. Die offenen Wohnbereiche fügen sich nahtlos in die Umgebung ein, während die hintere Spa-Terrasse Privatsphäre bietet. Glastüren in der Nähe der Küche öffnen sich zu einem abgeschirmten Raum, der sich perfekt für ruhige Kontemplation inmitten der Geräusche und Düfte der Berge eignet.

Située sur une pente boisée, cette résidence est surélevée sur pilotis pour atteindre la cime des arbres et capturer des vues sur la rivière, minimisant ainsi son empreinte au sol. L'espace abrité en dessous offre un lieu pour profiter de l'extérieur par tous les temps, tout en permettant à la nature de reprendre ses droits. Un monolithe en béton traverse le volume principal, et à l'intérieur, un vestiaire, une buanderie et une salle de bain offrent un refuge accueillant après une journée de ski ou de vélo. À l'étage, un escalier et un couloir assurent la transition entre les espaces de vie ouverts et les chambres privées. Revêtus de cèdre assorti à l'extérieur, ces espaces de circulation encadrent des vues sur les montagnes et la rivière. Les espaces de vie ouverts se fondent harmonieusement avec l'environnement, tandis que la terrasse spa arrière offre intimité et tranquillité. Les portes vitrées près de la cuisine s'ouvrent sur une pièce moustiquaire, idéale pour la contemplation paisible au cœur des sons et des odeurs de la montagne.

Situada en una ladera boscosa, esta residencia se eleva sobre pilotes para alcanzar las copas de los árboles y captar las vistas del río, minimizando su huella en el suelo. La zona protegida que hay debajo ofrece un espacio para disfrutar del aire libre con cualquier tiempo, al tiempo que permite que la naturaleza recupere el terreno. Un monolito de hormigón cruza el volumen principal, y en el interior, un cuarto de limpieza, un lavadero y un cuarto de baño ofrecen un refugio acogedor después de esquiar o montar en bicicleta. La planta superior cuenta con una escalera y un vestíbulo que sirven de transición entre las zonas de reunión abiertas y los dormitorios privados. Revestidos de cedro a juego con el exterior, estos espacios de circulación enmarcan las vistas de las montañas y el río. Las zonas de estar abiertas se funden a la perfección con el entorno, mientras que la terraza trasera con spa ofrece privacidad. Las puertas acristaladas cerca de la cocina se abren a una sala con mosquitera, perfecta para la contemplación tranquila en medio de los sonidos y aromas de la montaña.

Longitudinal section

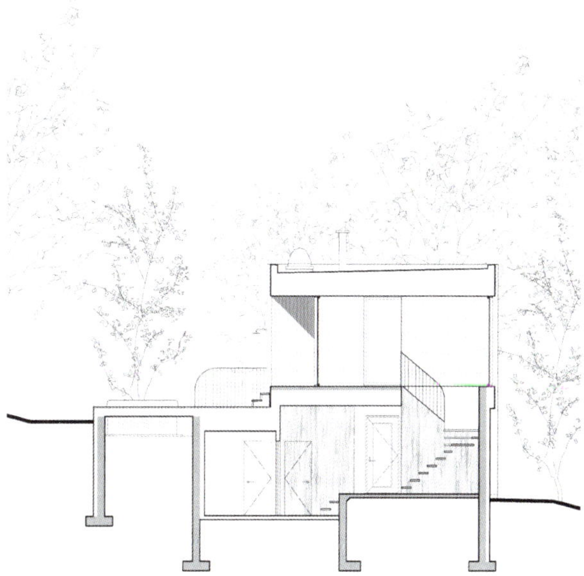

Cross section

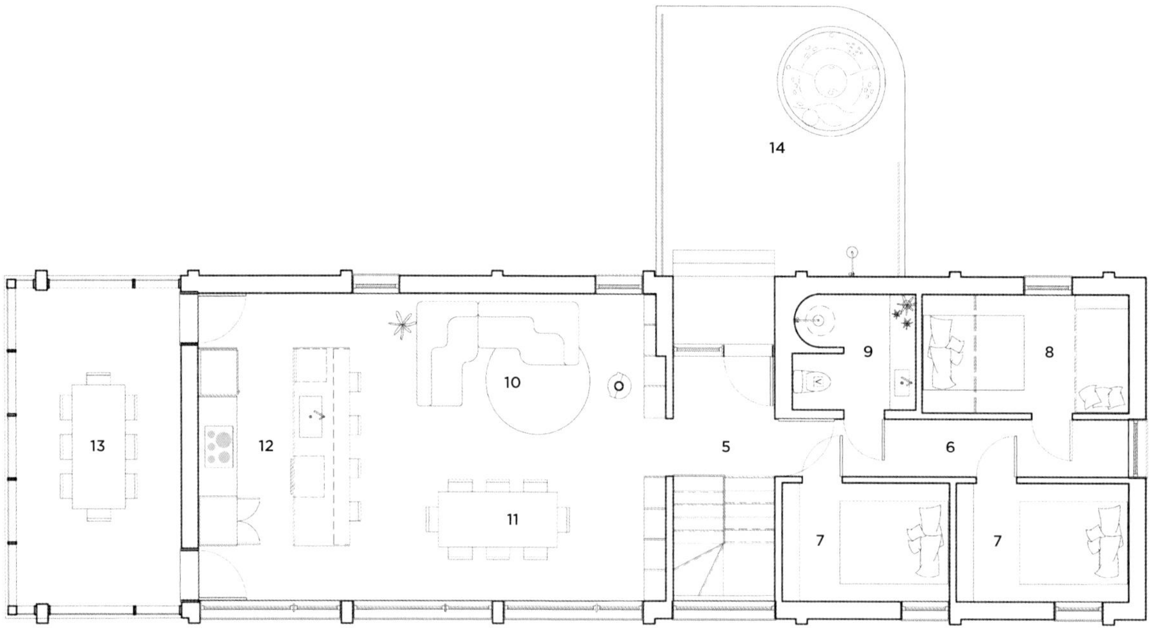

Upper level floor plan

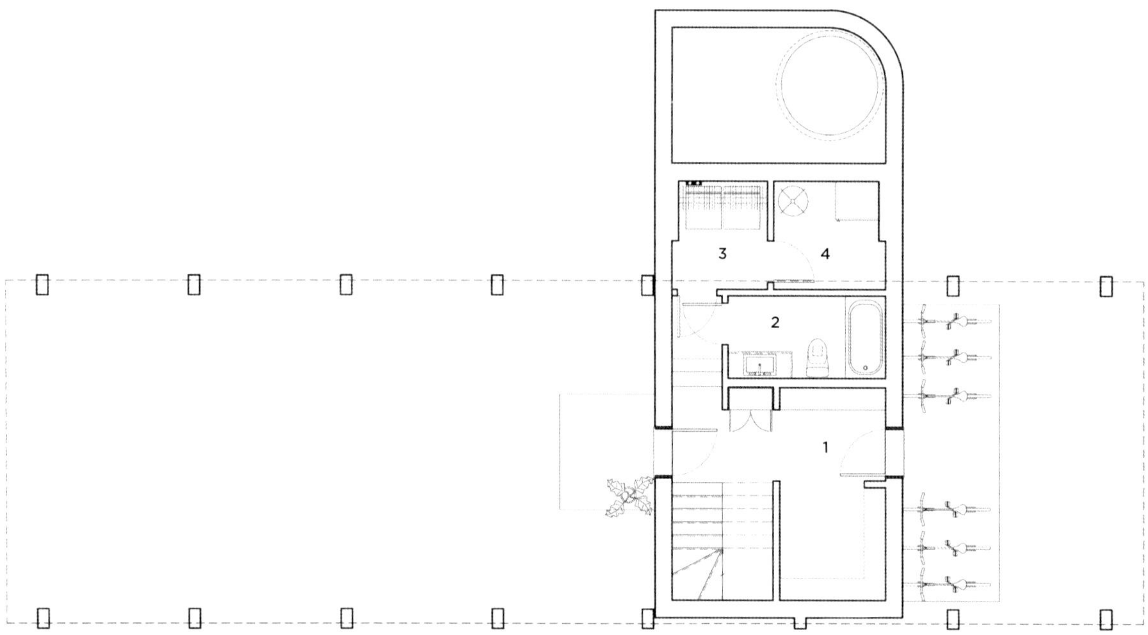

Lower level floor plan

1. Mudroom
2. Bathroom
3. Laundry room
4. Mechanical room
5. Hall
6. Bedroom corridor
7. Bedroom
8. Dormitory
9. Primary bathroom
10. Living area
11. Dining area
12. Kitchen
13. Screened room
14. Spa terrace

BoON ARCHITECTURE

"We design sustainable projects that resonate with the surrounding landscape."

BoON Architecture drives contemporary, sustainable solutions that focus on benefiting future generations through thoughtful and informed architecture. The studio designs buildings that harmonize with their natural, urban, and climatic environments, continuously innovating to achieve architectural excellence while minimizing ecological impact. With a strong foundation in bioclimatic and passive design principles, BoON ensures that its buildings are energy-efficient, durable, and resilient to shifting climates. The projects range from urban planning of eco-districts and residential complexes to community centers and landscape-integrated urban homes. BoON Architecture also possesses the resources to meet LEED and Passive House certification standards, positioning the firm at the forefront of ecological architecture in Québec.

BoON Architecture fördert nachhaltige Lösungen, die das Wohl zukünftiger Generationen durch durchdachte Architektur ins Visier nehmen. Das Studio entwirft Gebäude, die sich harmonisch in ihre natürlichen, urbanen und klimatischen Umgebungen einfügen, und entwickelt Innovationen, um architektonische Exzellenz mit minimalem ökologischen Einfluss zu erreichen. Mit einer soliden Grundlage in bioklimatischen und passiven Designprinzipien sorgt BoON dafür, dass seine Gebäude energieeffizient, langlebig und klimawiderstandsfähig sind. Die Projekte umfassen die Stadtplanung von Öko-Vierteln, Wohnkomplexen, Gemeindezentren und landschaftlich integrierten Stadthäusern. Zudem erfüllt BoON die Ressourcen, um LEED- und Passivhaus-Zertifizierungsstandards zu erreichen und positioniert sich damit an der Spitze der ökologischen Architektur in Québec.

BoON Architecture propose des solutions contemporaines et durables, axées sur le bien-être des générations futures à travers une architecture réfléchie et éclairée. Le studio conçoit des bâtiments qui s'harmonisent avec leur environnement naturel, urbain et climatique, en innovant continuellement pour atteindre l'excellence architecturale tout en minimisant l'impact écologique. Grâce à une solide maîtrise des principes de conception bioclimatique et passive, BoON garantit que ses bâtiments sont économes en énergie, durables et résistants aux changements climatiques. Ses projets vont de la planification urbaine des éco-quartiers et des complexes résidentiels aux centres communautaires et aux maisons urbaines intégrées au paysage. BoON Architecture dispose également des ressources nécessaires pour satisfaire aux normes de certification LEED et Maison Passive, plaçant ainsi le cabinet à l'avant-garde de l'architecture écologique au Québec.

BoON Architecture impulsa soluciones contemporáneas y sostenibles, enfocadas en el bienestar de las generaciones futuras a través de una arquitectura informada y reflexiva. El estudio diseña edificios que se armonizan con sus entornos naturales, urbanos y climáticos, innovando continuamente para alcanzar la excelencia arquitectónica mientras minimizan el impacto ecológico. Con una sólida base en los principios de diseño bioclimático y pasivo, BoON garantiza que sus edificios sean eficientes energéticamente, duraderos y resilientes a los cambios climáticos. Los proyectos abarcan desde la planificación urbana de eco-distritos y complejos residenciales hasta centros comunitarios y viviendas urbanas integradas en el paisaje. BoON Architecture también cuenta con los recursos necesarios para cumplir con los estándares de certificación LEED y Casa Pasiva, posicionando al estudio a la vanguardia de la arquitectura ecológica en Quebec.

boonarchitecture | boonarchitecture.ca

L'ALBAN

ARCTURUS

L'ALBAN

Lac Montauban, Québec, Canada // Lot area: 9 acres; building area: 3,590 sq ft

L'Alban takes full advantage of its lakeside setting, featuring a multi-level design with a garden level. The highlight is a west-facing outdoor pavilion with a screened room ideal for enjoying sunsets. Below, ample storage accommodates outdoor and water equipment. A bridge connects to the upper level, freeing the central level for large southern-facing windows that capture views and solar heat. Guest and children's areas have sun-shaded terraces, providing privacy and cooling, while the garden-level master suites open directly to the outdoors, ensuring a strong connection with nature. To address the steep terrain and weather, the design incorporates reinforced walls and cedar cladding, which will weather naturally and integrate with the landscape. Each detail is carefully crafted to enhance comfort and well-being in this scenic location.

L'Alban optimiert seine Lage am See mit einem mehrstöckigen Design, das ein Gartenniveau umfasst. Im Fokus steht ein nach Westen ausgerichteter Außenpavillon mit einem verglasten Raum, ideal für Sonnenuntergänge. Darunter befindet sich Stauraum für Outdoor- und Wasserausrüstung. Eine Brücke verbindet das obere Niveau, sodass das zentrale Niveau große, nach Süden ausgerichtete Fenster hat, die Ausblicke und Sonnenwärme einfangen. Die Gäste- und Kinderbereiche bieten mit Sonnenlicht geschützte Terrassen für Privatsphäre und Kühlung, während die Master-Suiten im Gartenniveau direkt ins Freie öffnen, um die Verbindung zur Natur zu stärken. Das Design berücksichtigt das steile Gelände und die Witterung mit verstärkten Wänden und Zedernverkleidung, die sich harmonisch in die Landschaft einfügen. Jedes Detail ist sorgfältig gestaltet, um Komfort und Wohlbefinden an diesem malerischen Standort zu fördern.

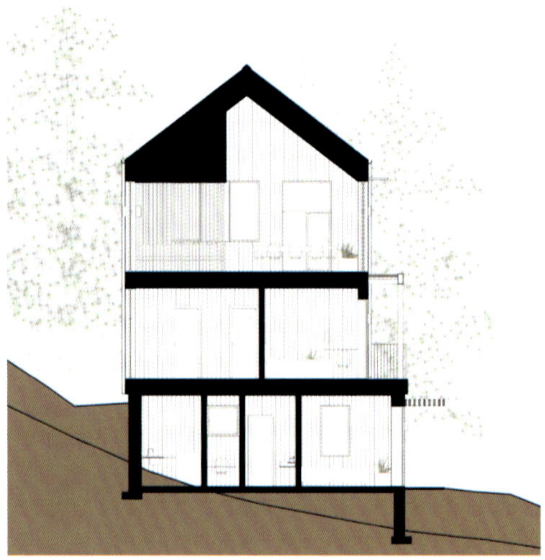

Cross section

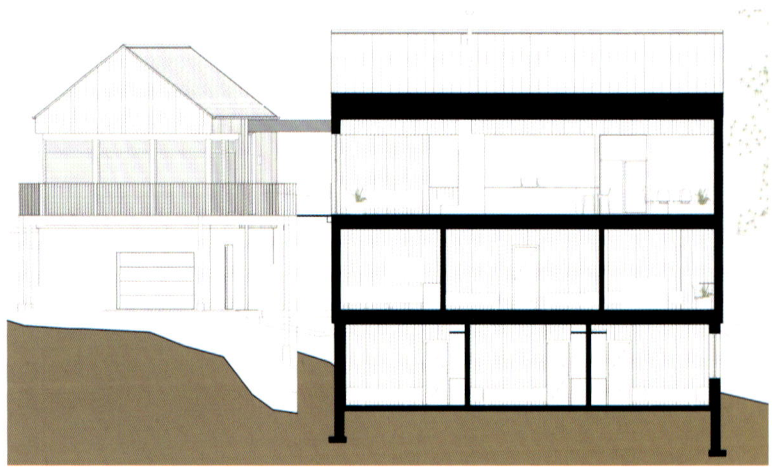

Longitudinal section

L'Alban profite pleinement de son emplacement au bord du lac, avec un design à plusieurs niveaux comprenant un jardin. Le point culminant est un pavillon extérieur orienté à l'ouest avec une véranda, parfait pour admirer les couchers de soleil. En dessous, un espace de rangement ample est prévu pour l'équipement de plein air et nautique. Un pont relie le niveau supérieur, libérant le niveau central pour de grandes fenêtres orientées au sud qui capturent les vues et la chaleur solaire. Les espaces pour les invités et les enfants disposent de terrasses ombragées, offrant intimité et fraîcheur, tandis que les suites principales au jardin s'ouvrent sur l'extérieur, renforçant la connexion avec la nature. Pour s'adapter à la pente et aux conditions météorologiques, le design intègre des murs renforcés et un revêtement en cèdre qui s'intégreront naturellement au paysage. Chaque détail est conçu pour améliorer le confort et le bien-être dans ce cadre pittoresque.

L'Alban aprovecha al máximo su ubicación junto al lago, presentando un diseño de varios niveles que incluye un nivel de jardín. El punto culminante es un pabellón exterior orientado al oeste con una sala cubierta, ideal para disfrutar de las puestas de sol. Abajo, un amplio espacio de almacenamiento acomoda el equipo de exterior y acuático. Un puente conecta con el nivel superior, liberando el nivel central para grandes ventanas orientadas al sur que capturan vistas y calor solar. Las áreas para invitados y niños cuentan con terrazas sombreadas, que proporcionan privacidad y frescura, mientras que las suites principales en el nivel del jardín se abren directamente al exterior, asegurando una fuerte conexión con la naturaleza. Para adaptarse al terreno inclinado y al clima, el diseño incorpora muros reforzados y revestimiento de cedro, que se integrará naturalmente con el paisaje. Cada detalle está cuidadosamente elaborado para mejorar la comodidad y el bienestar en este lugar pintoresco.

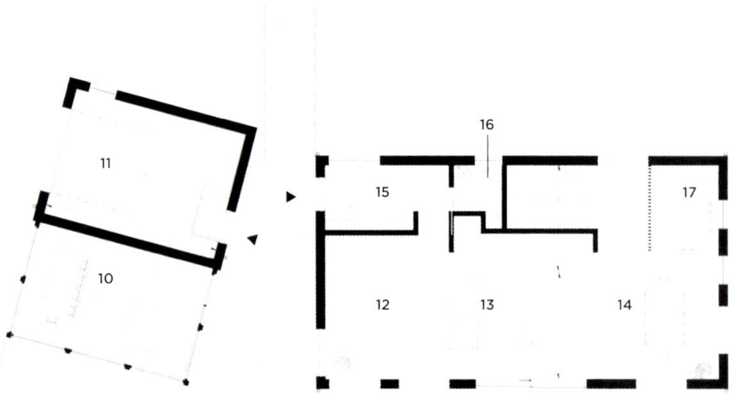

Upper level floor plan

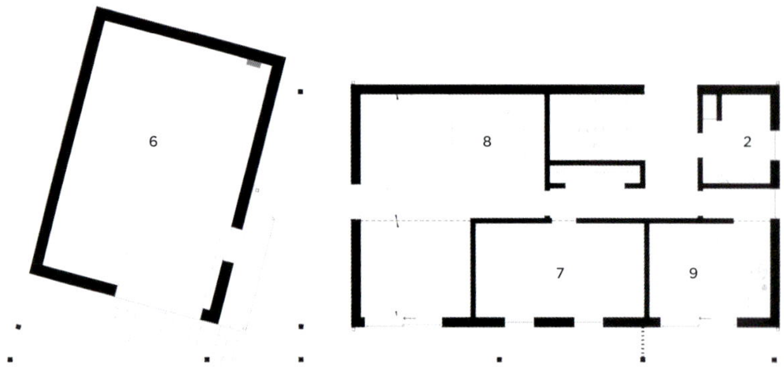

Ground level floor plan

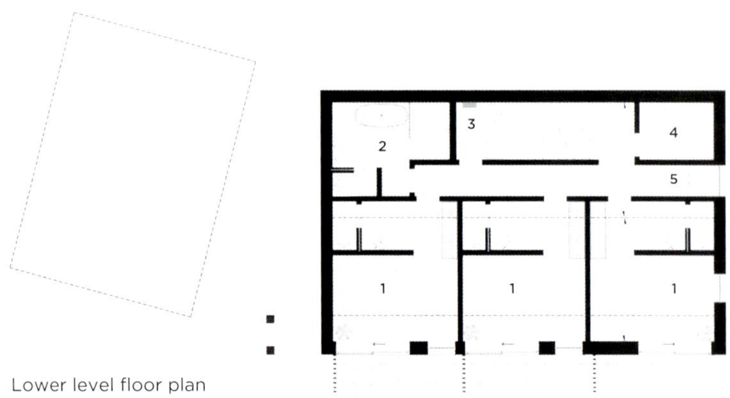

Lower level floor plan

1. Bedroom
2. Bathroom
3. Mechanical room
4. Laundry room
5. Home office
6. Storage
7. Dormitory
8. Family room
9. Guest bedroom
10. Screened living area
11. Garage
12. Living area
13. Kitchen
14. Dining area
15. Mud room
16. Powder room
17. Breakfast nook

ARCTURUS

Lac Sergent, Québec, Canada // Lot area: 12 acres; building area: 1,615 sq ft

Designed according to Passive House energy standards and located in a forested area near Lac-Sergent, the house is composed of three volumes—two simple black prisms, intersected by a third volume. The sloping roof that cuts through the house creates an inviting entry porch, linking the garage and the main living area, as well as a covered screened space. The contrasting materials emphasize the horizontal design, while wood accents in these sheltered areas add warmth and a sense of conviviality.

Entworfen nach den Energieanforderungen des Passivhauses und gelegen in einem bewaldeten Gebiet nahe Lac-Sergent, besteht das Haus aus drei Volumen—zwei einfachen schwarzen Prismen, die von einem dritten Volumen durchbrochen werden. Das geneigte Dach, das das Haus durchschneidet, schafft eine einladende Eingangsterrasse, die die Garage und den Hauptwohnraum verbindet sowie einen überdachten, geschützten Bereich bietet. Die kontrastierenden Materialien betonen das horizontale Design, während Holzakzente in diesen geschützten Bereichen Wärme und ein Gefühl der Geselligkeit hinzufügen.

Conçu selon les normes énergétiques des maisons passives et situé dans une zone boisée près de Lac-Sergent, la maison se compose de trois volumes : deux prismes noirs simples, entrecroisés par un troisième volume. Le toit en pente qui traverse la maison crée un porche d'entrée accueillant, reliant le garage et le salon principal, ainsi qu'un espace couvert et protégé. Les matériaux contrastants soulignent le design horizontal, tandis que des accents en bois dans ces zones abritées ajoutent de la chaleur et une atmosphère conviviale.

Diseñado de acuerdo con los estándares energéticos de las casas pasivas y ubicado en una zona boscosa cerca de Lac-Sergent, la casa está compuesta por tres volúmenes: dos prismas negros simples, intersecados por un tercer volumen. El techo inclinado que atraviesa la casa crea un porche de entrada acogedor, conectando el garaje con el área de estar principal, así como un espacio cubierto y protegido. Los materiales contrastantes enfatizan el diseño horizontal, mientras que los acentos de madera en estas áreas resguardadas añaden calidez y un sentido de convivialidad.

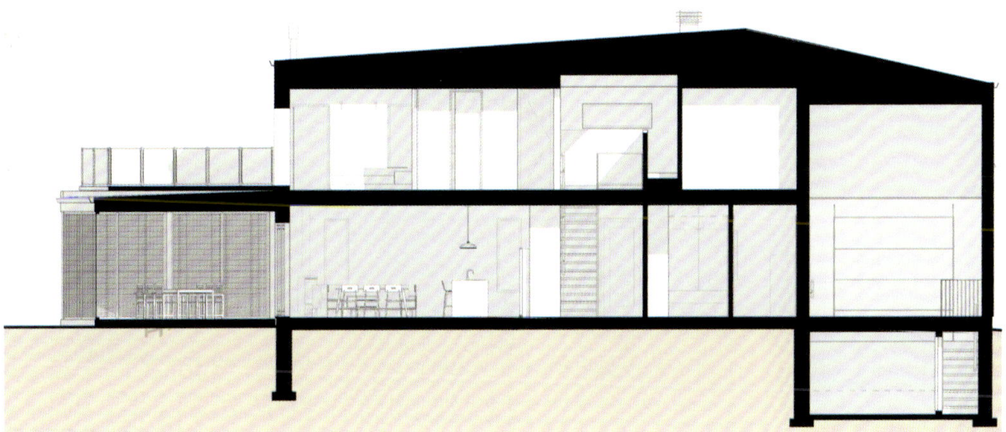

Longitudinal section

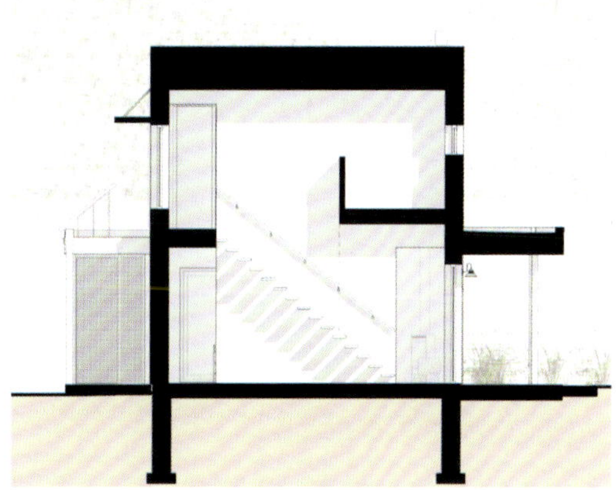

Cross section

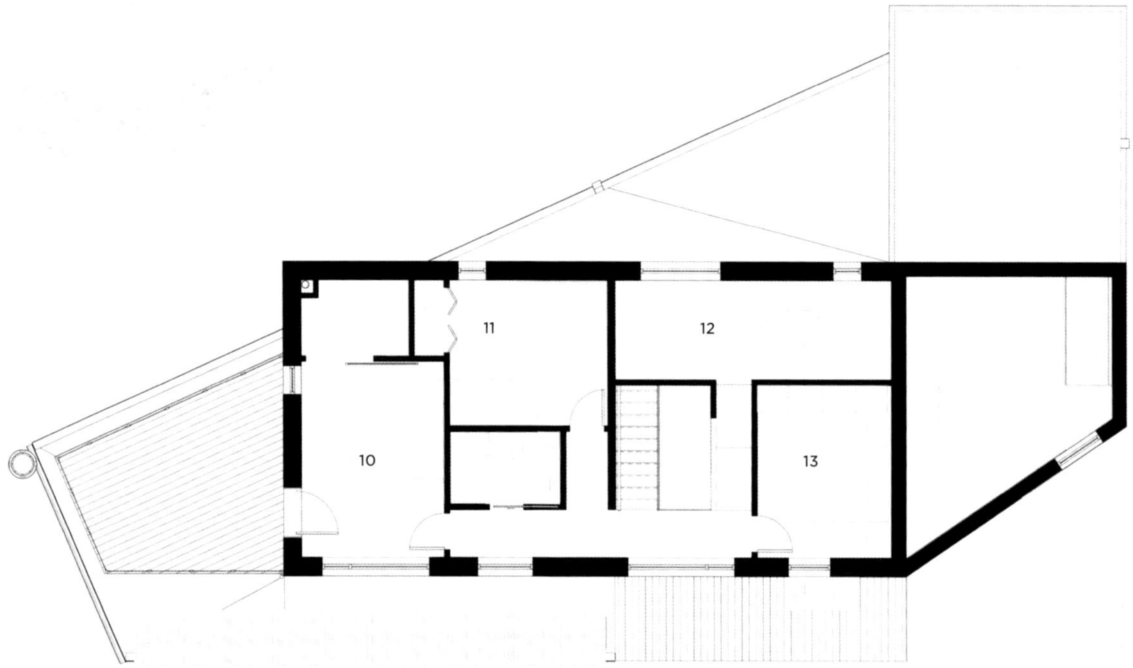

Second level floor plan

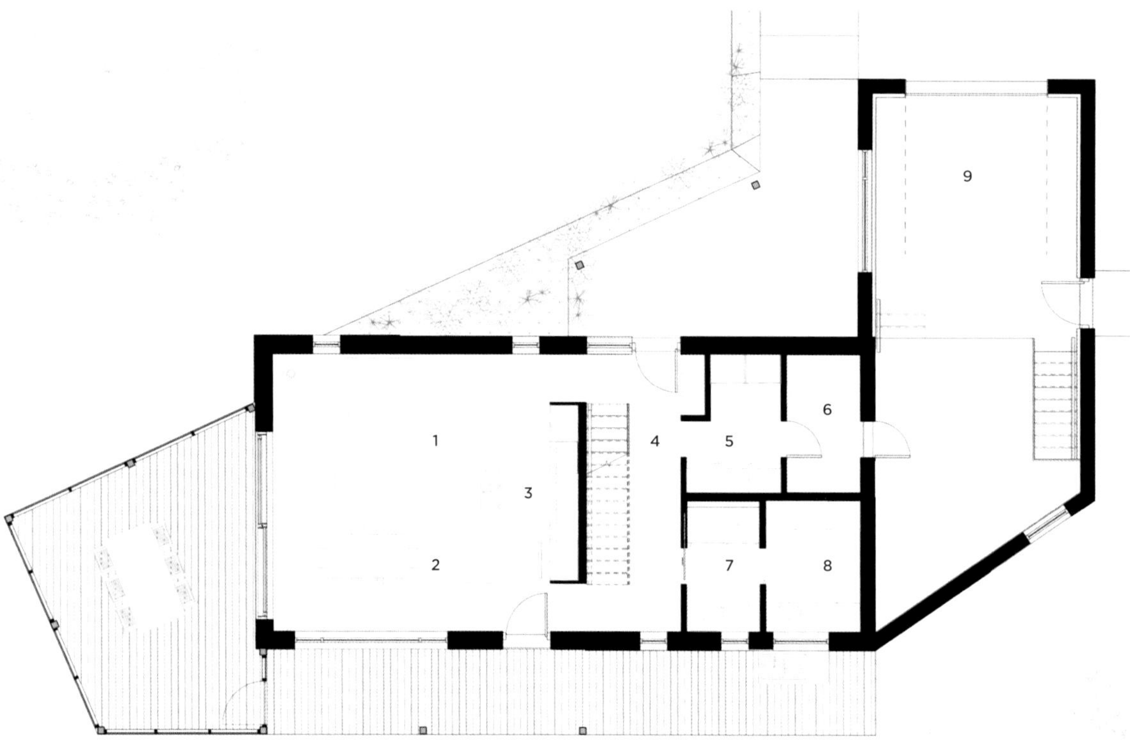

Ground level floor plan

1. Living area
2. Dining area
3. Kitchen
4. Entry
5. Mud room
6. Mechanical room
7. Bathroom
8. Laundry room
9. Garage
10. Primary bedroom
11. Dormitory
12. Exercise room
13. Guest bedroom

1628

"Our practice creates timeless living environments with a strong identity."

1628 is a creative firm that specializes in architecture, design, and landscape design. The company is located in Magog, Québec, Canada and was established in 1998 by François Parenteau, an architect, and Annie Charest, a designer, visual artist, and art historian. Since its inception, 1628 has prioritized the development of unique and enduring creations. The team members at 1628 view environmental respect not as a constraint, but as a wellspring of inspiration and innovation. In addition to their professional work, the firm dedicates significant resources to research and development to ensure ongoing evolution. 1628 undertakes projects both locally and internationally. The firm has received recognition through publications in various countries' media, participation in exhibitions, and awards in international architecture and design competitions.

1628 ist eine kreative Firma, die sich auf Architektur, Design und Landschaftsdesign spezialisiert hat. Das Unternehmen hat seinen Sitz in Magog, Québec, Kanada, und wurde 1998 von François Parenteau, einem Architekten, und Annie Charest, einer Designerin, bildenden Künstlerin und Kunsthistorikerin, gegründet. Seit seiner Gründung hat 1628 die Entwicklung einzigartiger und langlebiger Kreationen priorisiert. Die Teammitglieder von 1628 betrachten Umweltschutz nicht als Einschränkung, sondern als Quelle der Inspiration und Innovation. Neben ihrer professionellen Arbeit widmet die Firma erhebliche Ressourcen der Forschung und Entwicklung, um eine kontinuierliche Weiterentwicklung sicherzustellen. 1628 führt Projekte sowohl lokal als auch international durch. Die Firma hat Anerkennung durch Veröffentlichungen in den Medien verschiedener Länder, Teilnahme an Ausstellungen und Auszeichnungen bei internationalen Architektur- und Designwettbewerben erhalten.

1628 est une agence créative spécialisée en architecture, design et design de paysage. L'entreprise est située à Magog, Québec, Canada, et a été fondée en 1998 par François Parenteau, architecte, et Annie Charest, designer, artiste visuelle et historienne de l'art. Depuis sa création, 1628 a priorisé le développement de créations uniques et durables. Les membres de l'équipe de 1628 considèrent le respect de l'environnement non pas comme une contrainte, mais comme une source d'inspiration et d'innovation. En plus de leur travail professionnel, l'agence consacre d'importantes ressources à la recherche et au développement pour assurer une évolution continue. 1628 entreprend des projets tant au niveau local qu'international. L'agence a été reconnue par des publications dans les médias de plusieurs pays, sa participation à des expositions et des prix lors de concours internationaux d'architecture et de design.

1628 es un estudio creativo que se especializa en arquitectura, diseño y diseño de paisajes. El estudio está ubicado en Magog, Quebec, Canadá, y fue fundado en 1998 por François Parenteau, arquitecto, y Annie Charest, diseñadora, artista visual e historiadora del arte. Desde su creación, 1628 ha priorizado el desarrollo de creaciones únicas y duraderas. Los miembros del equipo de 1628 ven el respeto ambiental no como una limitación, sino como una fuente de inspiración e innovación. Además de su trabajo profesional, el estudio dedica importantes recursos a la investigación y el desarrollo para asegurar una evolución continua. 1628 lleva a cabo proyectos tanto a nivel local como internacional. El estudio ha recibido reconocimiento a través de publicaciones en medios de varios países, participación en exposiciones y premios en competiciones internacionales de arquitectura y diseño.

1628inc | 1628inc.com

S-PACE 1628

HOVEY RESIDENCE

S-PACE 1628

Magog, Québec, Canada // Lot area: 104,037 sq ft; building area: 4,898 sq ft

The project is a unified structure that combines the offices of an architecture and design firm with the residence of its directors. A light, sculptural, and continuous roof connects all these spaces, creating a three-dimensional plan that extends over the entire building, giving it a cohesive look and blending in with the surrounding hills. The interior spaces are divided into three flexible zones, allowing for easy transformation of spaces and circulation areas through the use of doors, removable partitions, and adaptable furniture. The open veranda serves as an extension of the living rooms, providing a seamless indoor-outdoor connection. All the rooms are designed to engage with the exterior and offer stunning views of Lake Memphremagog. Durable materials that require minimal maintenance were used, and the building's insulation, waterproofing, window orientation, and geometry were designed to minimize energy consumption in both winter and summer.

Das Projekt ist eine einheitliche Struktur, die die Büros einer Architektur- und Designfirma mit der Residenz ihrer Direktoren kombiniert. Ein leichtes, skulpturales und durchgehendes Dach verbindet all diese Räume und schafft einen dreidimensionalen Plan, der sich über das gesamte Gebäude erstreckt, ihm ein kohärentes Aussehen verleiht und sich in die umliegenden Hügel einfügt. Die Innenräume sind in drei flexible Zonen unterteilt, die eine einfache Umgestaltung der Räume und Zirkulationsbereiche durch den Einsatz von Türen, abnehmbaren Trennwänden und anpassbaren Möbeln ermöglichen. Die offene Veranda dient als Erweiterung der Wohnräume und bietet eine nahtlose Verbindung zwischen Innen- und Außenbereich. Alle Räume sind so gestaltet, dass sie mit der Außenwelt in Kontakt treten und atemberaubende Ausblicke auf den Lake Memphremagog bieten. Es wurden langlebige Materialien verwendet, die nur minimalen Wartungsaufwand erfordern, und die Dämmung, Abdichtung, Fensterorientierung und Geometrie des Gebäudes wurden so konzipiert, dass der Energieverbrauch sowohl im Winter als auch im Sommer minimiert wird.

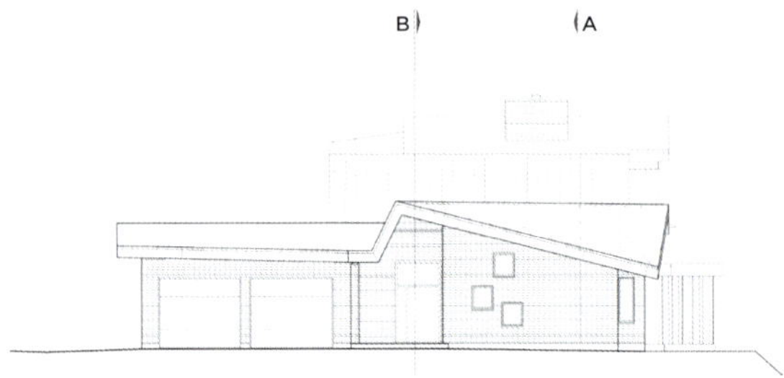

North elevation

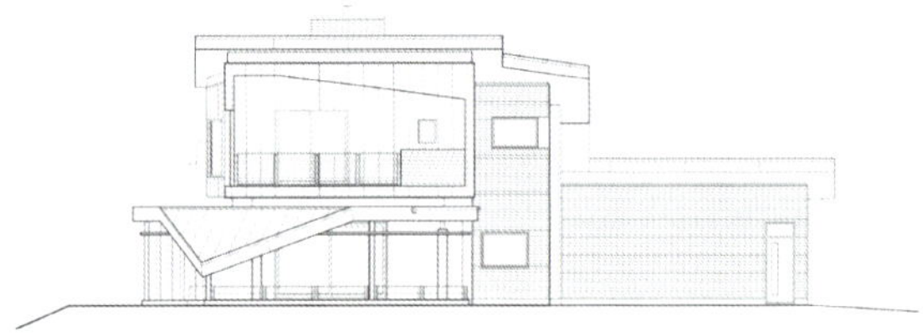

South elevation

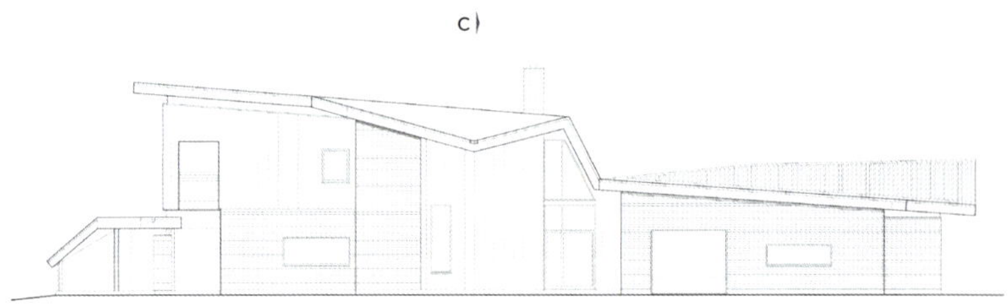

East elevation

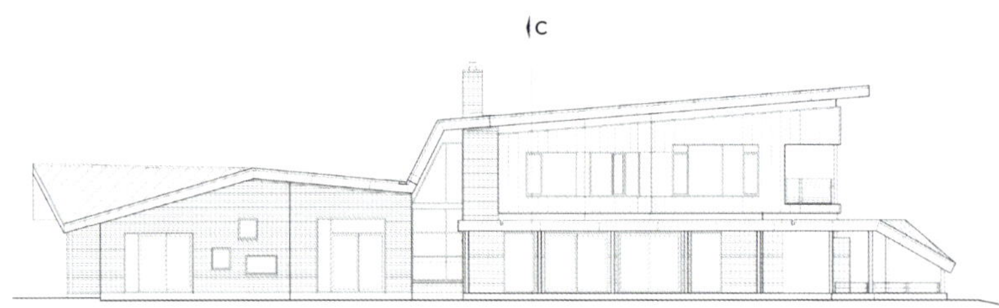

West elevation

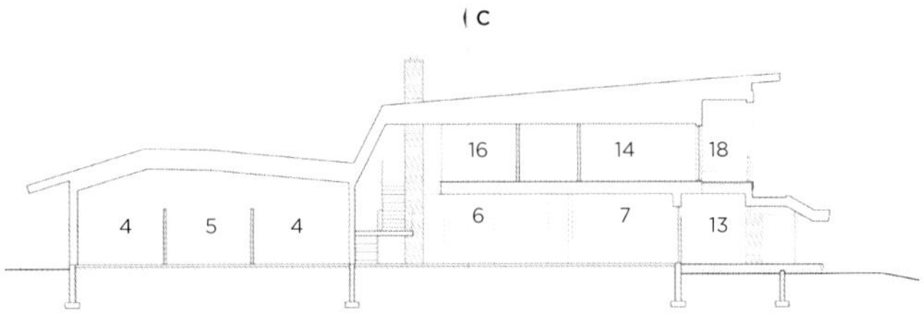

Section A

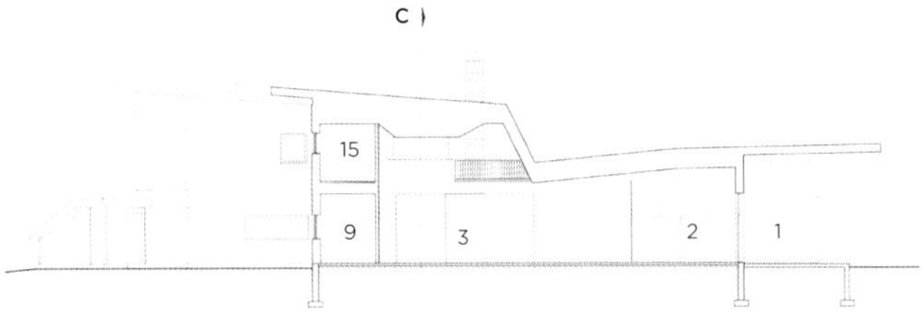

Section B

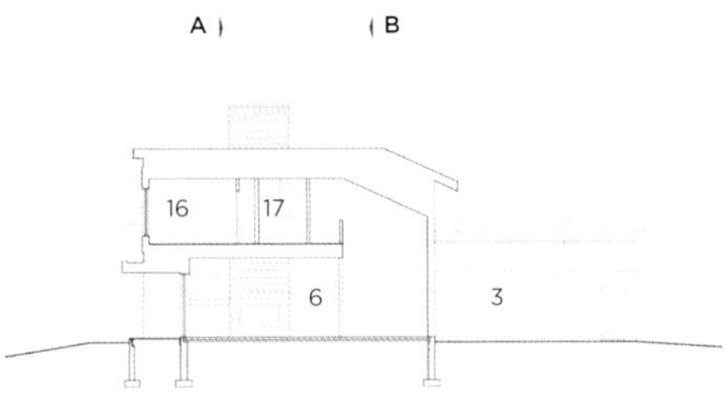

Section C

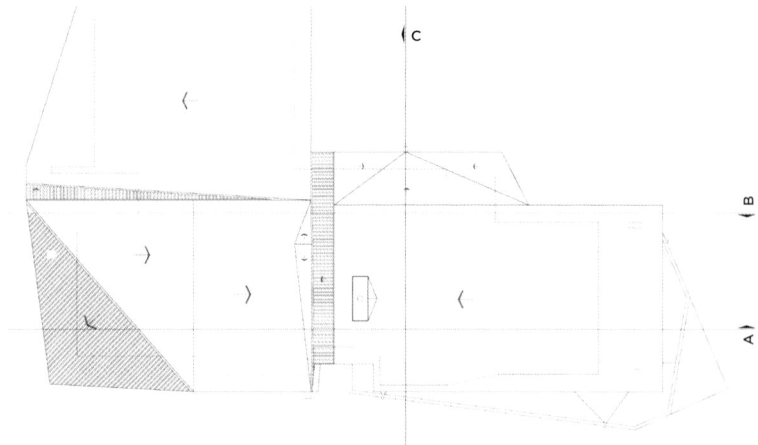

Roof plan

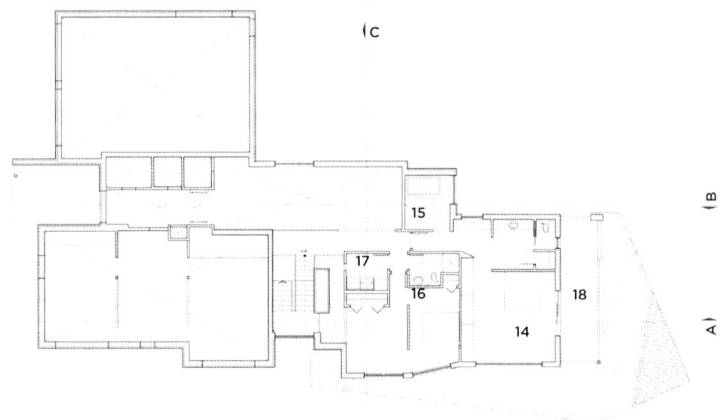

Second level floor plan

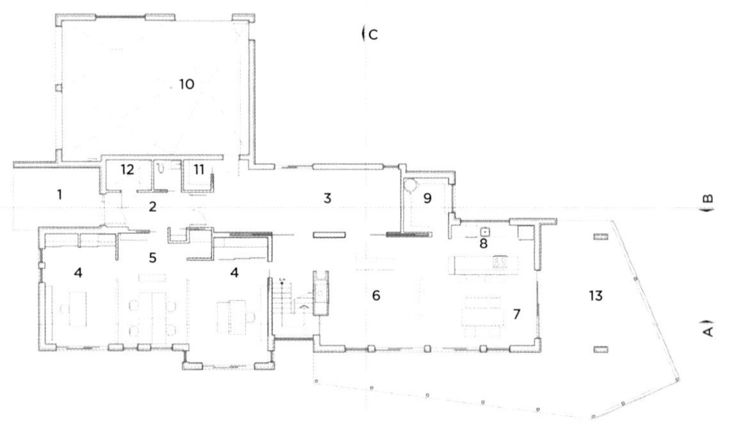

Ground level floor plan

1. Main entrance
2. Hall
3. Multipurpose room
4. Office
5. Library / drawing room
6. Living area
7. Dining area
8. Kitchen
9. Pantry
10. Garage
11. Storage
12. Mechanical room
13. Veranda
14. Primary bedroom
15. Bath / shower
16. Bedroom
17. Laundry room
18. Balcony

Le projet est une structure unifiée qui combine les bureaux d'une agence d'architecture et de design avec la résidence de ses directeurs. Un toit léger, sculptural et continu relie tous ces espaces, créant un plan tridimensionnel qui s'étend sur l'ensemble du bâtiment, lui donnant une apparence cohérente et s'intégrant dans les collines environnantes. Les espaces intérieurs sont divisés en trois zones flexibles, permettant une transformation facile des espaces et des zones de circulation grâce à l'utilisation de portes, de cloisons amovibles et de meubles adaptables. La véranda ouverte sert d'extension aux pièces de vie, offrant une connexion fluide entre l'intérieur et l'extérieur. Toutes les pièces sont conçues pour interagir avec l'extérieur et offrir des vues imprenables sur le lac Memphrémagog. Des matériaux durables nécessitant peu d'entretien ont été utilisés, et l'isolation du bâtiment, l'étanchéité, l'orientation des fenêtres et la géométrie ont été conçues pour minimiser la consommation d'énergie tant en hiver qu'en été.

El proyecto es una estructura unificada que combina las oficinas de una firma de arquitectura y diseño con la residencia de sus directores. Un techo ligero, escultórico y continuo conecta todos estos espacios, creando un plan tridimensional que se extiende por todo el edificio, dándole un aspecto cohesivo y mezclándose con las colinas circundantes. Los espacios interiores están divididos en tres zonas flexibles, lo que permite una fácil transformación de los espacios y las áreas de circulación mediante el uso de puertas, particiones removibles y muebles adaptables. La veranda abierta sirve como una extensión de las salas de estar, proporcionando una conexión sin interrupciones entre el interior y el exterior. Todas las habitaciones están diseñadas para interactuar con el exterior y ofrecen impresionantes vistas del lago Memphremagog. Se utilizaron materiales duraderos que requieren un mantenimiento mínimo, y el aislamiento del edificio, la impermeabilización, la orientación de las ventanas y la geometría fueron diseñados para minimizar el consumo de energía tanto en invierno como en verano.

HOVEY RESIDENCE

Eastern Townships, Québec, Canada // Lot area: 44,284 sq ft; building area: 5,490 sq ft

The Hovey Residence was designed to accommodate a couple of art lovers and their extended family. It is located near a lake, on sloping land surrounded by mature trees. The site was occupied by a house built in 1970. To reduce the environmental footprint of the project, the designers preserved, revisited, and expanded this building. The house is made up of two volumes connected by an interior corridor on the lower level and by an observation platform on the upper level. It is thus discreet on the street side and reveals itself on the lakeside. The platform ends with a cantilever directed towards the lake, which projects the observer into the landscape. Terraces and balconies were added to create exterior extensions. They accentuate the horizontality of the composition and counterbalance the height of the house. The goal was to create unique places that stand out and provide an experience for visitors. The house and the site are revealed in unexpected ways along the routes taken.

Die Hovey-Residenz wurde für ein Paar Kunstliebhaber und deren erweiterte Familie entworfen. Sie liegt in der Nähe eines Sees, auf abfallendem Gelände, umgeben von ausgewachsenen Bäumen. Das Grundstück war zuvor von einem Haus aus dem Jahr 1970 bewohnt. Um den ökologischen Fußabdruck zu verringern, haben die Designer dieses Gebäude erhalten, überarbeitet und erweitert. Das Haus besteht aus zwei Volumen, die im unteren Bereich durch einen Innenkorridor und im oberen Bereich durch eine Beobachtungsplattform verbunden sind. Auf der Straßenseite ist es zurückhaltend, während es sich zur Seeseite hin öffnet. Die Plattform endet mit einem Kragarm, der zum See hin ausgerichtet ist und den Betrachter in die Landschaft führt. Terrassen und Balkone wurden hinzugefügt, um Außenbereiche zu schaffen und die Horizontalität der Komposition zu betonen. Ziel war es, einzigartige Orte zu schaffen, die den Besuchern ein besonderes Erlebnis bieten. Das Haus und das Grundstück offenbaren sich auf unerwartete Weise entlang der genutzten Wege.

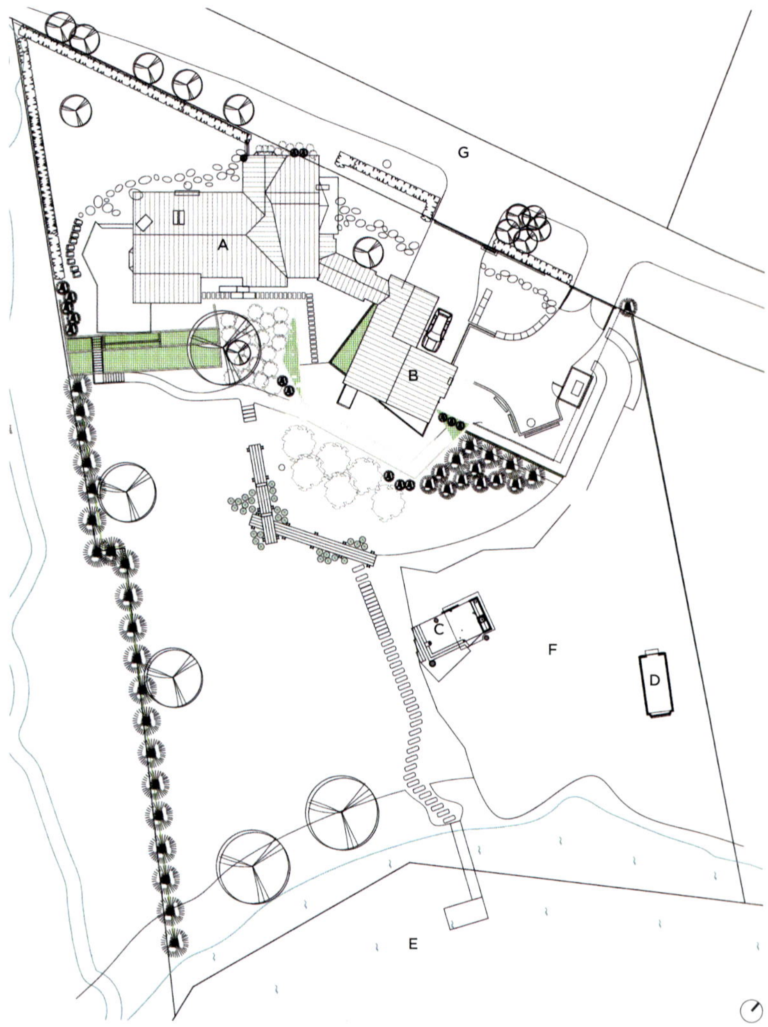

Site plan

A. Original wing
B. Addition
C. Outdoor pavilion
D. Storage pavilion
E. Lake
F. Forest
G. Street

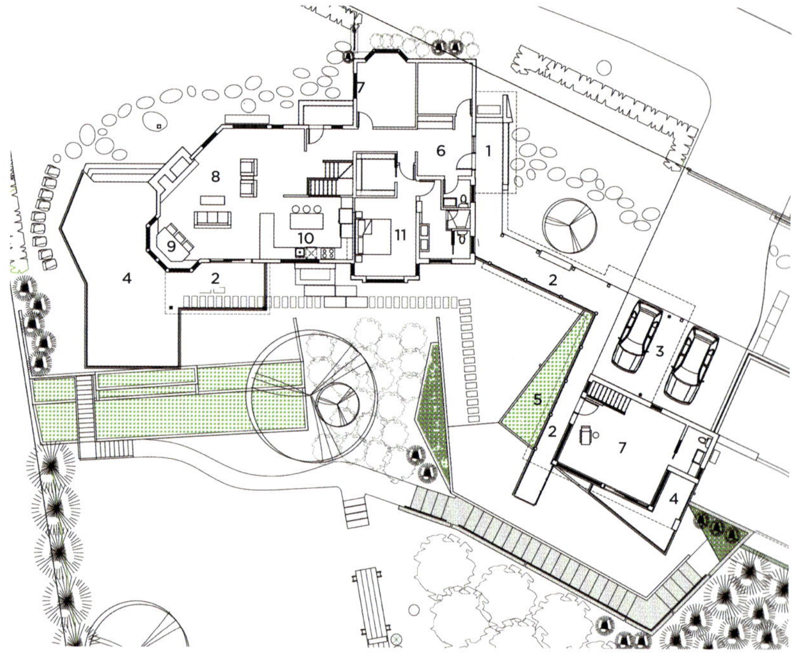

Upper level floor plan

La Résidence Hovey a été conçue pour accueillir un couple d'amateurs d'art et leur famille élargie. Elle est située près d'un lac, sur un terrain en pente entouré d'arbres matures. Le site était occupé par une maison construite en 1970. Pour réduire l'empreinte environnementale du projet, les concepteurs ont préservé, revisité et agrandi ce bâtiment. La maison est composée de deux volumes reliés par un couloir intérieur au niveau inférieur et par une plate-forme d'observation au niveau supérieur. Elle est ainsi discrète du côté de la rue et se révèle du côté du lac. La plate-forme se termine par un porte-à-faux dirigé vers le lac, qui projette l'observateur dans le paysage. Des terrasses et des balcons ont été ajoutés pour créer des extensions extérieures. Ils accentuent l'horizontalité de la composition et contrebalancent la hauteur de la maison. L'objectif était de créer des lieux uniques qui se démarquent et offrent une expérience aux visiteurs. La maison et le site se révèlent de manière inattendue le long des itinéraires empruntés.

La Residencia Hovey fue diseñada para acomodar a una pareja de amantes del arte y su familia. Está ubicada cerca de un lago, en un terreno inclinado rodeado de árboles maduros. El terreno estaba ocupado por una casa construida en 1970. Para reducir la huella ambiental del proyecto, los diseñadores preservaron, re visitaron y ampliaron este edificio. La casa se compone de dos volúmenes conectados por un corredor interior en el nivel inferior y por una plataforma de observación en el nivel superior. De este modo, es discreta en el lado de la calle y se revela en el lado del lago. La plataforma termina con un voladizo dirigido hacia el agua, que proyecta al observador hacia el paisaje. Se añadieron terrazas y balcones para crear extensiones exteriores. Estas acentúan la horizontalidad de la composición y contrarrestan la altura de la casa. El objetivo era crear lugares únicos que se destacaran y proporcionaran una experiencia para los visitantes. La casa y el lugar se revelan de maneras inesperadas a lo largo de las rutas tomadas.

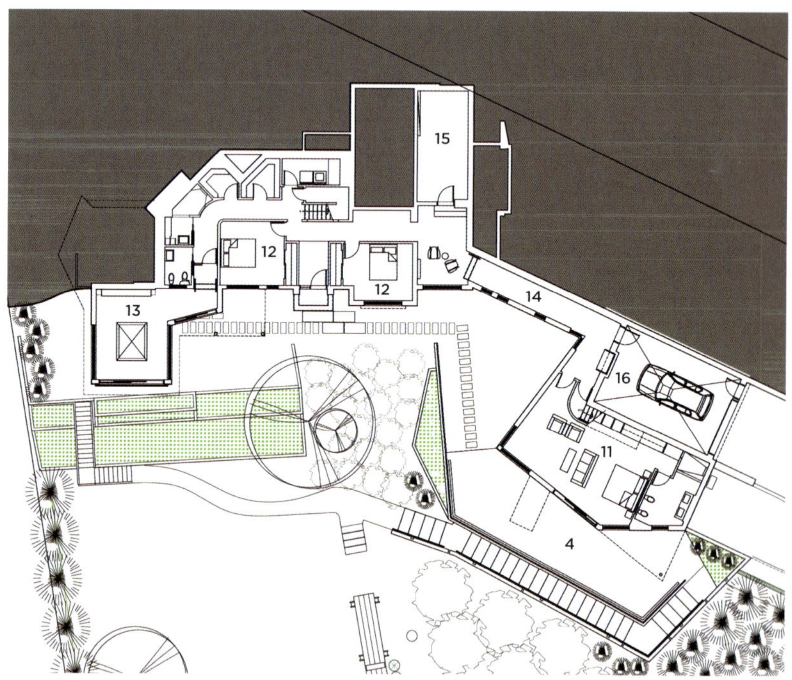

Lower level floor plan

1. Main entrance
2. Covered exterior corridor
3. Carport
4. Balcony/terrace
5. Green roof
6. Vestibule
7. Office
8. Living area
9. Dining area
10. Kitchen
11. Primary bedroom
12. Bedroom
13. Hot tub
14. Interior corridor
15. Mechanical/ electrical room
16. Garage

75

RUHL | JAHNES

"Our projects draw inspiration from the site, natural features, and our clients' unique lifestyles."

Ruhl | Jahnes combines pragmatism with visionary thinking, embracing renewable, sustainable, and site-specific design principles. Their process prioritizes maximizing views, sunlight, and airflow, emphasizing meticulous attention to detail and transparency in both practice and materials. The studio's diverse portfolio spans custom homes, lofts, apartments, and academic and commercial spaces, primarily in New England but extending as far afield as Hawaii and St. Croix. Ruhl | Jahne's award-winning designs are shaped by each project's unique natural context and their clients' lifestyles. As stewards of a shared built environment, the team aims to enhance it through innovation and expertise, one design at a time.

Ruhl | Jahnes kombiniert Pragmatismus mit visionärem Denken und setzt auf erneuerbare, nachhaltige und standortspezifische Designprinzipien. Ihr Prozess priorisiert die Maximierung von Ausblicken, Sonnenlicht und Luftzirkulation und legt besonderen Wert auf akribische Detailgenauigkeit und Transparenz in der Praxis und in den Materialien. Das vielfältige Portfolio des Studios umfasst maßgeschneiderte Häuser, Lofts, Apartments sowie akademische und gewerbliche Räume, hauptsächlich in Neuengland, aber auch bis nach Hawaii und St. Croix. Die preisgekrönten Entwürfe von Ruhl | Jahnes werden von den einzigartigen natürlichen Gegebenheiten jedes Projekts und den Lebensstilen ihrer Kunden geprägt. Als Verwalter einer gemeinsamen gebauten Umwelt zielt das Team darauf ab, diese durch Innovation und Fachwissen zu verbessern – ein Design nach dem anderen.

Ruhl | Jahnes combine pragmatisme et pensée visionnaire, en adoptant des principes de conception renouvelables, durables et spécifiques au site. Leur processus priorise l'optimisation des vues, de la lumière du soleil et du flux d'air, en mettant l'accent sur une attention méticuleuse aux détails et la transparence tant dans la pratique que dans les matériaux. Le portfolio diversifié du studio s'étend des maisons personnalisées, lofts, appartements, et espaces académiques et commerciaux, principalement en Nouvelle-Angleterre, mais s'étendant aussi loin qu'à Hawaï et St. Croix. Les designs primés de Ruhl | Jahnes sont façonnés par le contexte naturel unique de chaque projet et les modes de vie de leurs clients. En tant que gardiens d'un environnement bâti partagé, l'équipe vise à l'améliorer grâce à l'innovation et à l'expertise, un design à la fois.

Ruhl | Jahnes combina el pragmatismo con un pensamiento visionario, adoptando principios de diseño renovables, sostenibles y específicos del lugar. Su proceso prioriza maximizar las vistas, la luz solar y el flujo de aire, enfatizando una meticulosa atención al detalle y la transparencia tanto en la práctica como en los materiales. El diverso portafolio del estudio abarca casas personalizadas, lofts, apartamentos y espacios académicos y comerciales, principalmente en Nueva Inglaterra, pero extendiéndose hasta lugares tan lejanos como Hawái y St. Croix. Los diseños galardonados de Ruhl | Jahnes están moldeados por el contexto natural único de cada proyecto y los estilos de vida de sus clientes. Como administradores de un entorno construido de forma compartida, el equipo tiene como objetivo mejorarlo a través de la innovación y la experiencia, un diseño a la vez.

ruhljahnes

ruhljahnes.com

ESSEX BAY HOUSE

GAP COVE HOUSE

ESSEX BAY HOUSE

Gloucester, Massachusetts, United States // Lot area: 8 acres; building area: 2,236 sq ft

The Net-Positive House, overlooking Essex Bay in Gloucester, Massachusetts, replaces an existing house with antiquated systems and insufficient insulation. The owners are an artist and a computer scientist, and their new home reflects their passion for modern art, sculpture, technology, and sustainability. The design adheres to stringent local and State wetland regulations. The house has been positioned to maximize views, solar gain, and local topographic elements. The black exterior allows the house to blend in with the surrounding vegetation. The layout features a linear "bar" that houses the living space. Tall eaves and clerestory windows on the south side allow winter sunlight to filter into the main areas, while an ocean-facing porch wraps around an existing rock formation. Using a shed roof allowed for the accommodation of additional rooms while optimizing the orientation of rooftop solar panels.

Das Net-Positive-Haus mit Blick auf die Essex Bay in Gloucester, Massachusetts, ersetzt ein bestehendes Haus mit veralteten Systemen und unzureichender Isolierung. Die Eigentümer sind ein Künstler und ein Informatiker, und ihr neues Zuhause spiegelt ihre Leidenschaft für moderne Kunst, Skulptur, Technologie und Nachhaltigkeit wider. Das Design hält sich an strenge lokale und staatliche Vorschriften für Feuchtgebiete. Das Haus wurde so positioniert, dass es die Aussicht, den Solarertrag und die lokalen topografischen Elemente maximiert. Die schwarze Außenfassade lässt das Haus mit der umliegenden Vegetation verschmelzen. Das Layout verfügt über eine lineare „Bar", die den Wohnraum beherbergt. Hohe Traufen und Oberlichter auf der Südseite lassen das Wintersonnenlicht in die Hauptbereiche strömen, während eine zum Ozean gerichtete Veranda eine bestehende Felsformation umschließt. Die Verwendung eines Pultdachs ermöglichte die Unterbringung zusätzlicher Räume und optimierte gleichzeitig die Ausrichtung der Solarmodule auf dem Dach.

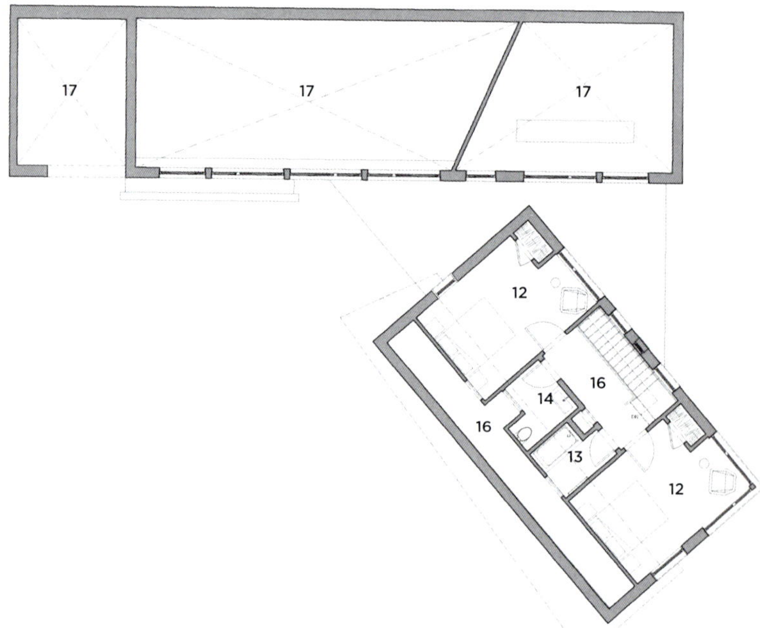

Second level floor plan

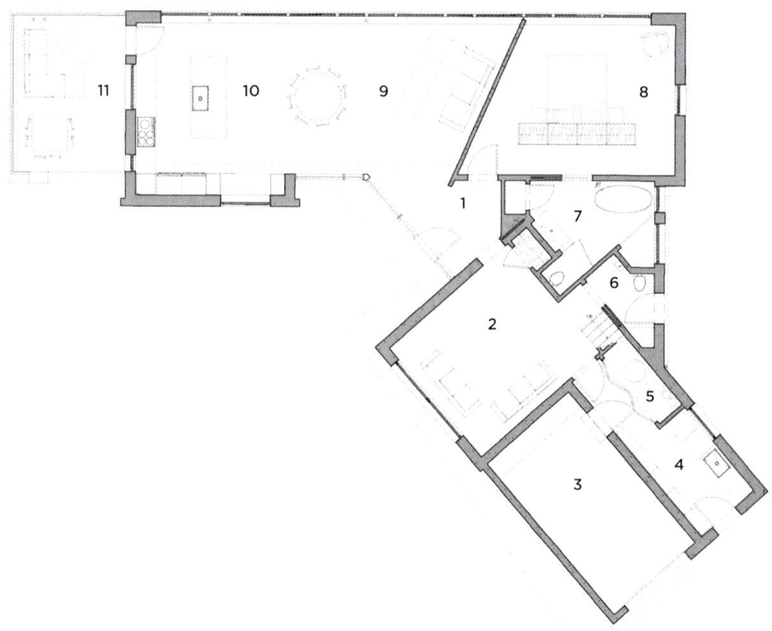

Ground level floor plan

1. Entry
2. Family room
3. Garage
4. Storage/ laundry room
5. Mechanical room
6. Powder room
7. Primary bathroom
8. Primary bedroom
9. Living/dining area
10. Kitchen
11. Dining deck
12. Guest bedroom
13. Shower
14. Bathroom
15. Hallway
16. Attic
17. Open to below

La maison Net-Positive, surplombant Essex Bay à Gloucester, Massachusetts, remplace une maison existante avec des systèmes obsolètes et une isolation insuffisante. Les propriétaires sont un artiste et un informaticien, et leur nouvelle maison reflète leur passion pour l'art moderne, la sculpture, la technologie et la durabilité. Le design respecte les réglementations locales et étatiques strictes en matière de zones humides. La maison a été positionnée pour maximiser les vues, les gains solaires et les éléments topographiques locaux. L'extérieur noir permet à la maison de se fondre dans la végétation environnante. Le plan présente une « barre » linéaire qui abrite l'espace de vie. De grandes avancées de toit et des fenêtres en clair-voie du côté sud permettent au soleil d'hiver de filtrer dans les espaces principaux, tandis qu'un porche face à l'océan entoure une formation rocheuse existante. L'utilisation d'un toit en pente a permis l'ajout de pièces supplémentaires tout en optimisant l'orientation des panneaux solaires sur le toit.

La Casa Net-Positive, con vistas a Essex Bay en Gloucester, Massachusetts, reemplaza una casa existente con sistemas anticuados y un aislamiento insuficiente. Los propietarios son un artista y un científico informático, y su nuevo hogar refleja su pasión por el arte moderno, la escultura, la tecnología y la sostenibilidad. El diseño cumple con estrictas regulaciones locales y estatales sobre humedales. La casa ha sido posicionada para maximizar las vistas, la captación solar y los elementos topográficos locales. El exterior negro permite que la casa se mezcle con la vegetación circundante. El diseño presenta una «barra» lineal que alberga el espacio habitable. Los aleros altos y las ventanas en forma de claraboya en el lado sur permiten que la luz solar invernal se filtre en las áreas principales, mientras que un porche orientado al océano rodea una formación rocosa existente. El uso de un techo inclinado permitió la incorporación de habitaciones adicionales mientras se optimizaba la orientación de los paneles solares en la azotea.

GAP COVE HOUSE

Rockport, Massachusetts, United States // Lot area: 25,000 sq ft; building area: 2,200 sq ft

Perspective section

This house, designed in dialogue with the local Conservation Commission, defies coastal trends with its modest size, net-zero energy status, and careful consideration of its environment. Situated in a rocky cove once home to a coast guard tower, it underwent a transformation involving pneumatic lifting and careful deconstruction and reconstruction. Its design prioritizes function over style, offering an open living space with panoramic ocean views and seven smaller spaces for living or sleeping. It features a ground-floor porch that allows severe winter storm surges to flow through durable exterior materials and exceeds FEMA regulations. Energy self-sufficiency is ensured through a substantial photovoltaic system, while accessibility is achieved with a flush entrance and elevator access. Innovative design elements include a solar chimney and carefully placed skylights that enhance daylighting and natural cooling.

Dieses Haus, entworfen im Dialog mit der örtlichen Naturschutzkommission, widersetzt sich den Küstentrends mit seiner bescheidenen Größe, seinem Status als Netto-Null-Energiegebäude und seiner sorgfältigen Berücksichtigung der Umwelt. Gelegen in einer felsigen Bucht, die einst einen Küstenwachtturm beherbergte, durchlief es einen Transformationsprozess, der pneumatisches Anheben und eine sorgfältige Dekonstruktion und Rekonstruktion beinhaltete. Sein Design priorisiert Funktion über Stil und bietet einen offenen Wohnbereich mit Panoramablick auf den Ozean und sieben kleinere Räume zum Wohnen oder Schlafen. Es verfügt über eine Veranda im Erdgeschoss, die es ermöglicht, dass schwere Wintersturmfluten durch haltbare Außenmateriallen fließen, und übertrifft die FEMA-Vorschriften. Die Energieautarkie wird durch ein erhebliches photovoltaisches System gewährleistet, während die Zugänglichkeit durch einen bündigen Eingang und einen Aufzug gewährleistet wird. Innovative Designelemente umfassen einen Solarkamin und sorgfältig platzierte Oberlichter, die die Tageslichtnutzung und natürliche Kühlung verbessern.

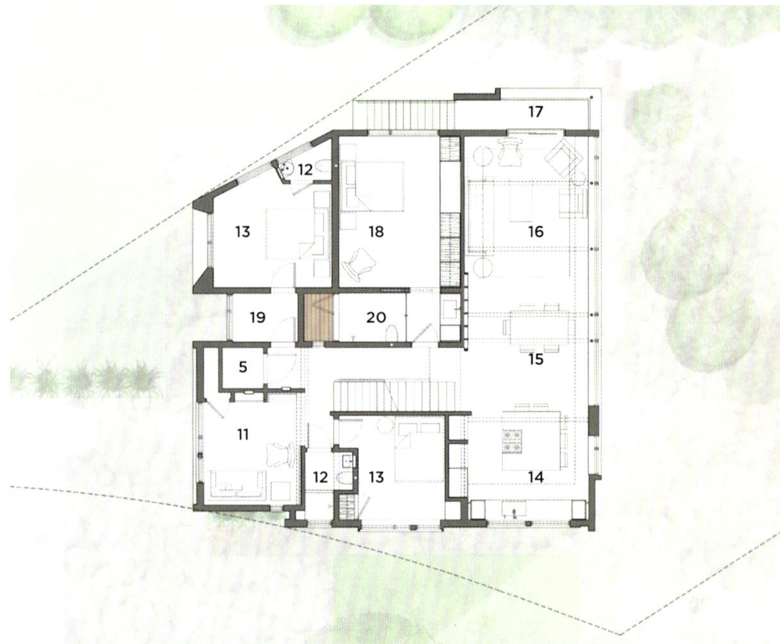

Second level floor plan

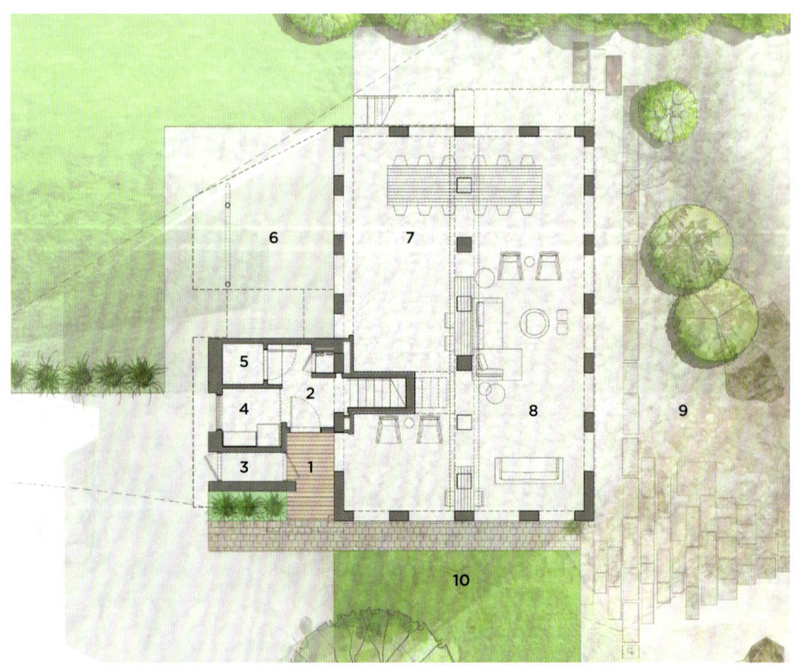

Ground level floor plan

1. Entry
2. Foyer
3. Recycling
4. Laundry room
5. Elevator
6. Shade garden
7. Outdoor dining area
8. Outdoor living area
9. Rock garden
10. Front yard
11. Media room
12. Bathroom
13. Bedroom
14. Kitchen
15. Dining area
16. Living area
17. Porch
18. Primary bedroom
19. Crib
20. Shower room

Cette maison, conçue en dialogue avec la Commission de conservation locale, défie les tendances côtières par sa taille modeste, son statut d'énergie nette zéro et son attention minutieuse à l'environnement. Située dans une crique rocheuse autrefois occupée par une tour de garde-côtes, elle a subi un processus de transformation impliquant un levage pneumatique et une déconstruction et reconstruction soigneuses. Son design privilégie la fonction au style, offrant un espace de vie ouvert avec des vues panoramiques sur l'océan et sept espaces plus petits pour vivre ou dormir. Elle dispose d'un porche au rez-de-chaussée qui permet aux violentes vagues de tempête hivernale de traverser des matériaux extérieurs durables et dépasse les réglementations de la FEMA. L'autosuffisance énergétique est assurée par un système photovoltaïque substantiel, tandis que l'accessibilité est facilitée par une entrée affleurante et un accès par ascenseur. Les éléments de conception innovants incluent une cheminée solaire et des puits de lumière soigneusement placés qui améliorent l'éclairage et le refroidissement naturel.

Esta casa, diseñada en diálogo con la Comisión de Conservación local, desafía las tendencias costeras con su tamaño modesto, estado de energía neta cero y cuidadosa consideración de su entorno. Situada en una cala rocosa que alguna vez albergó una torre de la guardia costera, pasó por un proceso de transformación que involucró levantamiento neumático, deconstrucción y reconstrucción minuciosas. Su diseño prioriza la función sobre el estilo, con un espacio de vida abierto con vistas al océano y siete espacios más pequeños para vivir o dormir. Tiene un porche en la planta baja que permite que las marejadas invernales fluyan a través de materiales exteriores duraderos, superando las regulaciones de FEMA. La autosuficiencia energética se asegura con un sistema fotovoltaico sustancial, y la accesibilidad se logra con una entrada al ras y acceso por ascensor. Los elementos de diseño innovadores incluyen una chimenea solar y tragaluces estratégicos que mejoran la iluminación y refrigeración natural.

53

FURTHER ARCHITECTURE OFFICE

"We are architects with a passion for telling compelling stories through progressive design."

FURTHER Architecture partners with clients who aim to elevate their everyday experience of home, work, and place. We craft custom and thoughtful solutions to sometimes complex problems using the power of design thinking and an optimistic belief in the emotional resonance of good design. Working closely and collaboratively with clients, we believe that good design has the power to create positive change and lasting value. Led by Principal Justin Towart, our team undertakes diverse projects of various scales and styles. To serve our clients, we leverage many years of professional experience realizing design across various project types, working together with a small team of collaborators as required on each project. Our office is located in Fairfield County, Connecticut, and we work in multiple states throughout the US on design-forward projects with an aim to produce thoughtful and well-executed design work that has a sense of timeless appeal while also speaking to the contemporary moment.

FURTHER Architecture arbeitet mit Kunden, die ihr tägliches Erlebnis von Zuhause, Arbeit und Raum verbessern möchten. Wir entwickeln maßgeschneiderte Lösungen für komplexe Probleme, indem wir die Kraft des Design Thinking und den Glauben an die emotionale Wirkung guten Designs nutzen. In enger Zusammenarbeit mit unseren Kunden sind wir überzeugt, dass gutes Design positive Veränderungen bewirken und bleibenden Wert schaffen kann. Unter der Leitung von Principal Justin Towart übernimmt unser Team Projekte verschiedener Größen und Stile. Mit langjähriger Erfahrung setzen wir Designprojekte um und arbeiten bei Bedarf mit einem kleinen Team zusammen. Unser Büro befindet sich in Fairfield County, Connecticut, und wir arbeiten in mehreren Bundesstaaten der USA an designorientierten Projekten. Unser Ziel ist es, durchdachte und gut ausgeführte Designarbeiten zu schaffen, die sowohl zeitlose Anziehungskraft besitzen als auch den zeitgenössischen Moment widerspiegeln.

FURTHER Architecture s'associe avec des clients qui cherchent à enrichir leur expérience de la maison, du travail et du lieu. Nous créons des solutions sur mesure pour des problèmes complexes, en utilisant le design thinking et en croyant à la résonance émotionnelle d'un bon design. En collaborant étroitement avec nos clients, nous croyons que le bon design peut créer des changements positifs et durables. Dirigée par Justin Towart, notre équipe entreprend des projets variés de différentes tailles et styles. Nous tirons parti de nombreuses années d'expérience dans la réalisation de designs divers, en collaborant avec une petite équipe selon les besoins. Basés dans le comté de Fairfield, Connecticut, nous travaillons sur des projets axés sur le design dans plusieurs états des États-Unis avec l'objectif de produire un design réfléchi et bien exécuté, intemporel et en phase avec notre époque contemporaine.

FURTHER Architecture se asocia con clientes que buscan mejorar su experiencia en el hogar, trabajo y entorno. Creamos soluciones personalizadas para problemas complejos, aplicando el pensamiento creativo y la convicción en la resonancia emocional de una buena propuesta. Creemos que un diseño bien ejecutado puede generar cambios positivos y duraderos, trabajando estrechamente con los clientes. Dirigido por Justin Towart, nuestro equipo aborda proyectos de distintas escalas y estilos. Aprovechamos años de experiencia profesional en diversos tipos de proyectos, colaborando con un pequeño equipo según las necesidades de cada proyecto. Nuestra oficina está en el condado de Fairfield, Connecticut, y trabajamos en varios estados de EE. UU. en proyectos innovadores con el objetivo de crear diseños cuidadosos y bien ejecutados, que combinen un sentido de atemporalidad con relevancia contemporánea.

further_architecture furtherarchitecture.com

COASTAL GABLES

PINE RIDGE RETREAT

COASTAL GABLES

New Shoreham, Rhode Island, United States // Lot area: 2.3 acres; building area: 3,480 sq ft

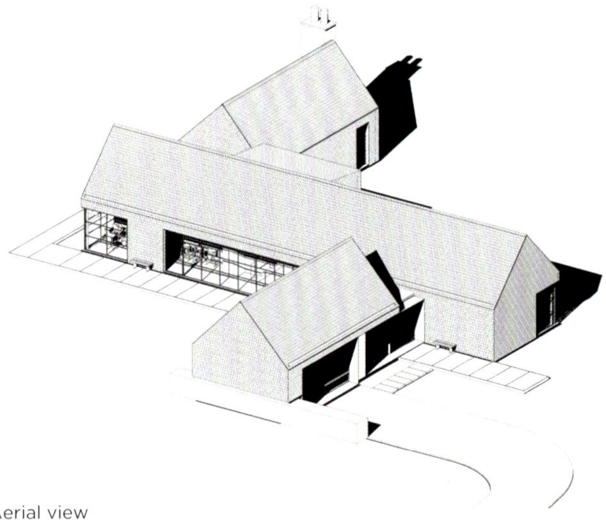

Aerial view

This project was envisioned as a compound of elemental forms juxtaposed against the low, coastal landscape of Block Island, west of Martha's Vineyard. A study in simplicity, the solid forms defer to the landscape of lanes, low stone walls, and grassy knolls of the island, emphasizing the poetic power of simple elemental forms. A contemporary interpretation of the barns and small cape cod style residences dotted along the coast, the house is a composition of simple gables with a 12/12 pitch. Set at twenty-one feet in width and height, three of these forms, rotated with respect to one another and clad in Western Red Cedar Shingles, slide along a glassy central spine. This configuration creates a series of courtyards around the residence, enhancing its integration with the natural surroundings. Inside, expansive black steel windows and doors appear as if 'carved out' of the wooden structures, seamlessly blending indoor and outdoor spaces.

Dieses Projekt wurde als ein Ensemble von elementaren Formen konzipiert, die der niedrigen Küstenlandschaft von Block Island westlich von Martha's Vineyard gegenübergestellt sind. Eine Studie in Einfachheit, die soliden Formen fügen sich in die Landschaft aus Wegen, niedrigen Steinmauern und grasbewachsenen Hügeln der Insel ein und betonen die poetische Kraft einfacher elementarer Formen. Eine zeitgenössische Interpretation der Scheunen und kleinen Cape Cod-Häuser entlang der Küste, das Haus ist eine Komposition aus einfachen Giebeln mit einer Neigung von 12/12. Mit einer Breite und Höhe von einundzwanzig Fuß rotieren drei dieser Formen zueinander und sind mit Western Red Cedar Shingles verkleidet, die entlang einer gläsernen zentralen Achse gleiten. Diese Konfiguration schafft eine Reihe von Höfen um die Residenz und verstärkt ihre Integration in die natürliche Umgebung. Im Inneren scheinen die großen Fenster und Türen aus schwarzem Stahl, als wären sie aus den Holzstrukturen 'herausgeschnitten', und verbinden nahtlos Innen- und Außenbereiche.

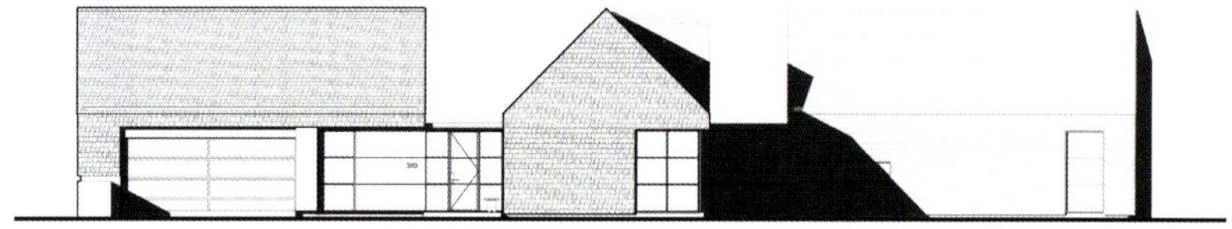

North elevation

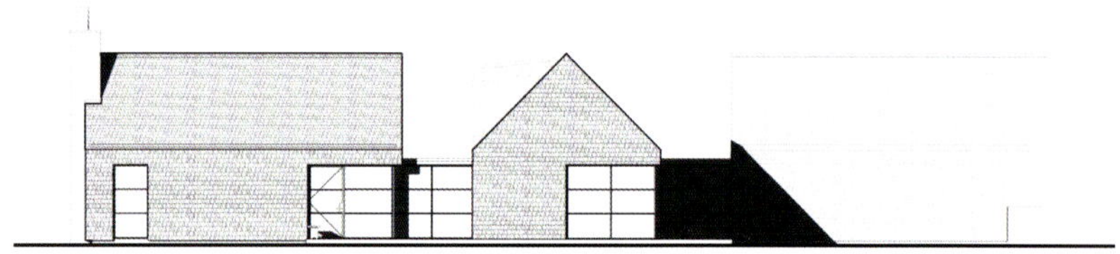

South elevation

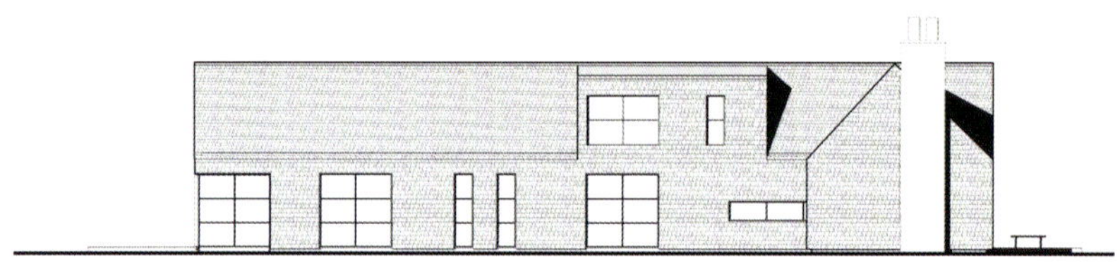

West elevation

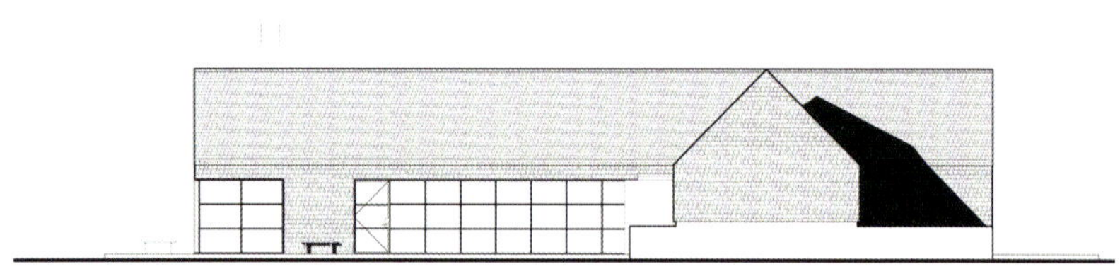

East elevation

Ce projet a été conçu comme un ensemble de formes élémentaires juxtaposées au paysage côtier bas de Block Island, à l'ouest de Martha's Vineyard. Étude de la simplicité, les formes solides s'effacent devant les chemins, murets en pierre et buttes herbeuses de l'île, mettant en valeur la puissance poétique des formes simples. Interprétation contemporaine des granges et petites maisons de style Cape Cod le long de la côte, la maison est une composition de pignons simples avec une pente de toit de 12/12. Mesurant vingt et un pieds de large et de haut, trois de ces formes, orientées différemment et recouvertes de bardeaux de cèdre rouge de l'Ouest, glissent le long d'une colonne vertébrale centrale vitrée. Cette configuration crée des cours autour de la résidence, renforçant son intégration dans le paysage naturel. À l'intérieur, de grandes fenêtres et portes en acier noir semblent 'taillées' dans les structures en bois, fusionnant harmonieusement les espaces intérieurs et extérieurs.

Este proyecto fue concebido como un conjunto de formas elementales yuxtapuestas contra el bajo paisaje costero de Block Island, al oeste de Martha's Vineyard. En un estudio de la simplicidad, las formas sólidas se subordinan al paisaje de caminos, muros bajos de piedra y colinas cubiertas de hierba de la isla, enfatizando el poder poético de las formas elementales simples. Como una interpretación contemporánea de los graneros y pequeñas residencias de estilo Cape Cod que se encuentran a lo largo de la costa, la casa es una composición de frontones simples con una inclinación de 12/12. Situadas a 7 m de ancho y alto, tres de estas formas, rotadas con respecto a sí mismas y revestidas con tejas de cedro rojo occidental, se deslizan a lo largo de una columna central acristalada. Esta configuración crea una serie de patios alrededor de la residencia, mejorando su integración con el entorno natural. En el interior, las ventanas y puertas de acero negro parecen estar 'esculpidas' en las estructuras de madera, fusionando sin esfuerzo los espacios interiores y exteriores.

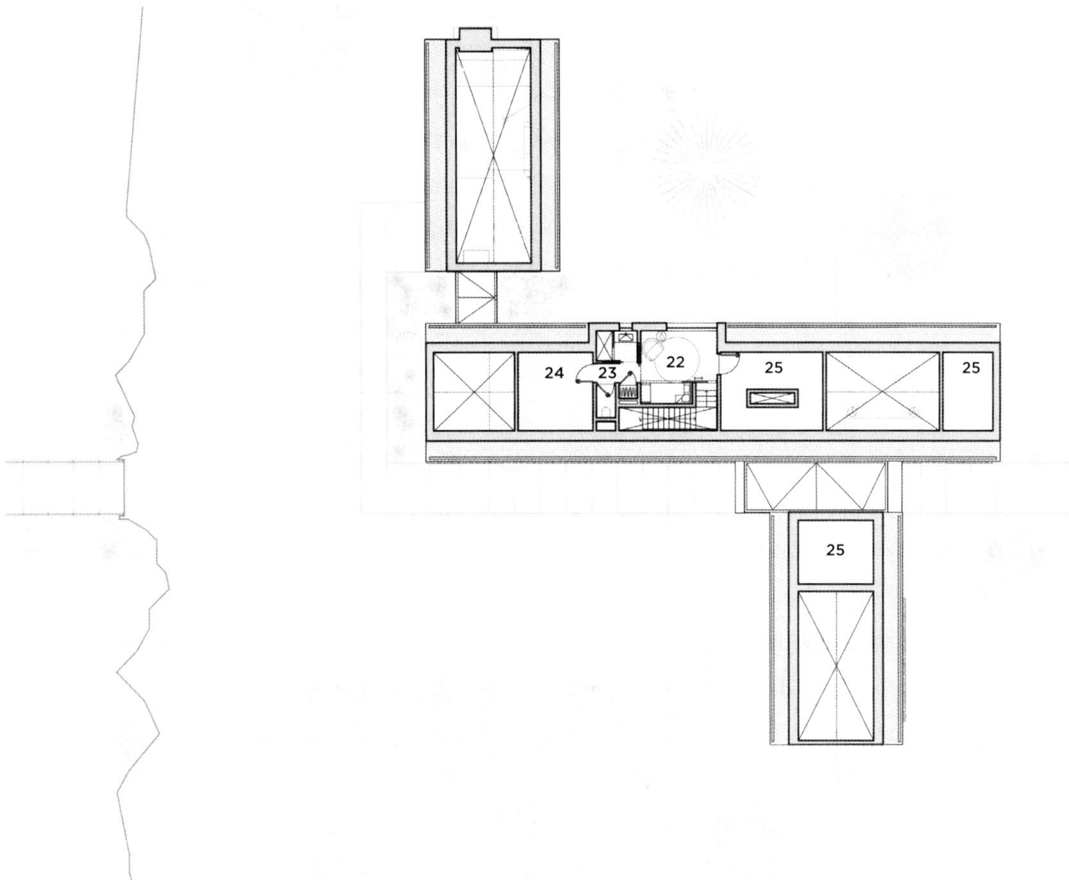

Second level floor plan

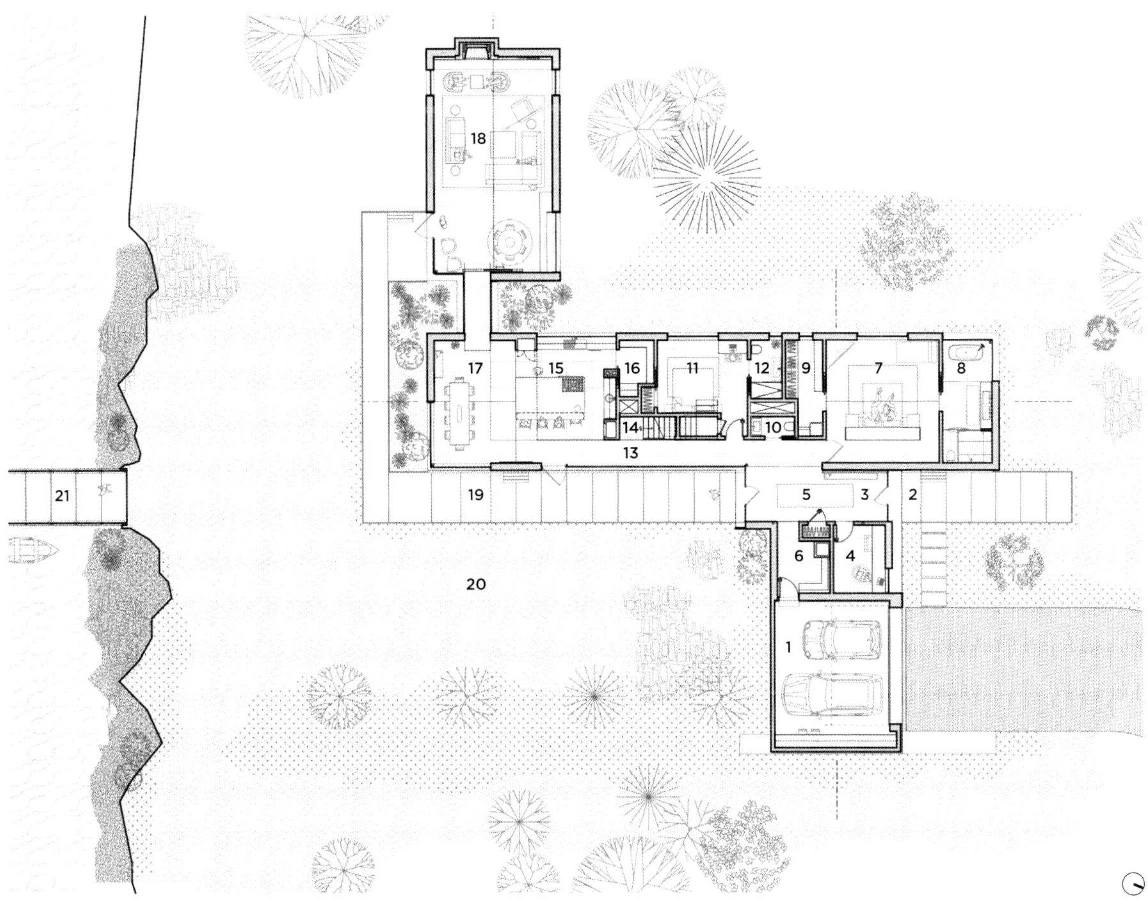

1. Garage
2. Front entry
3. Entry hall
4. Home office
5. Coat closet
6. Mud room/laundry room
7. Primary bedroom
8. Primary bathroom
9. Walk-in closet
10. Powder room
11. Guest bedroom
12. Ensuite bathroom
13. Main hall
14. Staircase to level 2
15. Kitchen
16. Pantry
17. Dining area
18. Great room
19. Outdoor deck
20. Yard
21. Pier
22. Bunk room
23. Pass-thru bathroom
24. Storage
25. Mechanical space

Site plan

PINE RIDGE RETREAT

Enfield, New Hampshire, United States // Lot area: 7.89 acres; building area: 950 sq ft

Nestled in the Pine forests of Western New Hampshire, Pine Ridge Retreat is an off-the-grid sustainable cabin with a small footprint. Designed to embrace the natural beauty of the surroundings, the cabin features a central room of glass and wood enclosed by a single soaring shed roof. Inside, the project takes advantage of the sweeping views via a large glazed central space. Within this single room, a simple monolithic wood-and-stone cube contains everything: a luxurious primary bedroom, full bathroom, kitchen, bar, and a media center. The bedroom is set adjacent to a flowerbed just beyond the glass wall, and light traces its way through the space from morning to evening, like a sundial. Formally, the project planning is a series of interlocking L-shaped walls and screens that are optimized relative to program, sun, and views — all intended to provide for moments of repose and reflection.

Eingebettet in die Kiefernwälder im Westen von New Hampshire ist Pine Ridge Retreat eine nachhaltige, netzunabhängige Kabine mit kleinem Fußabdruck. Die Kabine wurde entworfen, um die natürliche Schönheit der Umgebung zu umarmen, und verfügt über einen zentralen Raum aus Glas und Holz, der von einem einzigen hohen Pultdach umschlossen ist. Im Inneren nutzt das Projekt die weitreichenden Ausblicke durch einen großen verglasten zentralen Raum. In diesem einzigen Raum enthält ein einfacher monolithischer Holz-und-Stein-Würfel alles: ein luxuriöses Hauptschlafzimmer, ein komplettes Badezimmer, eine Küche, eine Bar und ein Medienzentrum. Das Schlafzimmer liegt neben einem Blumenbeet direkt hinter der Glaswand, und das Licht verfolgt seinen Weg durch den Raum von morgens bis abends, wie ein Sonnenuhr. Formal besteht die Projektplanung aus einer Reihe von ineinandergreifenden L-förmigen Wänden und Bildschirmen, die in Bezug auf das Programm, die Sonne und die Ausblicke optimiert sind — alle sollen Momente der Ruhe und Besinnung bieten.

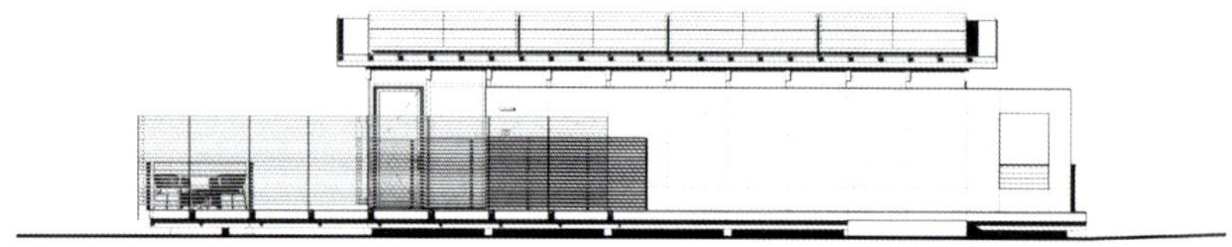

North elevation

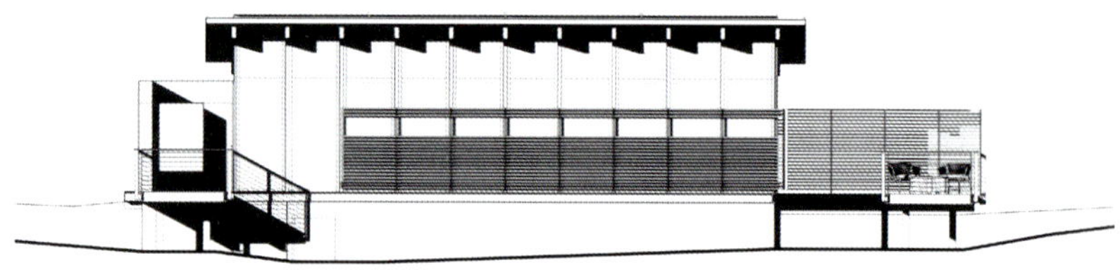

South elevation

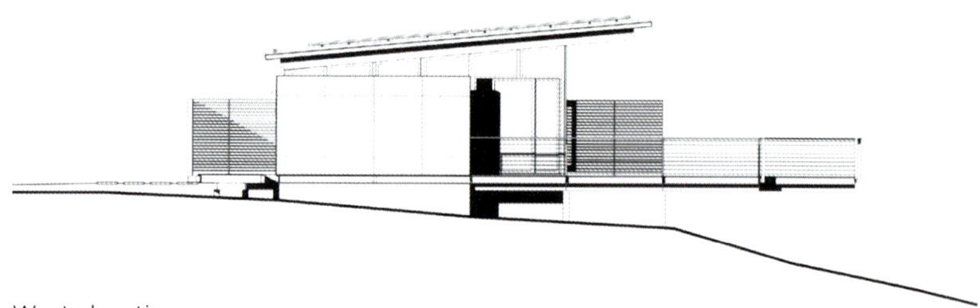

West elevation

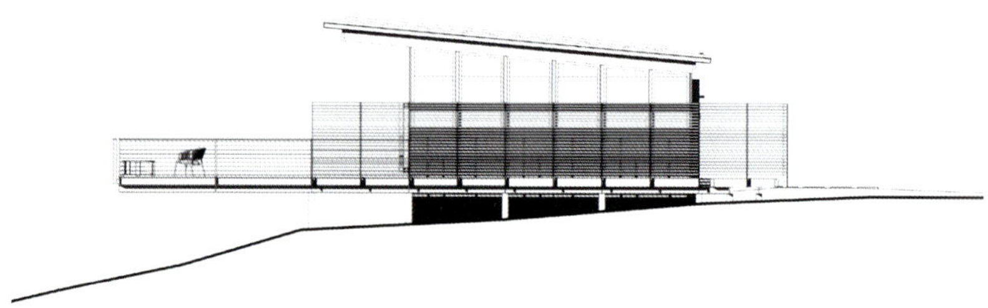

East elevation

Nichée dans les forêts de pins de l'ouest du New Hampshire, Pine Ridge Retreat est une cabane durable et autonome avec une empreinte écologique réduite. Conçue pour embrasser la beauté naturelle des environs, la cabane dispose d'une pièce centrale en verre et en bois, entourée d'un seul toit pentu s'élevant vers le ciel. À l'intérieur, le projet tire parti des vues panoramiques grâce à un grand espace central vitré. À l'intérieur de cette pièce unique, un cube monolithique en bois et en pierre contient tout : une chambre principale luxueuse, une salle de bains complète, une cuisine, un bar et un centre multimédia. La chambre est située à côté d'un parterre de fleurs juste au-delà de la paroi vitrée, et la lumière parcourt l'espace du matin au soir, comme un cadran solaire. Formellement, la planification du projet est une série de murs et de cloisons en forme de L imbriqués qui sont optimisés en fonction du programme, du soleil et des vues — tous destinés à offrir des moments de repos et de réflexion.

Ubicada en los bosques de pinos del oeste de New Hampshire, Pine Ridge Retreat es una cabaña sostenible y autónoma con una huella ecológica reducida. Diseñada para abrazar la belleza natural del entorno, la cabaña cuenta con una sala central de vidrio y madera, encerrada por un único techo inclinado elevado. En el interior, el proyecto aprovecha las vistas panorámicas a través de un gran espacio central acristalado. Dentro de esta única habitación, un cubo monolítico de madera y piedra contiene todo: un lujoso dormitorio principal, baño completo, cocina, bar y un espacio de entretenimiento. El dormitorio está ubicado junto a un parterre justo más allá de la pared de vidrio, donde la luz traza su camino a través del espacio desde la mañana hasta la noche, como un reloj de sol. Formalmente, la planificación del proyecto consiste en una serie de paredes y pantallas en forma de L entrelazadas que están optimizadas en relación con el programa, el sol y las vistas, todas destinadas a proporcionar momentos de descanso y reflexión.

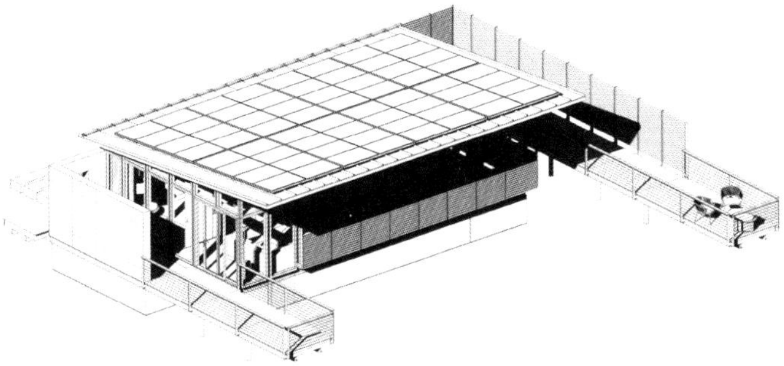 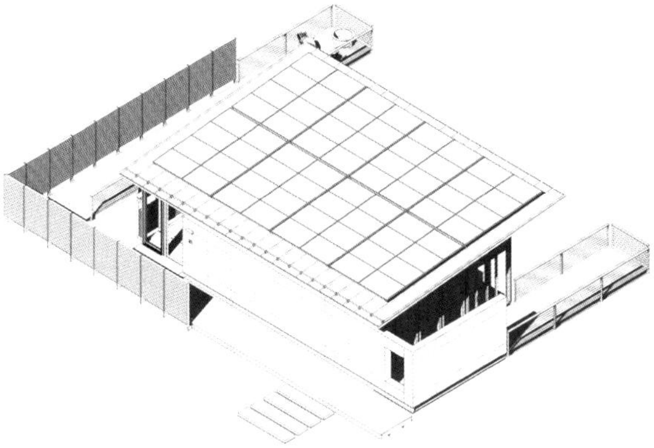

Aerial views

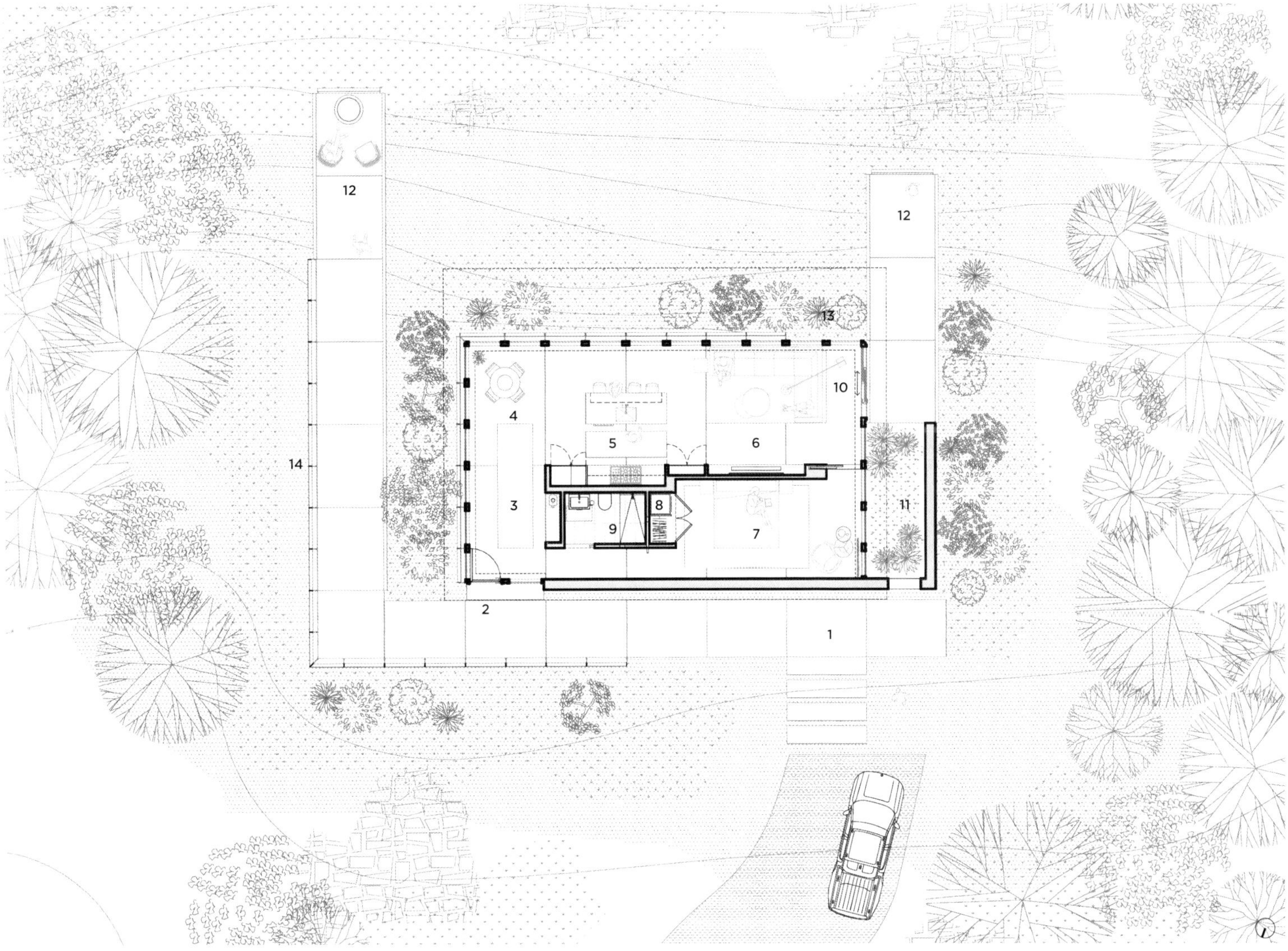

Floor plan

1. Raised entry walk
2. Main entry
3. Bar sink with storage
4. Dining/flex area
5. Kitchen
6. Living area
7. Bedroom
8. Washer/dryer closet
9. Bathroom
10. Sliders to viewing deck
11. "Sundial" flower garden
12. Viewing deck
13. Mechanical room access
14. Light louver scrim

GUILLAUME PELLETIER ARCHITECTE

"Culture, nature, and architecture form the DNA of our projects."

Guillaume Pelletier Architecte specializes in design, construction, and project management, focusing on residential and institutional projects. After many years in Japan working with Kengo Kuma & Associates and Yokomizo Makoto Architects, Mr. Pelletier returned to Canada to work at Atelier Pierre Thibault before founding his own architecture office in 2013. Drawing from his Japanese experience and the Québec context, "modesty" is central to his approach. The firm emphasizes simple design, natural materials, and the evocative use of light, aiming to create respectful and sustainable architecture. GPA has won several public commissions in Montreal and was recently chosen by Global Affairs Canada, along with a partner and a multidisciplinary team, to create the Canadian Pavilion for the International Exposition in Osaka 2025.

Guillaume Pelletier Architecte ist auf Design, Bau und Management spezialisiert und konzentriert sich auf Wohn- und institutionelle Projekte. Nach vielen Jahren in Japan, wo er mit Kengo Kuma & Associates und Yokomizo Makoto Architects zusammenarbeitete, kehrte Guillaume Pelletier nach Kanada zurück und arbeitete im Atelier Pierre Thibault, bevor er 2013 sein eigenes Architekturbüro gründete. Ausgehend von seiner japanischen Erfahrung und dem Kontext in Québec ist „Bescheidenheit" das zentrale Element seines Ansatzes. Das Büro legt den Schwerpunkt auf einfaches Design, natürliche Materialien und die eindrucksvolle Nutzung von Licht, um eine respektvolle und nachhaltige Architektur zu schaffen. GPA hat mehrere öffentliche Aufträge in Montreal erhalten und wurde kürzlich von Global Affairs Canada ausgewählt, zusammen mit einem Partner und einem multidisziplinären Team den kanadischen Pavillon für die Osaka 2025 International Exposition zu gestalten.

Guillaume Pelletier Architecte est spécialisé dans la conception, la construction et la gestion de projets résidentiels et institutionnels. Après avoir travaillé plusieurs années au Japon avec Kengo Kuma & Associates et Yokomizo Makoto Architects, Guillaume Pelletier est revenu au Canada pour travailler à l'Atelier Pierre Thibault avant de fonder son propre bureau d'architecture en 2013. S'inspirant de son expérience japonaise et du contexte québécois, la « modestie » est au cœur de son approche. Le cabinet met l'accent sur la simplicité du design, les matériaux naturels et l'utilisation évocatrice de la lumière, dans le but de créer une architecture respectueuse et durable. GPA a remporté plusieurs commandes publiques à Montréal et a récemment été choisi par Affaires mondiales Canada, avec un partenaire et une équipe multidisciplinaire, pour créer le Pavillon canadien de l'Exposition internationale d'Osaka 2025.

Guillaume Pelletier Architecte se especializa en diseño, construcción y gestión, centrándose en proyectos residenciales e institucionales. Después de muchos años en Japón trabajando con Kengo Kuma & Associates y Yokomizo Makoto Architects, el Guillaume Pelletier regresó a Canadá para trabajar en Atelier Pierre Thibault antes de fundar su propia oficina de arquitectura en 2013. Basándose en su experiencia japonesa y en el contexto de Quebec, la «modestia» es central en su enfoque. La firma enfatiza un diseño simple, materiales naturales y el uso evocador de la luz, con el objetivo de crear una arquitectura respetuosa y sostenible. GPA ha ganado varias comisiones públicas en Montreal y fue recientemente elegida por Global Affairs Canada, junto con un socio y un equipo multidisciplinario, para crear el Pabellón Canadiense para la Exposición Internacional en Osaka 2025.

gp_architecte | gp-architecte.com

LA CASCADE RESIDENCE

LAC SUPÉRIEUR RESIDENCE

LA CASCADE RESIDENCE

Wentworth North, Québec, Canada // Lot area: 170,000 sq ft; building area: 3,675 sq ft (including terraces)

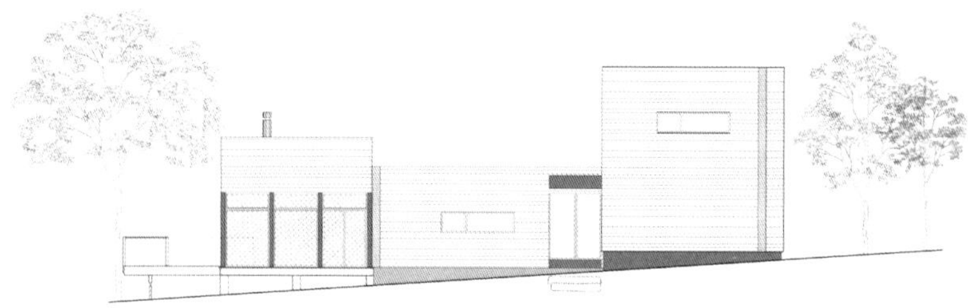

North elevation

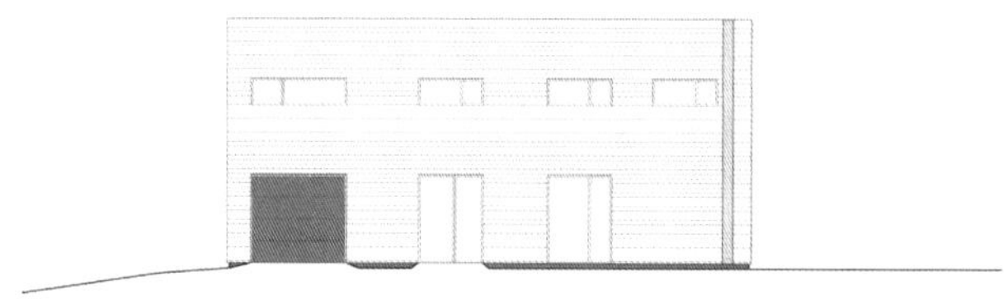

West elevation

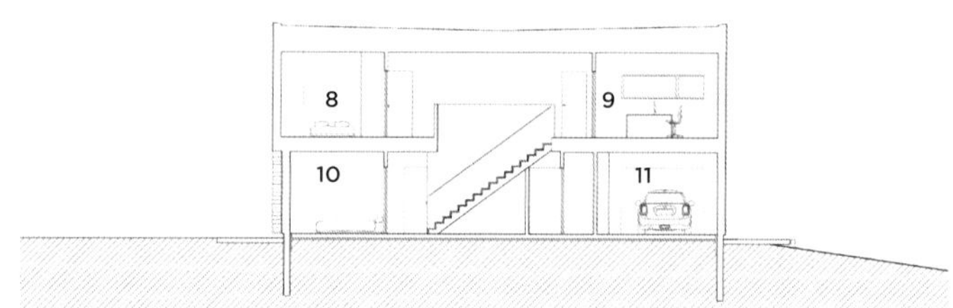

North-South section

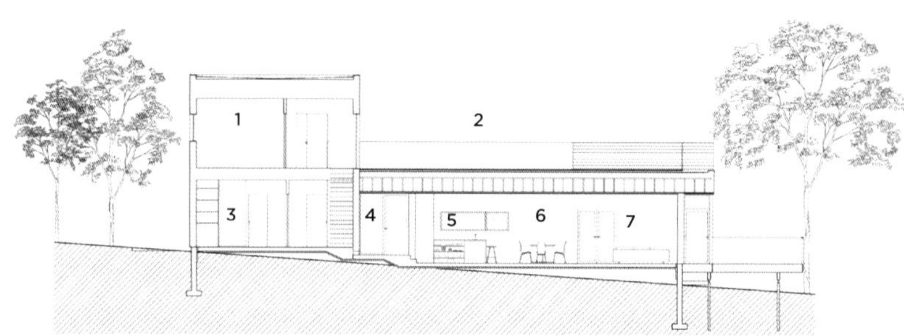

West-East section

1. Atelier
2. Roof terrace
3. Bathroom
4. Gallery
5. Kitchen
6. Dining area
7. Living area
8. Bedroom
9. Study
10. Primary bedroom
11. Garage

This house in the Laurentian mountains near Montréal is a work of art, with water playing a spectacular role in its design. Exposed vertical rain gutters create the gentle sound of a creek during light rain and form abstract ice sculptures in winter, showcasing water's fascinating parametric qualities. The clients, two graphic designers, envisioned their home as a contemporary sculpture inspired by the natural surroundings. The design process involved numerous models and iterations, culminating in a minimalist three-volume structure with a striking contrast: black exteriors, white interiors, generous fenestration, and fluid circulation. Perched on a rocky hill overlooking a lake, the house is designed to respond to sunlight, topography, and stunning views. Its asymmetrical layout enhances the spatial experience, seamlessly integrating interior and exterior spaces.

Dieses Haus in den Laurentinischen Bergen nahe Montréal ist ein Kunstwerk, bei dem Wasser eine spektakuläre Rolle im Design spielt. Offene vertikale Regenrinnen erzeugen während leichten Regens das sanfte Geräusch eines Baches und bilden im Winter abstrakte Eisskulpturen, die die faszinierenden parametrischen Qualitäten des Wassers zur Schau stellen. Die Kunden, zwei Grafikdesigner, stellten sich ihr Zuhause als eine zeitgenössische Skulptur vor, die von der natürlichen Umgebung inspiriert ist. Der Designprozess umfasste zahlreiche Modelle und Iterationen und führte zu einer minimalistischen Dreivolumenstruktur mit einem auffälligen Kontrast: schwarze Außenfassaden, weiße Innenräume, großzügige Fensteröffnungen und fließende Zirkulation. Auf einem felsigen Hügel mit Blick auf einen See gelegen, ist das Haus so gestaltet, dass es auf Sonnenlicht, Topographie und atemberaubende Ausblicke reagiert. Sein asymmetrisches Layout verbessert das räumliche Erlebnis und integriert nahtlos Innen- und Außenräume.

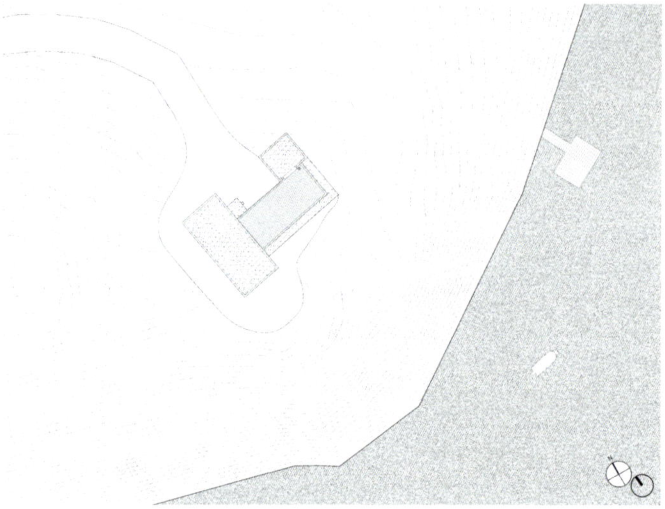

Site plan

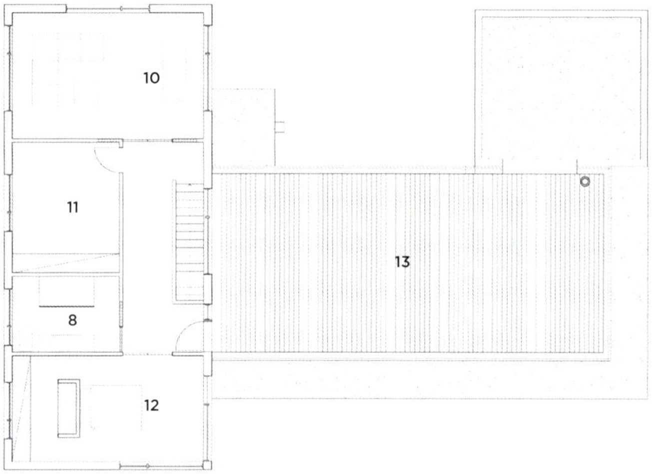

Second floor plan

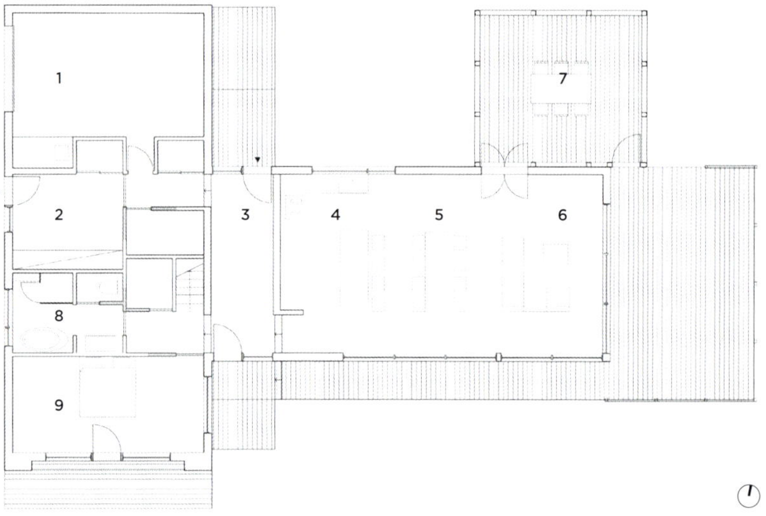

Ground floor plan

1. Garage
2. Entry
3. Gallery
4. Kitchen
5. Dining area
6. Living area
7. Screened room
8. Bathroom
9. Primary bedroom
10. Study
11. Atelier
12. Bedroom
13. Roof terrace

Cette maison dans les montagnes Laurentides près de Montréal est une œuvre d'art, avec l'eau jouant un rôle spectaculaire dans son design. Les gouttières verticales exposées créent le doux son d'un ruisseau pendant les pluies légères et forment des sculptures de glace abstraites en hiver, mettant en valeur les fascinantes qualités paramétriques de l'eau. Les clients, deux graphistes, ont imaginé leur maison comme une sculpture contemporaine inspirée par les environs naturels. Le processus de conception a impliqué de nombreux modèles et itérations, aboutissant à une structure minimaliste en trois volumes avec un contraste frappant : extérieurs noirs, intérieurs blancs, généreuses ouvertures et circulation fluide. Perchée sur une colline rocheuse surplombant un lac, la maison est conçue pour répondre à la lumière du soleil, à la topographie et aux vues imprenables. Sa disposition asymétrique améliore l'expérience spatiale, intégrant harmonieusement les espaces intérieurs et extérieurs.

Esta casa en las montañas Laurentinas cerca de Montreal es una obra de arte, con el agua desempeñando un papel espectacular en su diseño. Las canaletas de lluvia verticales expuestas crean el suave sonido de un arroyo durante las lluvias ligeras y forman esculturas abstractas de hielo en invierno, mostrando las fascinantes cualidades paramétricas del agua. Los clientes, dos diseñadores gráficos, imaginaron su hogar como una escultura contemporánea inspirada en el entorno natural. El proceso de diseño involucró numerosos modelos y repeticiones, culminando en una estructura minimalista de tres volúmenes con un contraste llamativo: exteriores negros, interiores blancos, generosas aberturas y circulación fluida. Situada en una colina rocosa con vistas a un lago, la casa está diseñada para responder a la luz solar, la topografía y las impresionantes vistas. Su disposición asimétrica mejora la experiencia espacial, integrando sin problemas los espacios interiores y exteriores.

LAC SUPÉRIEUR RESIDENCE

Lac Supérieur, Québec, Canada // Lot area: 30,000 sq ft; building area: 3,370 sq ft

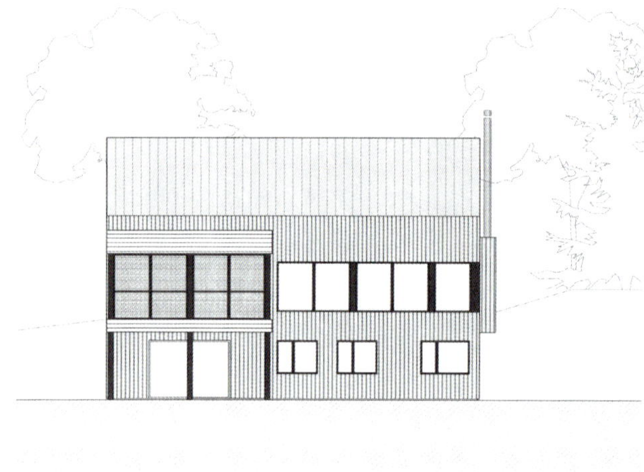

West elevation

Located near Mont-Tremblant in the Laurentides region of Québec, this project serves as a weekend residence for a family that enjoys skiing and outdoor sports. The site's long and narrow layout, following the slope of the mountain, as well as city by-laws dictating buildable area and house width, influenced the design of the residence. The main part of the house has a traditional pitched roof and dark wood cladding, reflecting the area's traditional architecture. A long horizontal section with lighter cladding and a flat roof intersects with the main part, adding a contemporary touch to the house. A carport leads to the entrance via an exterior bridge, and vertical rain gutters are unique architectural features. Inside, the design is clean yet cozy, focusing on an open layout for the common spaces and generous openings to take in the stunning views of the surrounding natural landscape. In the fall, the lake and mountains come into view, enhancing the overall experience.

Das in der Nähe von Mont-Tremblant in der Region Laurentides in Quebec gelegene Projekt dient als Wochenendhaus für eine Familie, die gerne Ski fährt und Sport im Freien betreibt. Der Entwurf wurde durch den langen, schmalen Grundriss des Grundstücks, der dem Hang folgt, sowie durch die städtischen Vorschriften, die die bebaubare Fläche und Breite des Hauses regeln, beeinflusst. Der Hauptteil hat ein traditionelles Giebeldach und eine dunkle Holzverkleidung, die die lokale Architektur widerspiegelt. Ein langer horizontaler Abschnitt mit heller Verkleidung und Flachdach fügt einen zeitgenössischen Akzent hinzu. Ein Carport führt über eine Außenbrücke zum Eingang, und vertikale Regenrinnen sind ein einzigartiges architektonisches Merkmal. Das Innere ist klar und einladend mit einem offenen Grundriss für die Gemeinschaftsräume und weiten Öffnungen, die die atemberaubende Aussicht auf die Naturlandschaft einfangen. Im Herbst erscheinen der See und die Berge, was das Gesamterlebnis verstärkt.

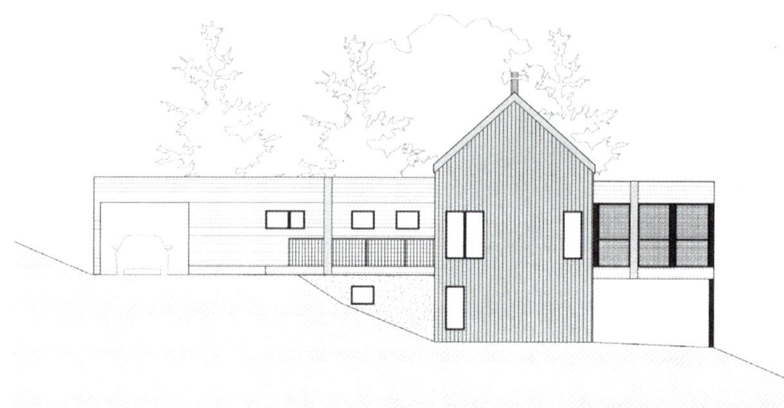

Northeast elevation

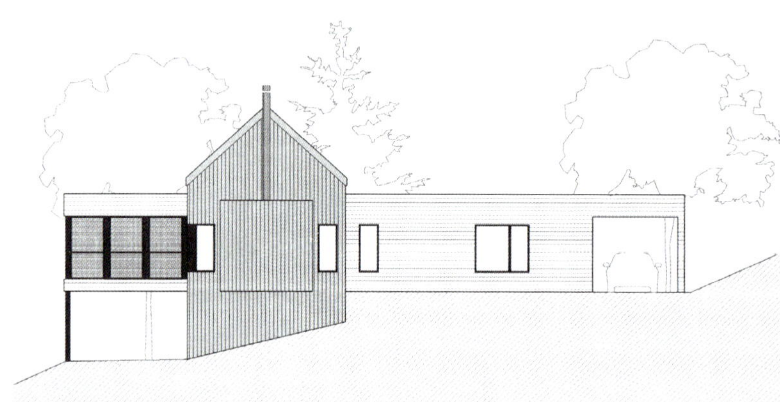

Southwest elevation

Situé près de Mont-Tremblant dans la région des Laurentides au Québec, ce projet sert de résidence de fin de semaine à une famille qui aime le ski et les sports de plein air. La conception de la maison a été influencée par le tracé long et étroit du site, qui suit la pente de la montagne, ainsi que par les règlements municipaux dictant la surface constructible et la largeur de la maison. La partie principale présente un toit à deux versants traditionnel et un bardage en bois foncé, reflétant l'architecture traditionnelle de la région. Une longue partie horizontale avec un bardage plus clair et un toit plat s'intercale avec la partie principale, apportant une touche contemporaine à la maison. Un abri à voitures permet d'accéder à l'entrée par un pont extérieur. Les gouttières verticales sont des éléments architecturaux uniques. À l'intérieur, le design est à la fois épuré et accueillant, avec un plan d'étage ouvert pour les espaces communs et de larges ouvertures pour capter les vues imprenables sur le paysage naturel environnant. En automne, le lac et les montagnes apparaissent dans les vues, améliorant l'expérience globale.

Ubicado cerca de Mont-Tremblant en la región de Laurentides en Quebec, este proyecto sirve como residencia de fin de semana para una familia que disfruta del esquí y los deportes al aire libre. El diseño de la vivienda se inspiró en las proporciones largas y estrechas del terreno, siguiendo la pendiente de la montaña, y por las ordenanzas municipales que dictan el área edificable y el ancho de la casa. La parte principal tiene un techo a dos aguas tradicional y un revestimiento de madera oscura que refleja la arquitectura local. Una sección larga y horizontal con revestimiento más claro y un techo plano se cruza con la parte principal, añadiendo un toque contemporáneo. Un cobertizo para coches que lleva a la entrada a través de un puente exterior y las canaletas verticales son elementos arquitectónicos únicos. En el interior, el diseño es limpio y acogedor, con un plano abierto para los espacios comunes y amplias aberturas para captar las vistas del paisaje natural. En otoño, el lago y las montañas aparecen en la vista, realzando la experiencia en su conjunto.

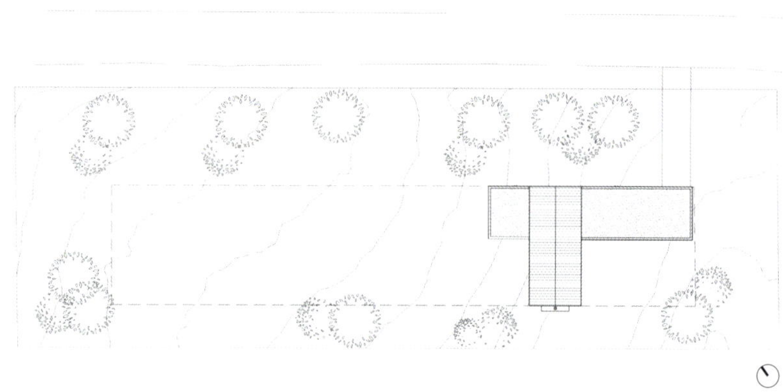

Site plan

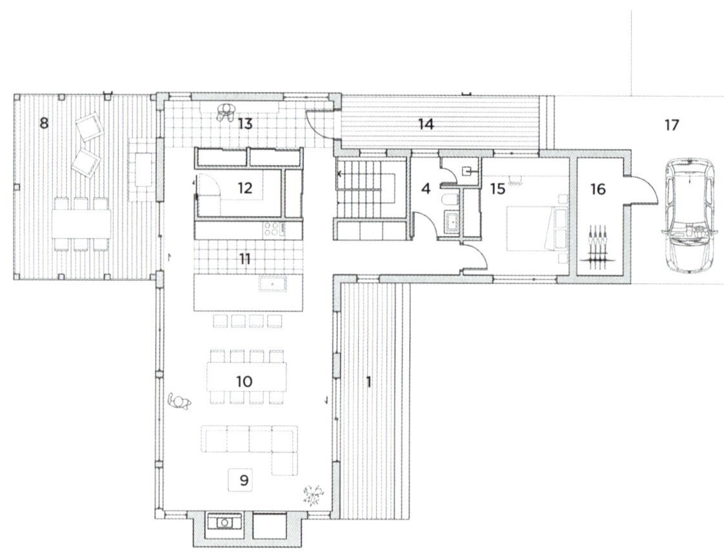

Ground floor plan

Basement floor plan

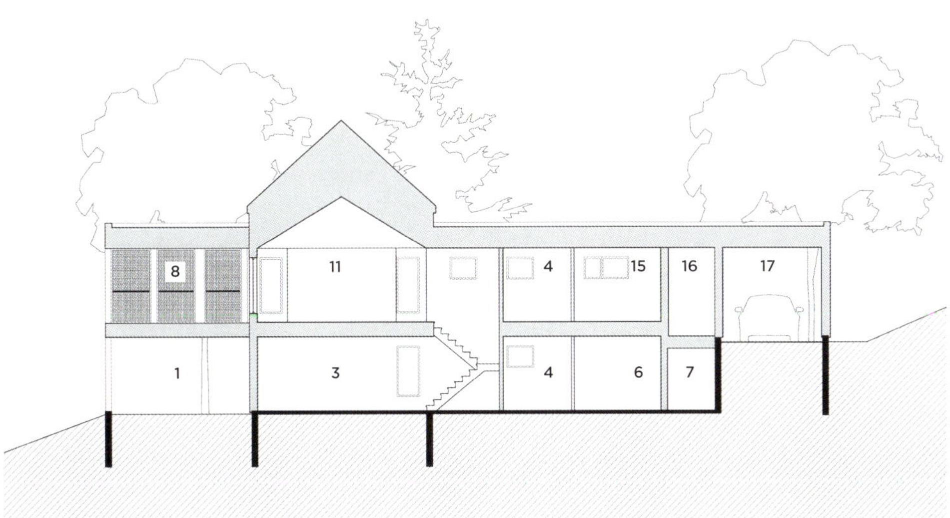

Building section

1. Terrace
2. Bedroom
3. Family room
4. Bathroom
5. Laundry room
6. Storage
7. Mechanical room
8. Screened porch
9. Living area
10. Dining area
11. Kitchen
12. Stock room
13. Entry
14. Entry bridge
15. Guest room/office
16. Exterior storage
17. Carport

ALEXANDRE BERNIER ARCHITECTE

"Thoughtful space, design with care."

Alexandre Bernier Architecte is a Montréal-based design studio that integrates architecture, furniture, interior design, and landscape across various scales. The studio blends refined contemporary aesthetics with traditional artisanal craftsmanship, focusing on material and spatial experience. Emphasizing societal and environmental concerns, the studio's philosophy centers on human dignity and meaningful connection to place, guided by themes like environmental appropriation, well-being, and local craftsmanship. Located in a former shoemaker's shop on Rue Notre-Dame in Montréal's Saint-Henri neighborhood, the studio merges creative design with community engagement, featuring a public front shop and workshop. Collaboration with local artists, craftsmen, and specialized manufacturers is central to the practice of Alexandre Bernier Architecte.

Alexandre Bernier Architecte ist ein in Montréal ansässiges Designbüro, das Architektur, Möbel, Innenarchitektur und Landschaftsgestaltung in verschiedenen Maßstäben integriert. Das Studio verbindet eine raffinierte zeitgenössische Ästhetik mit traditioneller Handwerkskunst und konzentriert sich auf Material und Raumerfahrung. Die Philosophie des Studios konzentriert sich auf die Würde des Menschen und eine sinnvolle Verbindung zu einem Ort, geleitet von Themen wie ökologische Aneignung, Wohlbefinden und lokale Handwerkskunst. Das Studio befindet sich in einer ehemaligen Schuhmacherei in der Rue Notre-Dame in Montréals Stadtteil Saint-Henri und verbindet kreatives Design mit gesellschaftlichem Engagement. Die Zusammenarbeit mit lokalen Künstlern, Handwerkern und spezialisierten Herstellern steht im Mittelpunkt der Arbeit von Alexandre Bernier Architecte.

Alexandre Bernier Architecte est un studio de design basé à Montréal qui intègre l'architecture, le mobilier, le design d'intérieur et le paysage à différentes échelles. Le studio allie une esthétique contemporaine raffinée à un artisanat traditionnel, en mettant l'accent sur l'expérience matérielle et spatiale. En se concentrant sur des enjeux sociétaux et environnementaux, la philosophie du studio est guidée par la dignité humaine et la connexion significative au lieu, avec des thèmes tels que l'appropriation environnementale, le bien-être et l'artisanat local. Situé dans une ancienne boutique de cordonnier sur la rue Notre-Dame dans le quartier Saint-Henri à Montréal, le studio fusionne design créatif et engagement communautaire, avec un atelier et une boutique en façade. La collaboration avec des artistes, artisans et fabricants locaux spécialisés est au cœur de la pratique d'Alexandre Bernier Architecte.

Alexandre Bernier Architecte es un estudio de diseño con sede en Montreal que integra arquitectura, mobiliario, diseño de interiores y paisajismo a varias escalas. El estudio combina una refinada estética contemporánea con la artesanía tradicional, centrándose en los materiales y la experiencia espacial. Haciendo hincapié en las preocupaciones sociales y medioambientales, la filosofía del estudio se centra en la dignidad humana y la conexión significativa con el lugar, guiada por temas como la apropiación medioambiental, el bienestar y la artesanía local. Situado en una antigua zapatería de la calle Notre-Dame, en el barrio de Saint-Henri de Montreal, el estudio fusiona el diseño creativo con el compromiso comunitario, y cuenta con una tienda y un taller públicos. La colaboración con artistas locales, artesanos y fabricantes especializados es fundamental en la práctica de Alexandre Bernier Architecte.

alexandrebernierarchitecte

ab-architecte.ca

BNV RESIDENCE

M RESIDENCE

BNV RESIDENCE

Montréal, Québec, Canada // Lot area: 2,040 sq ft; building area: 2,510 sq ft + basement

Street elevation

Alley elevation

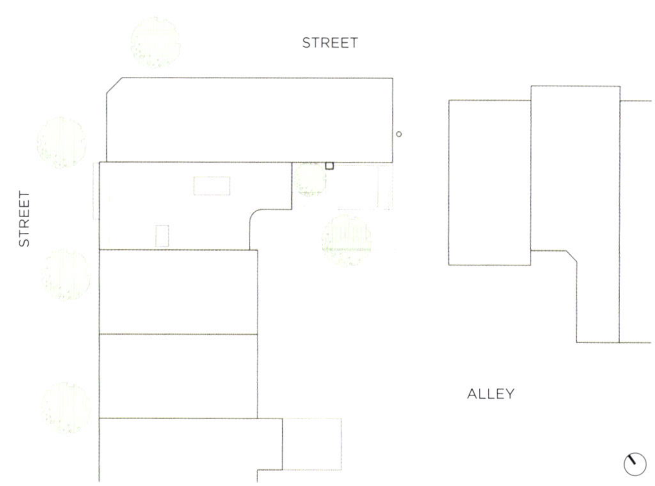

Site plan

The BNV Residence project explores how soft forms can enrich meaning and unity, creating a calming atmosphere amidst urban life's chaos. The building, originally simple and L-shaped, is renovated to blend seamlessly with its surroundings, emphasizing elegance and sensuality rather than standing out. The red brick facade, echoing Montréal's backyards, is reimagined with a curve that softens corner transitions and embraces the interior courtyard. Inside, a large skylight illuminates a gracefully curved staircase, leading to a light-filled living room and terrace. The pale, white-toned interior blurs spatial boundaries, enhancing the view of the urban landscape outside. A vintage garage/workshop, connected by a glass walkway around a small courtyard, becomes a contemplative secret garden. This courtyard, with a newly planted tree, adds light, air, and depth to the interior, marking the passage of time and seasons.

Das Projekt BNV Residence untersucht, wie weiche Formen die Bedeutung und Einheit bereichern und eine beruhigende Atmosphäre inmitten des Chaos des städtischen Lebens schaffen können. Das ursprünglich schlichte, L-förmige Gebäude wurde so umgebaut, dass es sich nahtlos in die Umgebung einfügt, wobei Eleganz und Sinnlichkeit im Vordergrund stehen, anstatt hervorzustechen. Die rote Backsteinfassade, die an die Hinterhöfe Montréals erinnert, wurde mit einer Kurve neu gestaltet, die die Eckübergänge weicher macht und den Innenhof einbezieht. Im Inneren erhellt ein großes Oberlicht eine anmutig geschwungene Treppe, die zu einem lichtdurchfluteten Wohnzimmer und einer Terrasse führt. Der helle, weiß getönte Innenraum lässt die räumlichen Grenzen verschwimmen und verstärkt den Blick auf die urbane Landschaft draußen. Eine alte Garage/Werkstatt, die durch einen gläsernen Steg mit einem kleinen Innenhof verbunden ist, wird zu einem kontemplativen, geheimen Garten. Dieser Hof mit einem neu gepflanzten Baum bringt Licht, Luft und Tiefe in den Innenraum und markiert den Lauf der Zeit und der Jahreszeiten.

Section through bridge

Le projet de la Résidence BNV explore comment des formes douces peuvent enrichir la signification et l'unité, créant une atmosphère apaisante au milieu du chaos de la vie urbaine. Le bâtiment, à l'origine simple et en forme de L, est rénové pour se fondre harmonieusement dans son environnement, mettant l'accent sur l'élégance et la sensualité plutôt que de se démarquer. La façade en briques rouges, évoquant les arrière-cours de Montréal, est réimaginée avec une courbe qui adoucit les transitions d'angle et embrasse la cour intérieure. À l'intérieur, un grand puits de lumière éclaire un escalier gracieusement courbé, menant à un salon baigné de lumière et à une terrasse. L'intérieur pâle, aux tons blancs, floute les frontières spatiales, rehaussant la vue sur le paysage urbain extérieur. Un ancien garage/atelier, relié par une passerelle vitrée autour d'une petite cour, devient un jardin secret contemplatif. Cette cour, avec un nouvel arbre planté, apporte lumière, air et profondeur à l'intérieur, marquant le passage du temps et des saisons.

El proyecto de la Residencia BNV explora cómo las formas suaves pueden enriquecer el significado y la unidad, creando una atmósfera tranquilizadora en medio del caos de la vida urbana. El edificio, originalmente sencillo y en forma de L, se renueva para fundirse a la perfección con su entorno, enfatizando la elegancia y la sensualidad en lugar de destacar. La fachada de ladrillo rojo, eco de los patios traseros de Montreal, se re imagina con una curva que suaviza las transiciones de las esquinas y abraza el patio interior. En el interior, una gran claraboya ilumina una elegante escalera curva que conduce a un luminoso salón y a la terraza. El interior, de tonos pálidos y blancos, difumina los límites espaciales y realza la vista del paisaje urbano exterior. Un garaje-taller antiguo, conectado por una pasarela de cristal alrededor de un pequeño patio, se convierte en un contemplativo jardín secreto. Este patio, con un árbol recién plantado, añade luz, aire y profundidad al interior, marcando el paso del tiempo y las estaciones.

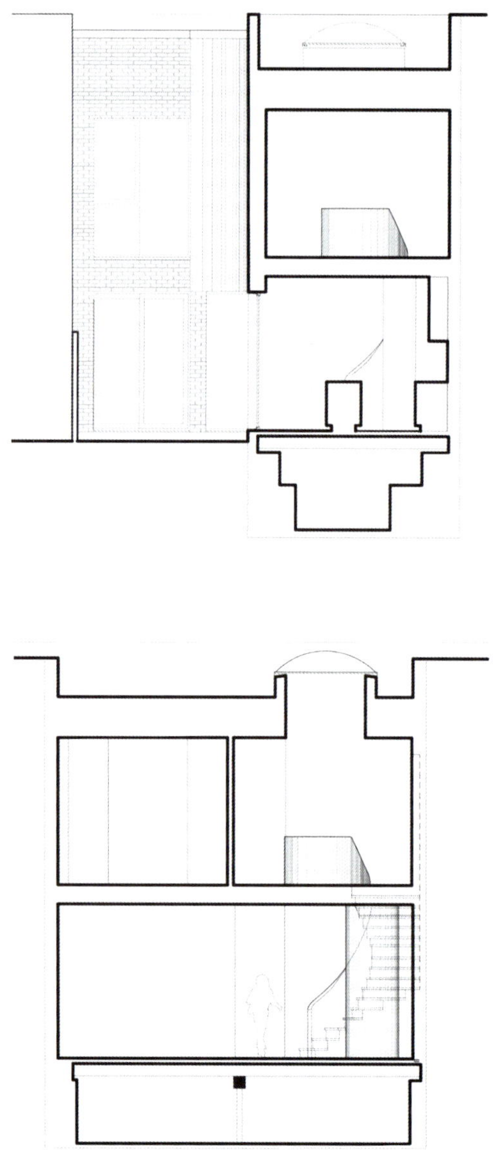

Cross sections

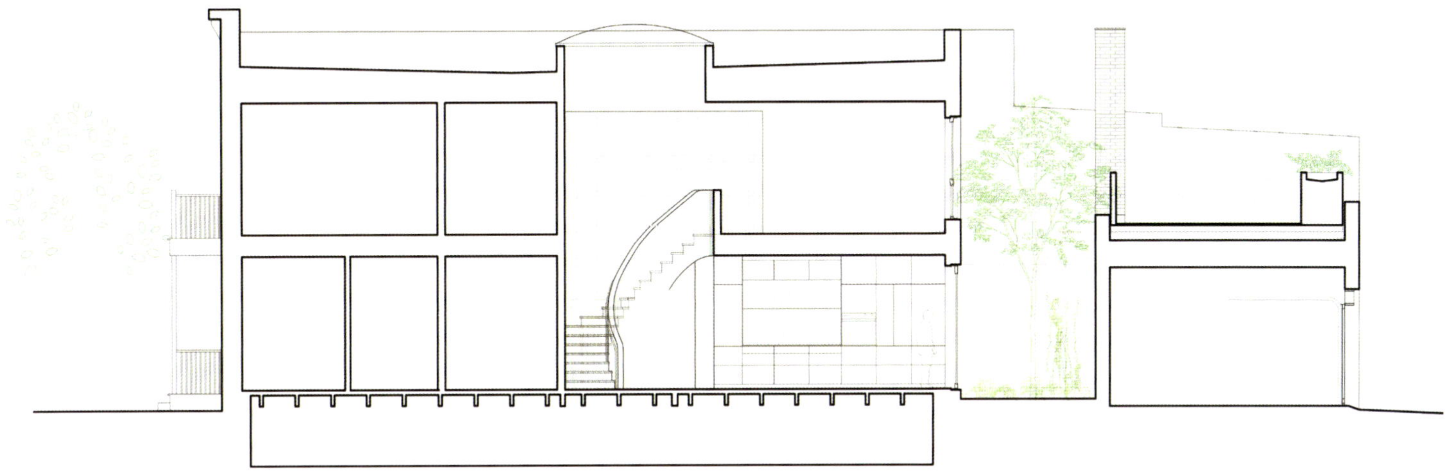

Longitudinal section

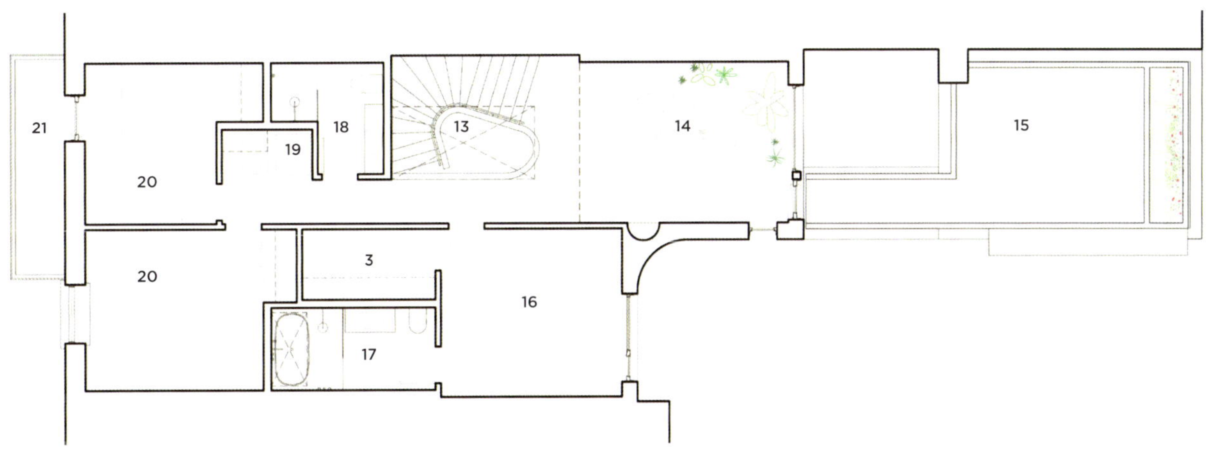

Second level floor plan

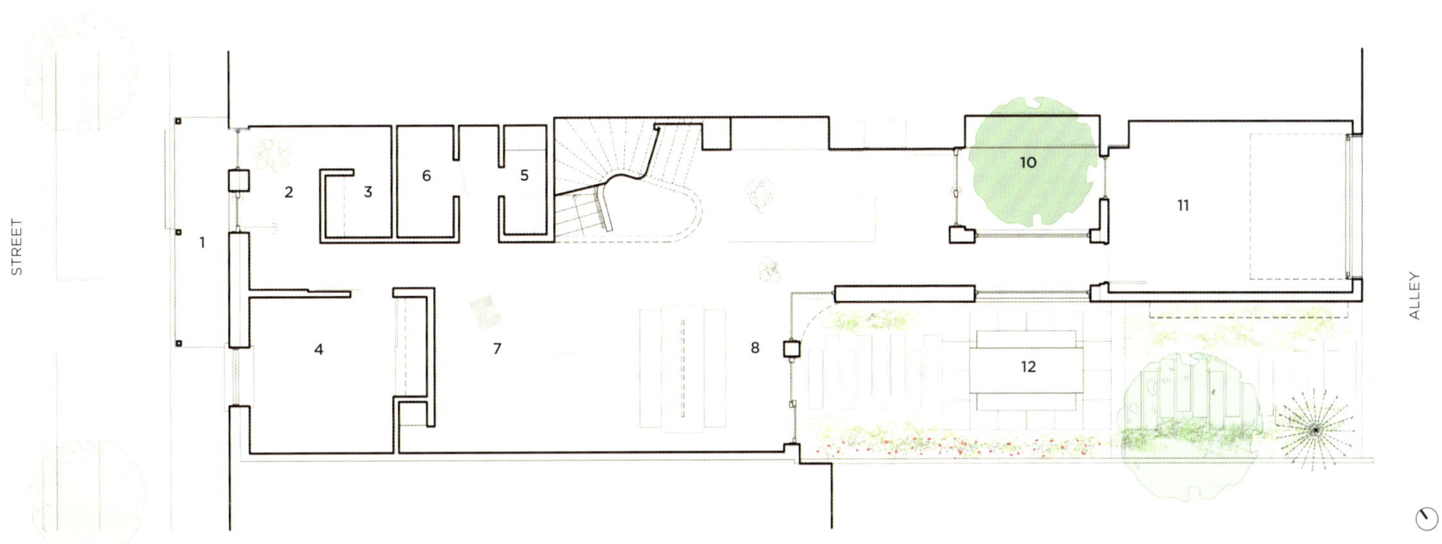

Ground level floor plan

1. Porch
2. Entrance
3. Walk-in-closet
4. Home office
5. Powder room
6. Mechanical room
7. Living area
8. Dining area
9. Open kitchen
10. Courtyard
11. Garage/workshop
12. Patio
13. Staircase and skylight
14. Family room
15. Roof terrace
16. Primary bedroom
17. Ensuite bathroom
18. Bathroom
19. Laundry closet
20. Bedroom
21. Balcony

M RESIDENCE

Montréal, Québec, Canada // Lot area: 2,625 sq ft; building area: 2,050 sq ft + basement

The M Residence project transforms a Montréal duplex into a single-family home for a couple with three children in the Rosemont neighborhood, known for its family-friendly urban environment. The design focuses on thresholds and transitions to enhance family life, expanding the entrance to accommodate the children and incorporating a skylight to brighten the space. The adjacent office provides semi-public access without intruding on privacy. Inspired by Alvar Aalto's concept of the garden as an integral part of the home, the design boldly opens the rear facade with a full-length sliding door, blending the courtyard and interior. This transformation creates a peaceful retreat from urban life. The parents' bedroom, with its glazed wall overlooking the courtyard, is a secluded retreat. Elevated like a treetop perch, it offers a private space for relaxation and reflection, seamlessly blending with the natural surroundings.

Das Projekt M Residence verwandelt ein Doppelhaus in Montréal in ein Einfamilienhaus für ein Paar mit drei Kindern im Viertel Rosemont, das für seine familienfreundliche städtische Umgebung bekannt ist. Der Entwurf konzentriert sich auf Schwellen und Übergänge, um das Familienleben zu verbessern. Der Eingang wurde vergrößert, um Platz für die Kinder zu schaffen, und ein Oberlicht wurde eingebaut, um den Raum zu erhellen. Das angrenzende Büro bietet einen halböffentlichen Zugang, ohne die Privatsphäre zu verletzen. Inspiriert von Alvar Aaltos Konzept des Gartens als integraler Bestandteil des Hauses, öffnet der Entwurf die hintere Fassade mit einer durchgehenden Schiebetür und lässt Hof und Innenraum miteinander verschmelzen. Diese Transformation schafft einen friedlichen Rückzugsort vom städtischen Leben. Das Elternschlafzimmer mit seiner verglasten Wand zum Hof ist ein abgeschiedener Rückzugsort. Wie eine Baumkrone hochgezogen, bietet es einen privaten Raum zum Entspannen und Nachdenken, der sich nahtlos in die natürliche Umgebung einfügt.

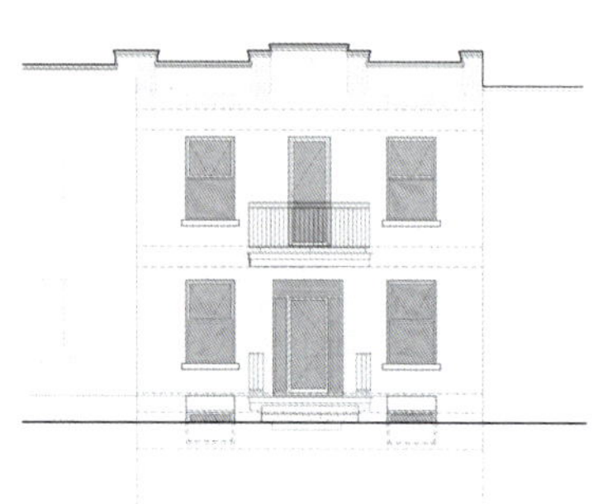

Street elevation

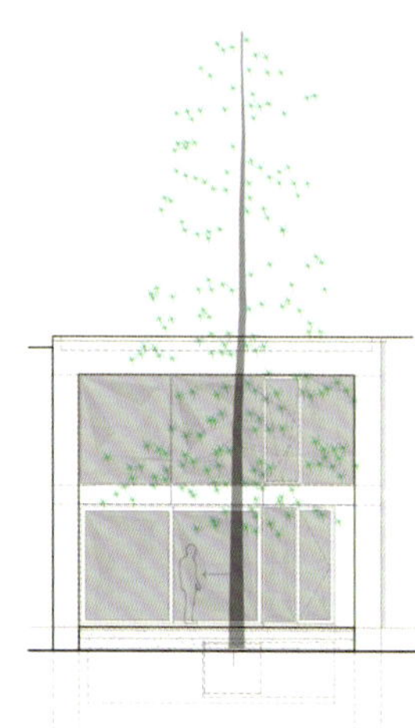

Rear elevation

Le projet Résidence M transforme un duplex montréalais en une maison unifamiliale pour un couple avec trois enfants dans le quartier de Rosemont, connu pour son environnement urbain propice à la vie de famille. Le design met l'accent sur les seuils et les transitions pour améliorer la vie familiale, en élargissant l'entrée pour accueillir les enfants et en incorporant un puits de lumière pour illuminer l'espace. Le bureau adjacent offre un accès semi-public sans empiéter sur l'intimité. Inspiré par le concept d'Alvar Aalto du jardin comme partie intégrante de la maison, le design ouvre audacieusement la façade arrière avec une porte coulissante sur toute la longueur, fusionnant la cour et l'intérieur. Cette transformation crée un havre de paix loin de la vie urbaine. La chambre des parents, avec son mur vitré donnant sur la cour, est un refuge isolé. Surélevée comme une perche dans les arbres, elle offre un espace privé pour la détente et la réflexion, se fondant harmonieusement avec l'environnement naturel.

El proyecto M Residence transforma un dúplex de Montreal en una vivienda unifamiliar para una pareja con tres hijos en el barrio de Rosemont, conocido por su ambiente urbano familiar. El diseño se centra en los umbrales y las transiciones para mejorar la vida familiar, ampliando la entrada para acomodar a los niños e incorporando una claraboya para iluminar el espacio. La oficina adyacente ofrece un acceso semipúblico sin invadir la intimidad. Inspirado en el concepto de Alvar Aalto del jardín como parte integrante de la casa, el diseño abre audazmente la fachada trasera con una puerta corredera de longitud completa, mezclando el patio y el interior. Esta transformación crea un apacible retiro de la vida urbana. El dormitorio de los padres, con su pared acristalada que da al patio, es un refugio aislado. Elevado como la copa de un árbol, ofrece un espacio privado para la relajación y la reflexión, en perfecta armonía con el entorno natural.

Longitudinal sections

Second level floor plan

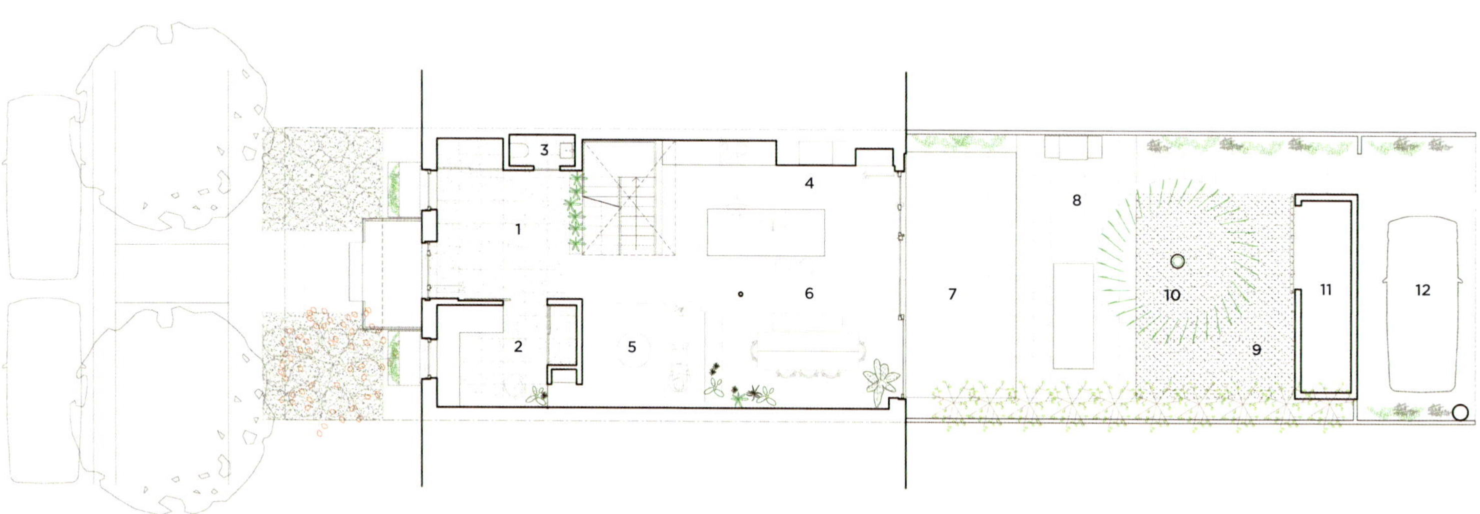

Ground level floor plan

1. Entry foyer
2. Home office
3. Powder room
4. Kitchen
5. Living area
6. Dining area
7. Gallery
8. Terrace
9. Playground
10. Tree
11. Shed
12. Parking
13. Skylight
14. Primary bedroom
15. Primary bathroom
16. Walk-in closet
17. Bathroom
18. Bedroom
19. Balcony

DIRECTORY

1628

S-PACE 1628
Architecture, Design, and Landscape
Design Team: Annie Charest and François Parenteau/1628
Structural Engineer and wood structure prefabrication: Usi-Home
Awards:
-Americas Property Awards 2022-2023 – Award in the category Mixed-use architecture
-Loop Design Awards 2023 – Nominated as a finalist for public's choice in the Architecture, mixed-use category.
Photographer: © Stéphane Groleau and Les Maxime

HOVEY RESIDENCE
Architecture, design, and landscape design Team: 1628
Structural Engineer: St-Georges Structure et Civil
Landscape Designer: Aménagement Éco-Trim
Awards:
-Americas Property Awards 2024 – Award in the category Residential architecture
-Loop Design Awards 2024 – Nominated as a finalist for public's choice in the Architecture, Residential and Houses category.
Photographer: © Stéphane Groleau and Pixel Nord

ALAN CHRIST ARCHITECTS

TAYLOR STREET RESIDENCE
Architect of Record: Alan Christ Architects, LLC
Architect: Scott Slarsky, Christopher Wortley, and Maryann Upton/SAS Design Build
Structural Engineer: Structures Workshop
Millwork: Jeong Lee Custom Cabinetry
General Contractor: The Holland Companies
Photographer: © Peter Vanderwarker

LAWRENCE ROAD RESIDENCE
Architectural Team: Alan Christ Architects, LLC
Interior Designer: PCA Architecture, Interiors + Planning
Structural Engineer: BERDI Consulting
HERS Rater: Sustainable Energy Analytics
Cabinetry: Metropolitan Cabinets & Countertops
General Contractor: Pessote Construction Inc.
Photographer: © Shelly Harrison Photography

ALEXANDRE BERNIER ARCHITECTE

BNV HOUSE
Architect: Alexandre Bernier Architecte
General Contractor: Construction Libersan
Photographer: © Maxime Brouillet

M HOUSE
Architect: Alexandre Bernier Architecte
General Contractor: Rénovation Mario Rufiange
Photographer: © Maxime Brouillet

AUSTIN PATTERSON DISSTON ARCHITECTURE & DESIGN

OLD STONE NEW LIGHT
Architecture and Interior Design: Austin Patterson Disston Architecture & Design
Landscape Designer: Rosalla Sanni Design
General Contractor: Eric Kotonski/EK Construction
Photographer: © Hulya Kolabas Photography

HOUSE ON THE POND
Architectural Team: Austin Patterson Disson Architecture & Design
Landscape Designer: Owner and installed by Krentzman Care
Interior Designer: Owner
General Contractor: Kyle Stokkers/Stokkers & Co
Photographer: © Hulya Kolabas Photography

BOON ARCHITECTURE

L'ALBAN
Architect: BOON Architecture
Interior Designer: Berthiaume Design
Photographer: © Drône Média

ARCTURUS
Architect: BOON Architecture
Photographer: © Marie H Rainville

DOYLE | COFFIN ARCHITECTURE

MODERN FARMHOUSE
Architectural Team: Peter T. Coffin, AIA, Principal in Charge, and Valmar T. Franca, Jr., AIA, Project Architect/Doyle | Coffin Interior Design
Landscape Designer: Brook Clark, PLA, ASLA, Principal in Charge, and Jackie Aylward, ASLA, Project Manager/Brook Clark Landscape Architects
Interior Designer: Paula Hamel Daher, Principal in Charge/Daher Interior Design
Photographer: © Neil Landino

WATERFRONT POST AND BEAM
Architectural Team: Peter T. Coffin, AIA, Principal in Charge, and Alex T. Bellina, AIA, Associate, Project Architect/Doyle | Coffin Interior Design
Landscape Designer: Brook Clark, PLA, ASLA, Principal in Charge, and Jackie Aylward, ASLA, Project Manager/Brook Clark Landscape Architects
Interior Designer: Jody Myers-Fierz, ASID, LEEP AP ID&C, Principal in Charge/Doyle | Coffin Interior Design
Photographer: © Neil Landino

FURTHER ARCHITECTURE OFFICE

COASTAL GABLES
Architectural Team: Justin Towart AIA Leed AP
Renderings: © Yuriy Bobak

PINE RIDGE RETREAT
Architectural Team: Justin Towart AIA Leed AP
Renderings: © Yuriy Bobak

GALE GOFF ARCHITECT

TRANQUILITY BASE
Architect: Gale Goff, Barret Borden, Pete Landis, and Jameson Ray/Gale Goff Architect
Landscape Architect: Martha S. Moore Landscape Architect
Masonry: Kevin Baker
General Contractor: Jacob Talbot Fine Homebuilding
Photographer: © Anthony Crisafulli Photography

TAPPENS BEACH HOUSE
Architect: Gale Goff, Barret Borden, Pete Landis, and Jameson Ray/Gale Goff Architect
Landscape Architect: Leslie Costa Landscape Architect
Interior Design: Kirby Goff Interior Design
General Contractor: Jacob Talbot Fine Homebuilding
Photographer: © Anthony Crisafulli Photography

GUILLAUME PELLETIER ARCHITECTE

LA CASCADE RESIDENCE
Architectural Team: Guillaume Pelletier, Samuel Gendron, Katerine McKinnon
General Contractor: Francis Bock, Groupe Marcillaud
Photographers: © Alain Lavergne and David Boyer

LAC SUPÉRIEUR RESIDENCE
Architectural Team: Guillaume Pelletier, Eveline Gagnon, Simon Fortier
General Contractor: France Bertrand & Serge Bujold
Photographer: © Alain Lavergne

MISIASZEK TURPIN

MEADOW RETREAT
Architectural Team: Sonya L. Misiaszek AIA and Jared A. Guilmett AIA/Misiaszek Turpin
Structural Engineer: Dubois and King, Inc.
Interior Consultant: Paul Lanoix Design
Lighting Designer: Light Positive
General Contractor: Sharpe Construction, LLC.
Photographer: © Misiaszek Turpin

MOUNTAIN HOME
Architectural Team: Sonya L. Misiaszek AIA and Robert K. Turpin AIA/Misiaszek Turpin
Structural Engineer: Rist-Frost Shumway Engineering, PC.
Mechanical Engineer: Yeaton Associates, Inc.
General Contractor: Twin Oaks Construction, Inc.
Photographer: © Joseph St. Pierre

NICHOLSON CERETTI ARCHITECTURE

SEAFORTH ARCADE

Architect: Nicholson Ceretti Architecture
Structural Engineer: Andrea Doncaster Engineering
General Contractor: MRB Contracting
Photographers: © All photos by Julian Parkinson except arcade photo by Darren Calabrese

NORWOOD

Architect: Nicholson Ceretti Architecture + Jordan Rice
Structural Engineer: Andrea Doncaster Engineering
General Contractor: MRB Contracting
Photographers: © Julian Parkinson

NORDAIS ARCHITECTURE

MAISON DU BOCAGE

Architectural Team: Mathieu Boucher-Côté, Marika Drolet-Ferguson/Nordais Architecture
Structural Engineer: STR, Trusko, Tank Shop
Kitchen Cabinetry: Armoires Qualitek
General Contractor: Jacques Gionet
Photographer: © Félix Michaud, Mylène Thériault, and Marika Drolet-Ferguson

SOMMARHUS

Architectural Team: Mathieu Boucher-Côté, Marika Drolet-Ferguson/Nordais Architecture
Lighting Designer: Luminaire Authentik
Solar Panels: Vertex Solutions
Kitchen Cabinetry: Armoires Qualitek
General Contractor: Mathieu Boucher-Côté
Photographer: © Félix Michaud

PAVLIDES STUDIO

BERKSHIRES LEGACY

Architect: Pavlides Studio
Interior Designer: Pavlides Studio
Landscape Designer: Walter Cudnohufsky Landscape Architect
Lighting Consultant: Evelyn Audet Lighting Design
Mechanical Systems: Allied Engineering
General Contractor: Lou boxer Builders
Photographer: © XXXX

FAMILY FARMHOUSE

Architect: Pavlides Studio
Interior Designer: Pavlides Studio
Structural Engineer: Camera/O'Neil Consulting Engineers
Stonework at Landscaping: Kevin Baker
General Contractor: Parker Construction
Photographer: © Nat Rea Photography

PRIESTLEY + ASSOCIATES ARCHITECTURE

MOUNTAIN ESCAPE

Architectural Team: Priestley + Associates Architecture
Landscape Architect: Terence J. DeWan & Associates
Structural Engineer: Albert P. Putnam, P. E.
Stonework: Maine Stone and Landscape and Freshwater Stone
General Contractor: Oliver Builders
Photographer: © Trent Bell

VILLAGE CONTEMPORARY

Architectural Team: Priestley + Associates Architecture
Structural Engineer: Albert P. Putnam, P. E.
General Contractors: Collins Builders and Michael Taylor, Builder
Photographers: © Susan Teare and Trent Bell

QUINZHEE ARCHITECTURE

LES FRÈRES TINO

Architect: Guillaume Fafard, founder and Principal architect, OAQ, AAPPQ, CPHD, and Camille Eustache, Candidate for the profession of architect/Quinzhee Architecture
Interior Designer: Par Lauzé
General Contractor: Menuiserie Elra
Photographer: © Maxime Messier

CHEZ LÉON

Architect: Guillaume Fafard, founder and Principal architect, OAQ, AAPPQ, CPHD, and Gabriel Lemelin, Architect OAQ/Quinzhee Architecture
Interior Designer: Quinzhee Architecture
Structural Engineer: MA-TH
General Contractor: KEVLAR Habitation in collaboration with Boreas Construction
Photographer: © Adrien Williams

REVERSE ARCHITECTURE

WAYLAND RESIDENCE

Architectural Team: Carl Solander, Principal; Tiandra Ray, Peter Zambelletti, Bridget MacKean, and Courtney Pope, Vivian Rulewich, Design and Graphics/Reverse Architecture
Surveyor: Summit Surveying, Inc.
Structural Engineer: Armando Plata
Custom Cabinetry: Windsor Architectural
General Contractor: Fresh Start Contracting
Photographer: © Heidi Solander

CAMBRIDGE TOWNHOUSE

Architectural Team: Carl Solander, Principal; Bridget MacKean, Designer; and Vivian Rulewich, Graphics/Reverse Architecture
Structural Engineer: Armando Plata
Surveyor: Summit Surveying, Inc.
HVAC Designer: Sun Engineering, Inc
Interior Decorator: Rachel Dunham Design
Custom Cabinetry: Herrick & White
General Contractor: Stack + Co
Photographer: © Heidi Solander

RUHL | JAHNES

ESSEX BAY HOUSE

Architectural Team: William T. Ruhl, FAIA; Sandra A. Jahnes, AIA, LEED AP; Dustin Tisdale AIA; Caroline LaFleche; and Shannon Sturm/ Ruhl | Jahnes
Landscape Designer: Laura Gibson
Structural Engineer: LJO Engineering, LLC.
HVAC Engineer: Zero Energy/Jordan Goldman
General Contractor: Jeff McMath
Photographer: © Nat Rea

GAP COVE HOUSE

Architectural Team: William T. Ruhl, FAIA; Nerijus Petrokas, LEED GA; and Jide Olanrewaju/Ruhl | Jahnes
Structural Engineer: Richmond So Engineers
General Contractor: Skinner & Watkins Inc.
Photographer: © Chris Becker Photo

SANIEE ARCHITECTS

LION HOUSE

Architecture: Saniee Architects
Interior Decoration: Busta Studio
General Contractor and Landscape Designer: Shoreline Pools
Photographer: © David Sundberg/ESTO

TUDOR HOUSE

Architecture: Saniee Architects
Landscape Designers: Rosalia Sanni Design and George Bridge Landscape
General Contractor: PDB Construction
Photographer: © David Sundberg/ESTO

SEVENTY2ARCHITECTS

IRON GREY HOUSE

Architect: seventy2architects
Landscape Architect: A2 Land Consulting
Structural Engineer: Preston Engineering
Photographer: © Janine Lamontagne Photography

SHERMAN LAKE HOUSE

Architect: seventy2architects
Landscape Architect: A2 Land Consulting
Structural Engineer: Preston Engineering
Photographer: © Janine Lamontagne Photography